---Traveling the---
-----Two-Lane-----

To Polly,

Who added much to
my days in Biddeford Pool,

Best Regards,

Marilyn

----Traveling the----
------Two-Lane------

a memoir and travelogue

marilyn berman

***BOOK*LOGIX**®
Alpharetta, GA

The author has tried to recreate events, locations, and conversations from her memories of them. She acknowledges that memories may not replicate actual events, and other participants may remember them differently. In some instances, in order to maintain their anonymity and protect privacy, the author has changed the names of individuals and places. She may also have changed some identifying characteristics and details such as physical attributes, occupations, and places of residence.

10 9 8 7 6 5 4 3 2   0 2 1 8 1 5

ISBN: 978-1-61005-558-1
Library of Congress Control Number: 2015902333

Printed in the United States of America

♾ This paper meets the requirements of ANSI/NISO Z39.48-1992 (Permanence of Paper)

This book is dedicated to Carol Fillman, Ruth Leutwyler, and Audrey Lowe, three women who have contributed to my journey and to this manuscript.

Make no little plans; they have no magic to stir men's blood and probably themselves will not be realized.

Daniel Burnham in *The Devil in the White City*

CONTENTS

Prologue – Bedside - 1

1. How It Began - 5

2. Working Out the Bugs - - - - - - - - - - - - - - - 11

3. New Beginnings - 15

4. Woman on a Ladder - - - - - - - - - - - - - - - - - - 23

5. Good Sleep to You - - - - - - - - - - - - - - - - - - - 33

6. Badlands - 39

7. Not All Who Wander Are Lost - - - - - - - - - - - 45

8. The Energizer Bunny - - - - - - - - - - - - - - - - - - 53

9. Dyke on a Bike - 59

10. Crossing the Border - - - - - - - - - - - - - - - - - - 67

11. The Reluctant Warrior - - - - - - - - - - - - - - - - 75

12. Conflict and Kindness - - - - - - - - - - - - - - - - 81

13. Courage - 91

14. The Soo - 99

15. Illusions -   103
16. Antonio and Danny - - - - - - - - - - - - - - - - - - -   109
17. Winter Is Coming -   117
18. Intermission -   123
19. Biddeford Pool -   129
20. Life in Maine -   135
21. Eleanor -   145
22. I Once Was Lost -   151
23. Weatherbeaten -   157
24. Good-Bye -   165
25. Transitions -   173
26. Evangeline -   177
27. Raising Consciousness - - - - - - - - - - - - - - - - - -   183
28. After the Storm -   189
29. Anna -   195
30. Sea-Change -   199
31. New, Old, and Ancient - - - - - - - - - - - - - - - -   205
32. Reflections -   211
33. From Mountains to Manhattan - - - - - - - - - -   213
34. Santa Fe Opera -   221
35. Don't Ask -   227
36. Curved Corners -   233
37. Strictly Rationed Chocolate - - - - - - - - - - - - -   241
Epilogue – "Where Have All the Flowers Gone . . ." - -   253
Acknowledgments -   257
About the Author -   261

UNITED STATES OF AMERICA

PACIFIC

OCEAN

MEXICO

Gul

CANADA

ATLANTIC

OCEAN

of Mexico

THE BAHAMAS

PROLOGUE
Bedside

My father stared at the hospital ceiling, unseeing. His jaw hung open as his lungs labored to move air in and out, the sound from obstructed passages like the raspy escape of air from a broken bicycle pump—the struggle apparent on his unconscious face.

We stood around his bed: Mom, me, and most of the family. More were on the way. With trembling fingers, my tiny mother traced the wrinkles on Dad's forehead, her mouth set and unmoving. This vigil seemed to go on forever, broken only by a trip to the bathroom, a dry sandwich from a machine, or a visitor from the hushed halls.

A tech in a white jacket and pants came in to manipulate the IV and other tubes that journeyed to various places inside my father. A few nurses came in, stood at the foot of the bed, and asked if we wanted to pray. We joined them in a hand-holding circle as they prayed Jesus would care for my Jewish father.

We didn't correct them. Prayer is prayer.

A doctor entered, his white coat unbuttoned, deep vertical furrows between his eyes. I asked if our father was in pain.

"We don't think so," he said.

"Does he know we're here?" my brother Jeff asked.

"Act like he does," he said, sounding like a recording. He spent more time looking at Dad's charts than at us. "Help him to know it's okay for him to leave you. It'll help him know you'll be fine without him. Then he can let go."

My sister Donna looked at the doctor. "If he's aware, then he's suffering. It must be unbearable. Is there anything you can do to speed this up?"

"No. Sorry."

And then he was gone. The doctor, not Dad. It would be a full day and night before the hideous wheezing ended.

The last day was a fitting end to the cheerless years that had gone before. Five years earlier, Dad drove past the end of the parking space and bumped into the Florida condo where he lived with my mother. That's when Mom took his car keys, replacing them with keys to their storage locker. When he tried to open the driver's door, he turned to her with a troubled expression and said, "Mom, there's something wrong with the lock."

She said, "Here, let me try." And then, when the door opened, she added, "I might as well drive. I'm already here."

Sometimes, when he took out the trash, he stood on the balcony wondering what he was supposed to do with the bag in his hand. But he could still talk, feed himself, and hug me with his well-muscled arms.

One day, he thought he had left his store unlocked.

He'd had stores—hardware, furniture, and appliance stores—but they had been in Chicago where I grew up, and were now long gone. He was agitated and couldn't relax. So, they left for "the store." Mom told him she couldn't remember where it was, asking him where to turn and following his directions until he forgot why they were out and asked for an ice cream cone.

Every time I visited them in Florida, some other part of him had disappeared or deteriorated. Before I left, I would just be getting used to this new dad. But the next time, something else would have vanished—until only his warm hug remained.

When he lay in his casket, my mom bent slowly—every muscle shaking—and kissed his cold, waxy forehead.

After the funeral, we bought Mom a new set of luggage, hoping she would travel. A few months later, I invited her to visit me in Atlanta, offering to go to Florida and fly back with her.

"No, darling, I'll be fine. I really don't need help to take a plane trip."

I fidgeted in my Atlanta office, watching my desk clock, anxious to pick her up and show her a good time. I jumped when the phone rang. Donna, my sister in Chicago, told me an airline employee phoned her. Mom had taken an earlier plane. When she arrived in Atlanta and no one was there to meet her, she found an attendant and said she was visiting her daughter in Chicago. So the attendant phoned Donna.

My heart pounded all the way to the airport, but I didn't get it yet. Nor did I understand the problem when my read-a-book-a-week mother asked me if she should spell *forty* with a "u." And it still didn't register when my friend Carol dropped us off at the Kiss-Ride stop at the transit station and Mom whispered, seriously asking me if she should kiss the driver.

After she returned to Florida, her neighbor called to tell me Mom was behaving strangely. She wouldn't agree to go out with friends and rarely left the house. When someone came to visit, she abruptly asked them to leave—unlike her usual self. Her friends were deeply concerned.

Only then did I understand the severity.

That's when she moved to an independent apartment in an assisted-living home. Her new life had begun, but not as we imagined. After caring for my father for five years, we hoped she would have some joy. Instead, my sweet, hardworking mother had begun to die—as she would for the next five years, just like my dad—a little bit at a time.

And I never told them my truth.

CHAPTER 1

How It Began

I sat fuming at a red light, waiting in a long line of cars, each green pulse freeing only a few. Inching toward my turn, with nothing better to occupy my mind, I asked myself how much longer I would inch through life. I was sixty-three; how many years did I have left? Would I follow in the path of my late parents, vitality slithering away in small, humiliating episodes, losing the ability to care for myself?

At that stuck-in-traffic moment, I decided to do something wonderful, something fantastic—now—while physically and cognitively intact. When I arrived at my office, I wrote a letter resigning my post-retirement job.

A few years earlier, I retired from a full career in academia, research, and health care and had taken a position as director of a Jewish-sponsored lesbian and gay help center. I liked my new job, but the fantasy of wandering far from home had been simmering in my still-fertile gray matter. I imagined driving up mountains, camping on lakes, shopping in quirky towns. Now, by damn, I would do it, alone, for at least a year—maybe eighteen months.

My friends thought I was crazy. "You're past sixty," said one. "And you're not even five feet tall. You'll be a target for any badass out there."

"Road kill," said another.

They feared I'd be lost more often than not. The ones who weren't confronting me directly muttered behind my back. "Think of it as thirty-six two-week vacations strung together," I suggested to my dubious friends while I returned to my plans.

Mom and Dad had encouraged independence and exploration, so unlike my newer friends, Donna and my brother Jeff were accustomed to my need for movement and adventure. They did, however, express concern for my safety. Life is short; the idea of this journey was fascinating. I would take reasonable care and enjoy every minute.

Where to go? What kind of vehicle? What to take? How to communicate with friends and family? How to find good tenants to care for my house?

Hunting for answers distracted me from fears of hereditary dementia.

The first question was easy. I'd always wanted to go to Alaska, land of *National Geographic* majesty. But how would I find my way? I could get around in flat cities laid out on a grid, but I lived in hilly Atlanta, where streets crossed each other more than once, sixty of them were called Peachtree, and I often felt like a rat running a maze with the promised cheese forever out of sight. I have considerable skill as a map reader and I'm good at left versus right and up versus down, but not every road is on the map. Besides, it's too hard to read a map while driving.

It was 2003. Navigation systems were just coming to the market. They were expensive in those early years, but how terrific it would be to have an invisible guiding voice. The first one I looked at operated with a computer under the driver's seat . . . twenty-one hundred dollars. Two months later, when I went back to buy it, a much better model was available. No computer under the seat, just a screen to be mounted on the dashboard and antennae to be wired from the screen to the hood of the vehicle. Price was now only thirteen hundred dollars.

So much progress in such a short time. I could never guess what would come in the near future. I bought it, had it installed, and got acquainted long before I left home.

As soon as I pushed the ON button, a map appeared on its screen and a woman spoke: "Proceed to the highlighted route. Then the route guidance will start."

Her voice was more like a news commentator than a computer—I was enchanted. She became my partner, my beloved companion, helping so much more than I could have imagined. When I was low on gas, she found the nearest station; when I wanted a book, she located the closest library.

When she said, "Take the next right turn—on Piedmont Avenue," and I was stuck in the left lane, I disobeyed and wondered what to do now that I was off-route. She knew I had not obeyed, but said, in a nonthreatening tone, "Recalculating . . ." and then displayed a new path. On the suggestion of my witty friend Lesley, I named her Mazie Grace—*I once was lost, but now am found.*

Deciding on the right kind of vehicle was more complex. I planned to stay in campgrounds more than hotels—more adventure and less expense—so I needed a vehicle big enough to live in. I went to RV centers, where salesmen showed me how to pull tubes and wires from hidden panels to set up for the night and how to put them all back when it was time to leave. I lifted my short legs onto tall steps to enter the driver's seat and wished for something smaller—a new VW Eurovan. Designed for weekend camping, it was the largest vehicle I could tolerate driving and the smallest home I could consider.

I selected an attractive silver gray, but the Eurovan was boxy—definitely not a sexy car.

All rear seats had to go—the rear-facing bench and one more forward facing—leaving only the two front passenger seats and a space five feet wide by eight feet long. I drew pictures of the van's interior, minus the rear seats I would remove to make room for a built-in bed, five feet by three. Then I cut pieces of cardboard to represent the bed, tiny fridge, dresser drawers, microwave, and porta-potty. Moving the pieces around the drawing, I found a place for each necessity. My friend Wade built a wooden base for a six-inch deep, foam-rubber mattress, cutting both to fit in the rear of the van. A small fold-out table held a desk lamp, an electric heater, and petite fan, each item velcroed to the table so I could drive without fear of projectiles. I put a miniature refrigerator under the table and a dresser against the front seat, drawers facing back for easy access. A microwave sat on top of the dresser. All this left a space just large enough for me to access everything I needed. Had I been any taller—or wider—I would not have fit in my tiny traveling home. I believed TV was essential. I found a fellow who installs them in limousines and asked him if he could do the same thing in my VW van.

"Yes," he said, "you can get local stations and you can use it for DVDs." Oh boy, oh boy! But after installation, I learned it totally depleted the car's battery in two hours unless the motor was running. And it rarely got a signal outside the city. It would have been great for kids to watch movies while mom drove, but I didn't have kids or family to entertain and had no wish to use it while on the road. I never used the TV, not even once.

I was long past the age where I could sleep all night without waking to pee, and I couldn't imagine creeping through unfamiliar paths in the rain or cold with a roll of paper in one hand and a flashlight in the other, perhaps slogging through mud in search of the communal bathroom. I wanted a system like they have in space where urine is processed to be used for drinking and washing while solid waste is burned when it re-enters our atmosphere. A toilet was a necessity, but what kind? The first one I found incinerated the waste—but it was over two thousand dollars.

Disappointed, but undaunted, I continued hunting for a solution to the middle-of-the-night problem. The answer was a simple, plastic contraption that folded up and looked like a briefcase. At night, I pulled the legs down, opened the top and exposed a seat and a mesh sack that held a disposable, biodegradable bag. At less than a hundred dollars, it always reminded me that the best purchase I *didn't* make was a waste-incinerating toilet.

Though sometimes the journey seemed far in the future, somewhat imaginary, I worked like an automaton, mindlessly performing computer-driven instructions until the house was empty, clean, and airy. As the work progressed, the trip left the realm of fantasy. It would happen! And as it became a reality, friends and family again expressed concern. How would they know where I was? How would I stay in touch? Smart phones didn't exist and calls were expensive, but I had a cell phone and laptop. Though Wi-Fi was new technology, it was rapidly becoming available at campgrounds and coffee shops, making it possible for me to describe my adventures in emails. I promised to be a regular correspondent.

I began to look for a renter. My friend Wendy, who owned rental property, taught me how to pre-check potential occupants for criminal records. Her partner, Cindy, offered to manage the property during my journey. Their contributions were essential to the rental process. After criminal background checks, I interviewed a promising couple who said they were a real estate agent and an artist. A quick Internet check indicated they were three months behind in their current rent. Another couple had used multiple social security numbers in several states, and the next pair had two bankruptcies and pages of unpaid debts. One bankruptcy and fewer debts would have been okay, but I'd have been a fool to rent to someone with so many unpaid obligations. But there were many callers; it took less than ten days to find appropriate renters.

The experience of meeting people with fake résumés was a good reminder: people can't always be trusted, and I was about to meet quite a few strangers.

Friends were still afraid for me and continued to give me instructions. Family, though not as fearful, added more advice. *Get an alarm for your car. Fill the tank when you hit half-full. Check your tires every time you get gas. Carry a spare battery. Keep a spare car key. Call me daily.* All of this advice—except "call me daily"—was valuable.

After months of preparation, it was time to go. Having abandoned my home, pots and pans, sofas, and bathtubs, I was transformed into a wanderer who lived in a van.

CHAPTER 2

Working Out the Bugs

I left home on May 1, 2004, with the intent of reaching Alaska by early July, allowing two months to reach my destination and then many weeks of touring before the roads could be treacherous. I headed north. My first stop: Chicago, city of my birth. Family members still living in the area took me to dinner. My brother Jeff and his wife Susie, their daughter Kim, nephew Gary, now an OSHA engineer, and his wife Krista, were concerned and had useful suggestions. But they were accustomed to my grand schemes and excited to send me off on the next one.

I had visited Chicago many times, but when I left this time, instead of heading back to Atlanta I traveled further north, not on the expressway, but on city streets leading to back roads and empty two-lane highways. Winding through Wisconsin, I adjusted to the relaxed pace of patchwork farmlands and small towns with butcher shops and real bakeries. The smell of fresh bread drifted through open car windows while the mundane problems of modern life floated out. The tiresome look-alike franchises, malls, and traffic vanished.

My plan was to take Interstate 2, a little four-lane that wanders across the northernmost United States under the Canadian border. Woodall's camping and travel guide would serve as Mazie's assistant and lead me to good campsites. It also described the touring highlights along the way. Since I had plenty of time to reach Alaska, I could drive a few hours each day and tour appealing towns, parks, and attractions. Little did I realize that two months was not much time for a wanderer.

In the past, my immediate surroundings had rarely entered my consciousness . . . I'd focused on drugs in our high schools, terrorism in Afghanistan, beheadings in Africa, or sometimes, dreams of riches and fame—seeing only what was necessary to reach my next "urgent" destination. But now, in no hurry, I kept three-by-five notecards handy in double-pocket shirts so I could stop and write. I would forget nothing.

A few hours out of Chicago, van idling at the side of a quiet road, I wrote about an Amish girl in a white cap and long-sleeved dress, pulling a red wagon carrying two small boys who looked like miniature men in wide-brimmed straw hats and suspenders. Because I took notes, I remembered the tiny town of Colby, population less than two thousand, and the mild cheese that bears its name. As I drove, I saw the road, the shops, the people, and I smelled the green growth of spring. Later, I would use the notes to write emails detailing my days and observations. Sometimes, while scribbling, I ached for all I'd missed in my distracted life in Atlanta, even on vacations.

The afternoon passed. I needed a place to sleep. Tired, I looked in my big book of campgrounds and found one nearby. I was excited, but a little anxious about spending the night in this unfamiliar way. My previous camping experience was only occasional, and never alone. Mazie and I approached the location—a small-town neighborhood, not picturesque, or even interesting—and I grimaced. I still hoped a wooded park would appear and reveal a lovely site to sleep in, but the campground was a bare parking lot on a residential hill—not what I had in mind, but it was too late to look for something else. There were a few other vans and RVs, so I certainly wasn't nervous, but I wasn't a "happy camper."

Resigned to a view of cement, I prepared to transform the van into a bedroom for the first time. I had purchased four privacy curtains, each designed for a specific section, indistinguishable from each other until fitted against the windows. The heavy gray fabric swirled around my shoulders and head as I struggled to find out which went where. I made a note to buy Velcro strips that would allow me to keep the material hanging, rolled up on their first snaps, out of the way, but ready.

After setting up my commode, the next task was to access a power source for the microwave and refrigerator, electric blanket, reading lamp, fan, and heater. A variety of grounding adaptors and converter plugs allowed me to attach everything to a campground receptacle. It looked like an infestation of snakes. Later, when the microwave and the heater were both on at once, the circuit breaker tripped. I went outside—in the half-light of dusk, in a cold drizzle, in my pajamas—to find the switch. I added a power strip to the shopping list.

The first night of my odyssey hardly matched my dreams, but the adventure had begun. I loved every problem, even as I planned the solutions. Knowing that most future sites would be lovely, I was undaunted.

With my battery-operated security alarm within reach, I slipped into bed. This alarm, unlike the kind I had at home, did not automatically connect to a security company. If someone should try to break in, this one needed human intervention. Based on the assumption that a burglar would make enough noise to wake me immediately, I would have ample time to push a button and generate a sound loud enough to wake the entire campground. Fortunately, this device was never needed. With deep satisfaction, I realized I was completely relaxed.

The TV, expensively installed in the ceiling and never used, stared at me in silent reproof—as it would every night and every morning—while I partook of the cherished ritual of words, reading delicious pages of courtroom drama, British detectives, and historical fiction. Unfortunately, these had to be purchased in physical form, books with covers—the kind with pages you could turn. And this meant that as the one I had brought with me was quickly completed, I had to find a store to purchase another.

I was as addicted to reading as I had once been to smoking. Being out of books was as intolerable to me as being hungry—and when it happened, I would get out of bed and drive to the nearest all-night convenience store to satisfy my need. Mazie knew how to find such places; night or day, we could find a book and return to the campsite without getting lost.

Although this first stop was no more than utilitarian, the bed was perfect. I was comfortable and slept soundly. My chamber pot, only one foot from my bed, served me well in the middle of the night. Liquid hand sanitizer, just inches away, allowed me the luxury of almost remaining asleep as I performed the routine two or three times each night. In the morning, I sipped microwaved tea with refrigerated cream and lay in bed until ready to dress. After folding up the potty, taking down the curtains, and pulling the plug out of the campground receptacle, I folded the curtains on the bed and left the cords on the floor. Then I shopped for the things needed to straighten my home: the Velcro to wrap each curtain and the power strip that would not only hold all of the plugs, but would also prevent me from killing power to an entire campground.

And it was time to leave this cement place.

Copper Falls State Park
Wisconsin

Colby ⊙
Wisconsin

CHAPTER 3

New Beginnings

On my second day out of Chicago, still early in May, I wandered through a few small towns and reached a real campground in Northwest Wisconsin, gray cement replaced by nature's green. With glorious spring weather, I joined hordes of RV tourists at Copper Falls State Park. Thick tree barriers divided the sites, giving each area a feeling of seclusion, but also of safety because people were on the other side of the trees. This time, turning my car into a home was simple. The curtains hung on their first snaps; all I had to do was release the Velcro, then unroll and secure the curtains to the remaining fasteners. The new power strip connected the entire van to the campground's power.

I slept soundly but awoke in these tranquil woods feeling lousy, struggling to recapture a dream. A remnant came back . . .

I'm nine, sitting at the top of the stairs with Henrietta, my live-in babysitter. I'm excited, telling her about my teacher—how pretty she is, her fancy necklace, her nice smile.

"Do you like her a lot?" she asks, staring at me with an unusually serious expression.

"Yes," I say, suddenly feeling bad about this conversation, somehow knowing that what I'm feeling isn't okay. "I think I want to go to sleep now."

I lie awake in my bed thinking Henrietta will tell my parents about our conversation, and for some reason I do not understand, this makes me uncomfortable. Other girls like our teacher a lot too, but I think my feelings are different. I worry for a while then fall asleep . . .

Fully awake, sipping tea in my van, I replayed this dream and my nine-year-old life. I know now that lots of little girls have crushes on their teachers, but I knew, even then, what I felt wasn't the same. Outwardly, I was a normal little girl, but I led a second life in my head, my thoughts filled with crushes on my teachers. The effort of silence overwhelmed me. *Damn it*, I thought. *I have to get over this.* Regrets swirled, my breathing became shallow, and the muscles above my abdomen stiffened, all so familiar—a lifetime of searching for peace and finding only turbulence.

And then another memory surfaced . . .

I'm twelve years old. It's 1957. I'm with friends, and we're riding our bikes. Mickey refers to an absent friend as "queer." I ask, "What's a queer?" He tells me, sneering and laughing: "Boys who like boys or girls who like girls." My breathing stops in midcycle; my eyes open wide and stick there. I think, Oh my God, I will never love a boy; I will never live like other people.

I have never considered this before. Now I have a name for it. I know now I'm queer. My easy childhood is over . . .

I remembered that long-ago bike ride, how the muscles in my chest and stomach tightened as if I were wearing my wide cinch-belt too tight. In the months that followed, shallow breathing and tight muscles became natural. Mental anxiety wrapped tentacles around my throat and body where they remained for more than half a century.

For the next decade, I lived one life—the queer one—in my head and the straight life in the real world. The only open homosexuals were, to our eyes, flamboyant: women who swaggered and looked like tough men and men whose hips swayed as they walked. Gay pride—not to be born for several decades—was just a gleam in their eyes.

Alone at night, I relaxed only when sleeping, terrified my parents would discover my mortifying secret: I was a freak.

Years later, longing for calm, I studied relaxation techniques and explored new modes of thought: existentialism, Taoism, Native American philosophy. These were intellectually satisfying and led to lively discussions with like-minded friends, but the knowledge never traveled from my brain down the nerves to my muscles. I was unable to translate mental truths to physical reality.

I learned to relax temporarily, but anxious or angry thoughts always returned. New upsets joined old, one after the other, like bugs drawn to an adhesive strip, refusing to die, sticking to me, wriggling and squirming.

That first morning in the Copper Falls campground, I meditated, as I always did when tense. First, deep breathing. In. Out. In . . . out . . . . *Stray thoughts disappear.* My neck relaxed, my shoulders, my back . . . muscles elastic. When fully relaxed, I imagined being on an elevator going down, deeper and deeper, to a safe room—one built in my head a long time ago to deal with a lifetime of distress.

In this meditative state, I realized I left home not only to go somewhere, but also to abandon something. I knew anger and irritation were useful only to motivate action; there is no purpose in being unhappy about something I cannot change. But ability doesn't necessarily follow knowing. I needed something else, something still elusive, to manage life's storms.

Free of past anguish, I was a passive recipient of tranquility, but wanted to achieve peace at will—not just as a chance result of my novel surroundings.

There was still plenty of time to get to Alaska. Copper Falls, with its rustic campground and rural one-street town, offered a respite. After all, the point was to enjoy the entire journey, not just Alaska. Instead of rushing to the road, I set off for a hike in the remote Wisconsin woods, carrying my pocket notecards. The notes were intended for email material, but they served another purpose. Writing kept me focused on sparkling rapids, spectacular waterfalls, and deep, rock-walled gorges. On returning to my campsite, my old thinking habits took over—again—emphasizing the sharp divide between my internal and external lives. My personal homunculus, an annoying little woman living in my head, pulled out her hammer and began to pound. She reminds me of the myriad of things I wish I had done differently . . .

Dad is declining; Mom does everything. He stands close to her, watching, wanting to help, but he can only do jobs with a single task. He can't remember or plan ahead. He hopes for an assignment. I think of a way to have him set the table.

Handing him three plates, I say, "Dad, would you please put these on the table?"

He sets them on the table and looks up at me expectantly.

"Now the napkins, please."

"Where, dear?"

"Like this, Dad."

He carefully places the three napkins to the left of our plates and smiles proudly, watching me put one fork on a napkin. He takes the other two from my outstretched hand, lips set, concentrating. He completes this task and nods in satisfaction . . .

As I prepare my breakfast—a microwaved ham sandwich and hot tea—and set my mug, a napkin, and paper plate on the picnic table, I think about my dad. These thoughts often come to me when I'm doing mindless tasks, but not so much as I focus on my surroundings. He was a loving father, giving his life for his family. He also opened his wallet and his heart to every worthy cause that presented itself. As Alice Sebold wrote in *The Almost Moon*, "Dementia, as it descends, has a way of revealing the core of the person affected by it." And, through it all, my parents' basic sweetness prevailed.

But when I had visited them, I didn't stay long.

Dad is near the end of his life; he lies in a nursing home bed with pneumonia. Mom is with him all day, every day. Her life is about him, all about him. Our conversations are focused on his incessant decline. She is highly anxious and desperately sad.

He won't walk. A physical therapist comes daily, but he refuses to get out of bed. When I arrive, I help him to a sitting position. Then Mom and I help him to move his legs, one at a time, until he's positioned on the side of the bed, legs hanging down. Mom takes his right arm and I take the left to keep him from falling; his feet slide to the floor, and he grabs the walker I've placed in front of him. He clamps his teeth together and takes a step, and then another. We all leave his room and, one painful step after another, walk the hall. I see a trickle of liquid running down Dad's leg. He has no idea he's peeing. Mom runs for a rag and follows us, wiping the floor. We do this every day for a week, but after I return to Atlanta he never walks again.

I leave Mom alone with him and return to my life, trying to forget their pain.

In this last year of his life, Mom is nervous, very nervous, and makes many little mistakes. My siblings and I think this is because she's watching her lifelong companion fall into ruin. But no. It's her turn now, the beginning of her dementia.

After my father dies, we know. When she visits me and doesn't know whether she is in Atlanta or Chicago, and asks if she should kiss the driver who drops us at the kiss-ride station, I try to deny it, but I know.

She declines and moves to an assisted living facility. When I visit, I try to find ways to entertain her. She once loved to paint my nails, so I buy her a paint-by-numbers set and we do it together. I look up at her and see that set of the jaw, that jutting lower lip Dad used to help him set the table. It's her turn to try to hold on each day to whatever remains of herself.

It's unbearable to watch her eyes, opened wide and frightened, as she tries to figure out how to put on her shoes. I repeat the answers to the same questions, over and over, and too often, I lose patience. She is still physically present, but we can no longer converse. The Mom of just a few years ago is gone.

And I live with the ever-present fear that this is my future . . .

Dementia has a way of testing the tolerance of even the kindest people. And I was hardly in that category. The effort it took to be serene with my parents, each in their turn, was so great that I often behaved poorly . . .

I'm staying in Mom's room in the assisted living home. At five thirty in the morning, a caregiver arrives, enters the room without knocking, and then shouts, "Wakey wakey!"

"Is this how you wake her every morning?" I yell, jumping from my bed. "What a terrible way to wake up! You can't keep doing this to my poor mom." And I keep going until I realize I'm behaving like an ass. The surprised caregiver stands there, mouth slightly open; Mom is trembling.

The caregiver leaves and my mom, still tremulous, comforts me. "I hate the way they wake me. Thank you for telling her. I really appreciate it. But darling," she adds, shivering, "next time could you do it without yelling?"

Often, when my mind wandered over the past, the hammer-wielding maniac in my head pounded out disturbing memories. This journey was providing a clearer awareness of how I allowed her to dominate quiet moments. I had only glimpsed the fresh buds of spring and water gleaming in sunlight and briefly heard the sound of waterfalls. Now I returned to my old habits: re-living countless mistakes, a life lived imperfectly, the past haunting the present, my notecards mostly blank. These thoughts not only drowned out the sounds of nature and haunted my present, but have always distracted me from the beautiful and good.

But as Alexander McCall Smith said while writing about the sky in Botswana, "Out in the open, under such a sky as this, misdeeds [are] reduced to their natural proportions—small, mean things that [can] be faced quite openly, sorted, and folded away." And indeed, with this reminder from a favorite author, I found myself able to focus on this setting in this, my current world. I stood still and looked around me. As my surroundings swelled in my consciousness, the importance of my history diminished. The habit of dwelling in the past was deeply ingrained, but I had recently experienced days of calm. I could use my current freedom, gorgeous surroundings, and the notecards, to regain peace. The homunculus would return, but I now had tools to deal with her, the most powerful being awareness of the habit. For many years I heard the instruction, "Be in the here and now." In Copper Falls, I began to understand it.

I returned to my campsite and began to prepare my supper—a tuna sandwich—not noticing a white-tailed deer relaxing under my picnic table. I stood and saw her looking at me, absorbing my presence, staying with me as I ate, silent except for her soft breathing. She wasn't waiting for food; she was resting, graceful even in repose, her fur golden in the waning light.

My first thought—that I was sharing my home with her—was replaced with the certainty that she was allowing me to share hers. Huge brown eyes gazed at me unblinkingly, so gentle I could imagine she loved me. There's hunting in these Wisconsin woods, but my deer felt safe with me—and I with her.

Night falls early in the north woods. As the sun began to sink, I heard the sorrowful song of loons, loud with lengthy cries like wild laughter. Settled in my van with windows open and reading light shining on my treasured pages, I heard sounds unknown in enclosed, air-conditioned spaces: the clicking of crickets, howls of wild creatures, passionate music of loons, and soft wind combined to define the country night. This was not a familiar world, and if I had been outside the safety of the van, those sounds would have frightened me. But in my hard-shelled home, I felt a part of creation, yet safe from a rattler's bite or a grizzly's claws.

Sweet peace, how rare this was for me.

Solway •.•..............
Minnesota **Bemidji** ...•.........
Minnesota ◎**Copper Falls State Park**
Wisconsin

CHAPTER 4

Woman on a Ladder

The next night, still early in May of 2004, I slept at a lakeside campsite in eastern Minnesota. When I awoke, my first thought was that if I didn't get to Alaska by early July, there wouldn't be enough time to tour leisurely before winter made the roads impassable. I wanted to drive all day to get some miles behind me.

A hurried breakfast and then I got on the road—no time to waste.

There were no signs pointing to the campground exit, but Mazie Grace put a map on the dashboard with a symbol showing the relation of my car to the road and said in a helpful monotone, "Proceed to the highlighted route—then the guidance will start."

But I wasn't feeling well, coughing, sniffling, and breathing through my dry mouth. Forty-five minutes later, a Hampton Inn appeared on the edge of Lake Bemidji—comfort beckoned. My plan to drive all day disintegrated, replaced by an irresistible urge to pamper myself. The van, as if on its own volition, drove into the parking lot. I sighed in acceptance, requested a lake view, and registered. Opening the door to my room, I faced a wall-to-wall, floor-to-ceiling window overlooking the lake. And almost as striking were the prints on the walls depicting the local north woods of Minnesota.

This place was perfect, and I could use a several-day stay to cure this cold, but my budget didn't allow it. Though my net worth was in the plus column, I was far from wealthy. When I was young, my parents tried to teach me to manage money, but it seemed like we had an unlimited supply—and I spent whatever was available . . .

It's Charity Day at my grade school. We're about to divide my class into two teams. The team that donates the most money wins. My allowance is ten dollars a week, and my purse is always full. Just as a coach wants the best athletes, the fund-raising captain wants the best donators. I'm always the first selected for this event—my team wins every year.

The captain collects the first round of donations, and the totals are tallied on the board. If we're behind, I just pull out more money for the next round. I don't run out.

Dad owns four large furniture, television, and appliance stores. He advertises on TV; his delivery trucks run all over the city. One of the manufacturers gives annual awards to the companies that sell the most TVs. He refuses to take a profit on items he sells to friends, charging only the wholesale price. I learn the art of giving from his example. And yet, Dad's company sells enough to win eight tickets for a South American cruise; he and Mom invite the top performing salesman, his wife, and two other couples to join them as their guests.

Mom and Dad want their children to have more than just things. They sign us up for lessons in everything: horseback riding, ballet, piano, dramatics, swimming. Thanks to dramatic lessons, I win an oratory contest, but I'm a pathetic piano student. In ballet class, when the teacher says, "Down on floor," I misunderstand and sit on the polished wood. Everyone laughs. I take the lessons but don't always excel. My sister Donna is better at piano and more graceful on the dance floor. There is no parental upset when we want to quit one in which we do poorly. They want only to provide opportunity.

Mom teaches us to send valentines to everyone in our home rooms. About a hundred kids—all the kids we know from school, temple, and the neighborhood— are invited every year to a Halloween party. I love to watch Dad supervise as we bob for apples, his efforts causing his usually neat hair to fall on his sweaty forehead.

He donates a giant television to my school, the first one many kids have seen. Always wanting something, I spend most of my allowance, every week. Everyone knows we have money . . .

A few years later, Dad would lose everything. The year was 1955, and bankruptcy was not accepted as it is today. It was almost as bad as homosexuality. With few exceptions, their social life disappeared along with their money. After bankruptcy, old friends loaned him money to buy a small hardware store. He did pay for my out-of-state tuition in undergraduate school—looking back, I don't know how he did this. I had a part-time job to help with my other expenses, and in graduate school, I always had a clinical fellowship providing enough to pay tuition and the basics. Although he never complained during the undergraduate years, I'm now sure he was happy I supported myself through the advanced degrees. I learned to live on whatever came in, but often had to borrow five dollars near the end of the month. In those days, that was enough for a full week's groceries.

I drove the short distance to downtown Bemidji: street parking, no meters. At a glance, the parked van looked like any suburban mini-van, so I attracted no special attention. I walked to several art galleries, college coffee shops, and a live theater. Even that short distance tired me, so I stopped at the Uptown Café and sipped a cappuccino while scanning paintings with accompanying philosophical statements on peace, loss, and friendship.

All over town, campus sculptors had large pieces on display—a shock. Didn't artists live in big cities or at famous universities with discerning patrons and appreciative pedestrians? I had a lot to learn.

My nose was stuffed. I pressed one tissue after another to my face. After only eleven days on the road, I wanted to rest—in a real bed, in a room that wouldn't move in the morning. But this lovely hotel was too expensive for more than a night or two. A drive around town, looking for a cheap bed-and-breakfast, was unproductive.

Wondering what to do, I parked and walked into a renovated building with a two-story atrium, antique shops, and art galleries on each floor. A middle-aged woman stood on a tall ladder painting a mural of the local woods. It covered the long wall, twenty feet high. It was so real I felt as though I had wandered into the painting and found someone touching up the leaves.

Though attractive, the artist obviously didn't put appearance high on her list of priorities. Her hair looked as if she had been standing under a ceiling fan—and makeup was the last thing on her mind. She looked down, saw me watching, and smiled.

"Hi," she said, and after a pause continued, "Shopping for art or just looking around? I'm Maureen, by the way."

"I'm Barilyn," I mumble, my cold preventing the nasal consonants. "Just browsing." I thought she was going to try to sell me something. She continued painting as we chatted about the university and about this building—an artists' co-op.

She turned to me, brush aloft, and asked, "How do you happen to be in Bemidji? Have someone in college here?"

"Doe," I said. "I'm actually on an eighteen-bunth trip. I left home three weeks ago. I wanna get to Alaska by early July. That'll leave six weeks with passable roads. If you don't get out by bid-August, you cad get stuck there all witter."

"Are you enjoying the gorgeous weather we have now?"

"I'd be enjoying it bore if I could breathe through my dose, I'm looking for a good bed and breakfast. Do you doe of one?"

She shook her head. Then she said, "I have an extra room at my farm in Solway. It's just outside Bemidji. Would you like to be my guest for a few days?"

I was stunned and uncomfortable with an offer from someone I just met. I declined. We exchanged a few more pleasantries before I picked up her brochure and left—still sick and with a too-expensive place to sleep, but touched by her offer of hospitality.

Returning to the Hampton Inn, I read the signature on the lobby paintings—Maureen O'Brien, the woman on the ladder. The prints in my room, the ones I admired earlier, were hers as well. Her phone number was on the brochure, so I called and left a message with her son saying how much I enjoyed her art in my hotel. She returned the call and invited me to lunch at her farm. This time I accepted.

In the van, Mazie said, "Follow the road for twelve miles." And fifteen minutes later, "Turn left in a quarter of a mile." Mazie easily found the farm and the house, guiding me sweetly on these country roads to my bucolic destination and generous host.

An artist and a real farm! I had only been to one other working farm . . .

I'm a graduate student invited to a housewarming party at the new home of one of my professors. Her husband, Doc, has given me an idea for a gift by complaining about mowing the full acre of lawn.

I search the countryside and find a scrubby, dry farm with an obvious he-goat for sale, put a pretty ribbon around his neck, and bring him to their garden party. Well-dressed older ladies stare as I lead the well-endowed goat down the long driveway.

Doc breaks the silence, saying, "Look at the goat on those balls!"

Beyond this brief pastoral experience, I had seen distant cows from the highway and pigs in a petting zoo, but that was about it.

At Maureen's farm, goats and horses wandered near the fence; chickens clucked in a nearby shed. Ducks and turkeys ambled around the yard. Pear, apple, and plum trees promised edible fruit. The large garden allowed her, as she wrote in her brochure, "to enjoy all aspects of planting and nurturing and harvesting food from the land."

Her studio, in a building behind the house, overflowed with finished art on walls and art in progress on tables. Our lunch was in the kitchen nook. On every wall was an open window, bird feeders outside of each.

Before we ate, Maureen dragged a sack of seeds to the wall, reached into the bag and filled the feeders. While I watched plump wrens and bluebirds with their bright blue wings and tan breasts fluttering around their meal, my hostess repeated her invitation to stay a few days. This time, I accepted.

We talked for hours that first day, strangers sharing intimacies. I told her about my sexual orientation, thinking it was important before spending the night. She listened intently, but seemed to absorb the information without judgment.

Years ago, when still in hiding, I occasionally failed to mention my sexual orientation until a friendship was fully developed. By then it was uncomfortable to find the right time and the right words. Fortunately, my instincts prevented me from ever becoming close to someone who recoiled in horror—but I never knew for sure until the subject came up.

I was in my mid-sixties as I sat at Maureen's kitchen table. It seemed odd that I would think about whether to tell, or when. But given my history, perhaps it wasn't so remarkable . . .

I'm thirteen, sitting in the backseat of the car with my siblings. Mom and Dad are up front. We're going out to Sunday dinner in downtown Chicago.

We pass the corner of Dearborn and Division, an intersection some people call Queerborn and Perversion. Two boys cross the street, arms around each other as we sit at a light. They walk with swaying hips; one grins and waves at a passerby.

"Wouldn't you hate to be the parents of one of those fairies? Always afraid for them?" my father asks Mom. She adds, "What a horrible life. On the streets at night, no family life. Their parents must be so worried and sad."

I worry about my future. I'll never love a man. I'll be a spinster. But there's no way I can live the odd life of the few fairies and queers I've seen. And once again, I think that my parents can never know . . .

Maureen told her story, a life pockmarked with unpleasant events. Her mother left when she was a child. The father of her first three children asked for a divorce. Her second husband gave her two more children. She left him after several difficult years and experienced the satisfaction of creating a life for herself and her five offspring. Her art was not only her passion, but also her livelihood.

While Maureen worked to support her family, she used everything she'd learned to counsel women in challenging marriages. Whether she was talking or listening, she looked directly at me, eyes wide open and soft. I think anyone would want to unload—and to hear what she had to say.

Watching her paint and feed the birds, I would not have guessed she suffered. Maureen showed remarkable ability to accept whatever came her way, loving life in spite of its intermittent, appalling cruelties.

I asked her how she coped.

"Painting feeds a part of me that nothing else can. It's nourishing beyond any material thing. And I find great solace in my woods—the forest always provides a sense of balance that gives me calm."

Happiness is not always possible, but acceptance of reality, and the resultant peace, has always been the choice for Maureen. She was my teacher, the first on this journey.

I spent a week with her, just enough time to fully recover from my cold. One afternoon we went to a barnlike store. The only resemblance to a Walmart or even a Home Depot was its size. This store was functional. Period. It sold everything one might need on a farm.

Our mission: to buy two-day-old peeping chicks to raise for food. For me, it was like going to look at a new litter of baby kittens, tiny and sweet. Maureen had to be of two minds: baby chicks were adorable, but they were also part of the business of food production.

Back at the farm, Maureen put these little peeps in a warming box in her shed. She was their mama now. Like all babies, they examined everything—and then plopped down to sleep. Maureen, with the help of friends, would later do her own butchering.

My groceries have always come from the store, foods far removed from their origins. At the meat counter, when I would look at poultry in Styrofoam trays and plastic wrappers, I didn't think of chickens as recently living, adorable creatures, but rather as I would a can of beans. Those few days with Maureen taught me what happened before chickens got to the store, the activities that brought food to my table.

My brother Jeff called one afternoon as I sat in Maureen's kitchen. When I told him where I was, he asked, "How can you trust her? Why does she trust you?" I said I was learning to have faith in my instincts.

After we hung up, I looked at my new friend, puttering around the kitchen, and I asked myself, *Do I have to leave home to connect with strangers?*

As I was drifting off to sleep that night, I remembered Jeff as a little boy . . .

Jeff is playing in the tub, splashing water on the floor. Mom comes in, sees the mess, and gets mad. Mom and Dad don't hit us. When they're annoyed, they tell us and then explain why what we did was bad.

This time though, she picks up a towel and snaps it at him. He jumps out of the tub and begins to run around the house, naked and dripping water as he escapes her menacing towel. I watch, trying to be inconspicuous.

Mom catches up with him as he cowers, soaking wet and shivering, dead-ended in a corner of the dining room. She stares for a moment . . . then bursts out laughing and walks away, towel skimming the floor . . .

Mom and Dad didn't believe in spankings . . . a disapproving look followed by silence was enough. This towel-snapping incident was the only time either of them came close. How could I ever think of telling these kind and loving people that I would never marry, never give them grandchildren, but instead live what they would consider a fearful life.

Maureen used my visit as an excuse to take a rare few days off.

She took me to meet her eighty-six-year-old friend, Amos, who lived on a lake, in a log cabin owned by three generations of his family. His one-room guest cottage was the model for one of Maureen's paintings at the Hampton Inn.

Amos prepared a picnic lunch, and we ate moist, flavorful chicken sandwiches at a wooden table on the banks of his lake. Then back in the house, I saw another of Maureen's murals, this one covering an entire wall and depicting Amos's woods.

He spoke of his wife, with whom he'd shared a long and close relationship. She had died a few years earlier, leaving him alone. She was a master quilter, and he kept a room dedicated to her work. As he showed me a few of her quilts hanging on the walls, he caressed the fabrics. Opening a book displaying all of her work, he turned the pages with care as he told me about her and their life together, explaining that they were a perfect mix—an artist and a scientist.

Amos had been an engineer working as an independent consultant in solar and wind energy in the world of ecology, long before anyone worried about global warming. He purified water in Third World countries and developed energy-efficient systems for heat and pumping water from deep wells. This was a man with a lifetime commitment to alternative energy. I thought about his choice to live his retirement years in a serene setting, far from the bustle of city life or even small town activity. He needed only himself and his memories. When we met, he lived alone on his lake in the woods, his genius known only to a few.

Maureen wanted me to see the headwaters of the Mississippi in Itasca State Park. She told me to dress in something I wouldn't mind getting wet and dirty.

We went first to the rental dock where a tanned fellow brought us two kayaks. We gripped his hand and cautiously stepped into our personal boats and settled onto our cushions. We could have gone faster, but the idea was to be in the water, feel the slight breeze, and look at the sky—a sky so pale that it merged seamlessly with the nearly transparent clouds above a thick horizon of dark green trees.

The lake flows over a twenty-foot rock formation where the headwaters of the Mississippi—only three-feet deep—begin their more than two-thousand mile journey to the Gulf of Mexico. When these waters reach Wisconsin, they widen to four miles across, and near New Orleans, they swell to two hundred feet deep.

We reached the spot where lake ends and river begins. A crowd of barefoot adults and children played in the water and walked on the slippery rocks connecting the two. Like everyone else, I took off my shoes and began the short walk. The kids scrambled across, reaching the other side in seconds. The parents were more sedate, but still nimble. After the first few steps, realizing my balance on the wet surface was inadequate, I got down on all fours and crawled.

I never want to miss an experience merely because the years have changed my body. I can still find a way to navigate a few rocks.

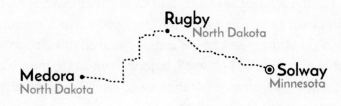

CHAPTER 5

Good Sleep to You

Maureen offered a wonderful transition between a life surrounded by people and the solitary life on the road. She gifted me with her small painting of the rocks at the mouth of the Mississippi—a poignant reminder of my visit. And she asked to join my family and friends on my list of email recipients. I left her home ready to enjoy nature and my independent travels. During the next few months, I met people only to share an event or a meal, making no new friends until I settled in for the winter.

After leaving Maureen in late May, I meandered across western Minnesota and eastern North Dakota on modest US 2, accompanied by Mazie and entertained by XM Radio, everything familiar drifting farther and farther away. Mazie could take me anywhere in this unknown land; I could follow any whim with no fear of being lost. Only a few years earlier, the only available resource would have been silent maps, strewn around the passenger seat and floor.

About sixteen hundred miles from my Atlanta roots, I approached Rugby, North Dakota, the geographic center of North America, population less than three thousand. A fifteen-foot-tall rock monument, located in the parking lot of a gas station, marked this distinction.

It once stood beside Highway 2, but the town had to move it when they widened the highway. Inhabitants of Rugby care only that the monument remains in their town.

I grew up in Chicago, far from Rugby in size and customs. What would it have been like to grow up gay in sleepy Rugby in the 1940s and 1950s? I would certainly have felt I was the only person to love someone of my own sex and would have been even more frightened of discovery than in Chicago. But, in addition to my well-guarded secrets, I had another problem—one that needed big city medical care . . .

I'm in the seventh grade, sitting in the first seat of the first row, the seat reserved by the teacher for the best reader in the class. In other classes, seating is arranged by height or in alphabetical order. I am the shortest in the class, and my last name begins with B, so I always sit in this seat. I'm writing an essay about a story we've just read and trying to spell "drive," an easy word— but I can't. And something is wrong with the vision in my right eye. The image is blurry on the right. I blink, but it doesn't help. My face begins to tingle, then the fingers of my right hand. Within a few minutes, the sensation crawls up my hand and arm, tightening as if I have slept on it funny. My right side is going to sleep.

I slide from my desk and walk toward Mrs. Peterson. The tight tingling sensation goes down my body until the entire right side is numb. I can't think clearly. When I try to speak, my words are nonsense.

Someone calls my parents, and I go home, crawl into bed and wait. Within a few hours, the symptoms recede, but I have a terrible pain on the left side of my head, unbearable for one full day before it disappears.

A month later, it happens again—approximately once a month for a year— until our doctor suggests hospitalization for tests. I'm relieved they will find out what's wrong with me and fix it. They X-ray my head and take blood samples. They tell me nothing. I read and eat and wait.

Then a nurse puts me in a wheelchair, and I roll down a long corridor to a room where a technician tells me she will give me an EEG exam. This is meaningless to me. I see a dark machine and a set of thick wires. She puts something circular on the end of each wire, and then she sticks each on my head. Soon I look like Medusa, a monster from the Greek mythology I'm studying in school, wires like snakes traveling from every part of my head to the machine. They're reading my mind, I think in horror. Now they will know everything, all of my thoughts, my secrets.

But all they know is I probably have a form of migraine.

I'm released from the hospital at ten in the morning with a prescription for codeine to take when the nightmarish numbing recurs, followed by the terrifying inability to talk and the blinding headache. But my secrets are safe.

At four in the afternoon I get dressed for a boy-girl party at a friend's house. We sit in a circle and play spin-the-bottle. One of the boys spins it, and when it stops, he kisses the girl closest to where the bottle's neck is pointing. Then that girl spins, and she repeats the process with the boy selected by the bottle.

I don't mind kissing boys—but I'm still in love with Mrs. Peterson . . .

Leaving tiny Rugby, I shook myself out of this reverie and returned to my new life. I had been gone long enough to know this trip wasn't only a vacation, but a new way of existing. My van was no longer just a place to sleep and wake up. It was my home, and though tiny, it felt like a protective cocoon.

In normal driving, it would have taken me three days to reach western Minnesota and the Dakotas from Atlanta. Instead, I had been gone for three weeks—and a few reincarnations. I continued to remember upsets and regrets, but the associated ache was receding—as flames in a fireplace turn to embers when you stop adding fuel.

My mind and body were taking new journeys . . . journeys that encouraged me into tranquility.

Medora, North Dakota, a frontier town abandoned in the early 1900s and restored a half-century later, was my next stop. With its wooden boardwalks and old-timey shops, Medora provided the first of many opportunities to travel into the past. Transported to another era, without a personal history, I could walk in the footsteps of those who lived far from an expressway, an airport, a hospital. I was exploring their shops and streets, pretending I belonged.

If I had been speeding down the road, focused on my destination, I would have missed Medora and Rugby and all the little towns represented in white letters on green signs. Life has gone by that way.

Slow down, slow down, I told myself.

My ability to find scenic campgrounds improved. Near Medora, I camped in a valley between two clay-and-sandstone buttes. I closed the curtains, seeing nothing but blackness until, after several hours of good sleep, I walked outside to see first light spreading across a backdrop of tan and orange.

An hour later, in the campground office, I found a poster for a "pitchfork" fondue dinner and *The Medora Musical* in an outdoor amphitheater. My experience with fondue had been the big-city kind—a restaurant where a maître d' shows you to a cloth-covered table with a bowl of heated oil in an elegant chafing dish. Raw food arrives in bite-sized pieces, ready for you to spear with silver skewers and drop in the hot oil to cook exactly to your taste.

With this history, I could hardly imagine "pitchfork" fondue.

While signing up for a seat on a van that would take me to the show and fondue, a pleasant couple told me they were going to the same event and invited me to join them. I don't recall their names or what they looked like. They were just company for the evening to share the unique food preparation and the humor and skill onstage. These were the first of many with whom I would spend a few hours, conversing briefly before moving on in different directions.

We arrived at an outdoor picnic area called Tjaden Terrace, where bare wooden tables seated a dozen people each. A soft breeze floated by as the sun set, changing the colors of the surrounding buttes. The evening began with the fondue, prepared frontier style. Humongous metal pots on the ground replaced the dainty bowls of oil, actual pitchforks supplanted the slim skewers I had known, and thick steaks took the place of tiny pieces of meat. Much as one would delicately place a graceful fork into a small bowl of hot oil, cowboys stabbed several steaks on each pitchfork and submerged the tines into the huge pots of bubbling grease.

As we feasted on steaks, baked potatoes, beans, coleslaw, and double-chocolate brownies, we listened to live music performed by cast members—an appetizer for the production we would see later.

After dinner, we descended on a steep escalator to the Burning Hills Amphitheater. Hundreds of steeply pitched seats looked down on a stage nestled in the valley between the buttes, the real sky as backdrop.

In the middle of the show, two elk wandered onto a hill beyond the stage as the entertainment continued below, unpaid extras beneath a sky changing from crisp evening blue to royal blue to deep navy.

My companions and I returned to the campground in the van, speaking about the unique food, the uncommon amphitheater, and the enjoyable show. When I returned to my tiny domicile, I first thought it was sad to spend such an unusual evening with strangers, but later reasoned that some of those with whom we spend time always remain strangers. We only speak our true thoughts and feelings when we are confident they are acceptable to our companions. Only a few send signals that they wish to know us and be known.

Good night—good sleep I wish for you,
my fellow wanderers.
We stop our song and part our ways—so what
if we never meet again…
—DAN ANDERSSON, Epilogue in Posthumous poems, 1920

CHAPTER 6

Badlands

I left Medora on June 20. July 1 was coming up fast and Fairbanks, Alaska, was still twenty-six hundred miles away—about eight days of steady driving. *No more playing around, Marilyn. It's time to get to work and drive.*

But soon after I got on the road, I hit the famed Badlands. Badlands? I had always heard this was a picturesque part of the country but never stopped to think about its pejorative label. *How could this gorgeous land be "bad"?*

At a gas stop, I asked the cashier about the name. She thought it might be because it's so hot in summer and so cold in winter. Customers, overhearing, added that the bright sun on bedrock can cause temporary blindness and men have been known to disappear while attempting to cross this land. My guidebook told me the Lakota called it "Mako Sico," which means "the land that is bad."

I chose not to resist. Giving up my agenda, I drove into historic Theodore Roosevelt National Park—and gasped at the sight of this vast, stark wilderness, all vegetation burned away ages ago, leaving only the exotic landscape and wild colors. In these Badlands, I saw a panorama of ragged peaks and corkscrew gorges, curved roads twisting through buttes and mesas that changed from black to blue then orange and magenta as the sun moved in the sky.

The source of this beauty was only erosion, volcanic ash, petrified wood, wind, and rain—together sculpting and painting sand and clay to thrill the soul.

Having given up my plans for the day, I went into nearby Makoshika State Park, a sanctuary created to preserve this exquisitely harsh wilderness. Here I saw more buttes, even larger and more jagged. *Aha.* Makoshika—the Lakota "Mako Sico," land that is bad. Some say these are the most impressive of the Badlands. Some geologists think an ancient grassfire removed all growth, leaving only ethereal boulders, with wildflowers and evergreens providing glorious flashes of color.

Sixty miles down the road, I chanced upon Glendive, Montana, population around five thousand. It had been a long time since I drove through anything larger. Most buildings were one or two stories, providing only essential services and shops. Yet the four-lane main street testified that this was a town with some traffic.

An even smaller oasis appeared on a road between Glendive and Fort Peck, my next stop on the get-to-Alaska itinerary. A building, indicating food and shopping, appeared like a mirage. Once again, I couldn't resist—didn't want to resist—stopping for refreshment of body and soul. It was not on a plan, not even on a map, but appeared suddenly out of nowhere. Alaska was a destination, somewhere down the road. This was here, right now.

On the way to a café in the back, I passed beautifully displayed cattle medicines near designer clothing. A decorative fountain added to the appeal. While waiting for a tuna melt, I studied this unique shop with everything needed by local farmers and ranchers, not haphazardly strewn on tables and available for expedient shopping, but presented to please the eye. No plastic-wrapped sandwiches, but rather gourmet meats and breads. The owner of this market had obvious respect for his or her neighbors and a belief in the value of beauty in everyday life.

Unusual, in fact unique, these stops added excitement to the long moments of driving. Like an oasis in the desert, to avoid them felt risky; they were necessary for the continuation of the journey.

I had never heard of Fort Peck, Montana, but soon learned it's far from unknown. The first cover of *Life* magazine, published three years before I was born, featured a photo of the three-and-a-half-mile Fort Peck Dam, built by government workers during the Great Depression. Established in the late 1800s as a fur-trading post, it swelled to a boomtown of ten thousand in the 1930s. Now, the one-gate local airport welcomes travelers from neighboring states and Canada intent on seeing not only one of the largest man-made lakes in the world, but also to enjoy the fine tourist amenities.

I stayed in the vintage Fort Peck Hotel, a wooden structure on the National Register of Historic Places. Of its thirty-three rooms, only one was still available. Since it lacked an en suite bathroom, my portable toilet, now closed to look like a large plastic attaché, would have to serve. As I sauntered through the early-twentieth-century lobby, swinging my "briefcase," I was secure in the knowledge I would not have to toddle down the hall and greet other disheveled residents in the bathroom.

The hotel's casual restaurant offered both fine dining and comfort food. My dinner was a piece of homemade apple pie. Not since my mother rolled her piecrust had I tasted such an exquisite dessert. The fruit was hot—cooked, but not mushy—and with just enough sauce to cover each chunk of apple. The crust was flaky and lightly browned. The perfect remedy for this road-weary traveler . . .

I'm ten. I come home from school, open the door, and walk into our large kitchen to see Mom wearing a flowered housedress while standing by our Formica-topped table. She dips her hands in and out of a bowl of flour and sprinkles it on a glass cutting board, preparing to knead dough for a pie crust.

Evelyn, the woman who comes in daily to help Mom with housework, is a few feet away ironing one of Dad's shirts. She stops to spray water on the collar before giving it the last touch. She joined us when I was two and Donna was a newborn. Jeff was born five years later. As they work, Mom and Evelyn listen companionably to One Man's Family, *a favorite radio soap opera. I feel welcome and know that I'm wanted.*

Evelyn turns off the radio. I sit at the table, and Mom joins me, asking about my day. She listens intently as I tell her about art class with Mrs. Peterson and my latest painting, a watercolor of our house. I wish I could tell her how I feel about Mrs. Peterson.

Yesterday, Mom, the room-mother for my fifth-grade class, brought homemade chocolate chip cookies to school. Last night, there were ten couples at our house for a dinner party. Tonight, she will preside over the synagogue's B'nai B'rith meeting. She can't wait for her presidency to end. She likes to serve, but isn't sufficiently assertive for an executive position. The other women elected her because she's well-known, pretty, and popular. The Mahjong club will meet tomorrow in our living room.

No matter how busy she is, she always makes time for her children. Only the dark shadow of my secret mars my life . . .

Mom had gone from activity to activity, caring for her family and community. She continued until it was time for others to care her.

When I considered what to do with my evening, I stumbled upon a flyer for the Fort Peck Summer Theater, which was a short distance from the hotel. While government workers built the dam and lodging, others created this venue to entertain those who were constructing the dam.

Unemployed artisans designed the handcrafted appointments, blown-glass lighting, and massive hand-hewn beams. Though intended to be temporary, no one has ever been willing to tear it down. Instead, the Fort Peck Fine Arts Council was formed to care for and restore the building to its original splendor. It was reborn as a summer theater.

The show that night was *The King and I*. Waiting for it to begin, I looked around at the enthusiastic audience who filled the huge auditorium. My jeans and light sweater harmonized with the casual clothes worn by other spectators—an occasional sports jacket the dressiest. Couples spoke softly to each other, everyone well-mannered and at ease in a theater setting.

A cultured audience, talented performers, and creative costumes, lighting, and sets—a surprising and perfect evening in a town I never knew existed.

As my evening ended, I returned to my historic hotel and reflected on what I'd done in the last few weeks. I'd left Atlanta for Alaska, but the thrill had been in the wandering—gorgeous scenery, quality entertainment, delicious food, and unexpected towns, like tiny Rugby and Medora, with their irresistible pull into the past. Drawn by instinct, there was no reason to pass these villages and race down the road.

I stood looking at my room, so unlike a Holiday Inn, shocked to realize that this was what I left home for. Planning a trip around a destination was an ingrained habit—not what I wanted now. I had lived my life from one objective to the next: small tasks such as projects due, meetings to attend, and larger ones, like *be in Boston on Tuesday* defined my minutes, days and years.

Alaska was another destination, another responsibility, another deadline.

No. No more.

CHAPTER 7

Not All Who Wander Are Lost

As I drove toward Glacier National Park, I realized my hair needed a cut, my clothing needed a washer and dryer, and I needed supplies. Since I rarely cooked, sandwiches were a mainstay, so I was almost out of bread, lunch meat, and peanut butter. The light bulb in my lamp had burned out, and a few new books would be nice. The little town of Glasgow was on the way, and now, with no deadlines, I took advantage of the local facilities.

Routine tasks in a strange place become part of the adventure. At home, I knew where to find any service; here I would have to search or ask. And once there, the atmosphere would be less slick—far homier than in my familiar big city.

A short drive down the main drag brought me to a small hair salon where a well-coifed woman said, "Be with you in about five minutes." While waiting, I wondered if she would be as stubborn as most Atlanta stylists—beauticians who did whatever they wanted, no matter what I asked for.

She returned and invited me to the sink for a wash.

"Oh, no thanks," I said. "It's clean, and these hard sinks hurt my neck."

"Okay then," she said, waving me into her chair with one hand while flipping open a pink shawl with the other. "And how would you like it cut?"

I told her about the idiosyncrasies of my hair and how to flatten my cowlick—and hoped she was listening. Then I sat back, trying not to worry, trying not to watch, and reflecting instead on my next stop.

Ten minutes later, she blew it dry, then turned my chair around and handed me a mirror. The cowlick lay flat; the fringe on my neck was perfect—a great cut—and only ten dollars! In Atlanta it would have been at least fifty.

The laundromat wasn't far. While I folded my clothes, I asked the attendant about the nearest grocery store. He gave me directions to my last errand in Glasgow. And then, ready to move along, I continued west on Highway 2.

Two and a half hours later, I stopped for coffee and found another unexpected treasure—the remains of a buried town. In my earlier days, I would have sipped my coffee with no awareness of anything but the cup, cream, sugar, and spoon. Even if I noticed my surroundings, the time would have prevented a stop. But now, I could explore anything that caught my attention. And Havre, Montana, definitely drew me in.

When a 1904 fire destroyed this town, all of the businesses had adjoining basements. As building supplies were unavailable, shopkeepers moved everything that hadn't burned into this underground area and re-opened for business. For many years, a shopper could walk down the stairs and then go from one dirt-walled store to the next—dentist, bakery, pharmacy, soda fountain, butcher, and more—never returning to the street above.

As the town gradually moved back aboveground, much of the equipment and furnishings remained entombed below—now open for tourists to visit an earlier century.

The dentist's chair looked a bit like a torture seat and the baker's oven was built into the wall. If you didn't see the handlebar mustaches and leather suspenders on the costumed actors, you might think the oven was a microwave.

In another portion of this subterranean town was a dormitory built for Chinese laborers. Overhead, a rectangle of muted light from glass blocks imbedded in the sidewalk illuminated this unusual underground chamber, the gentle glow softening ugly living conditions.

Railroad moguls brought the Chinese to Havre to lay miles of tracks needed for ever-expanding transport of people and goods. Because white workers persecuted Asians, the town forced them to live—segregated from the provincial attitudes of the white citizenry—beneath the streets in the dark and plain caves built as housing for them. *What a horrible way to begin life in a new country,* I thought, staring at the bunk beds. America, where incomparable opportunity coexists with obscene servitude. While shifting to a less blatant form, racism—and sexism—certainly still exists, though perhaps supported by fewer people.

As I peered into a physical manifestation of America's dour potential, I realized I witnessed this remnant of Havre only because I opened my eyes to what was around me. Ordinary traveling events—like a road sign—could bring the unexpected into my journey.

Late that afternoon, weary after the drive from Havre to the outskirts of Glacier National Park, I reserved a spot at a campground—a large, grassy, treeless backyard—just to have a place to sleep, and then went on to get a foretaste of the fifteen-thousand-square-mile preserve.

I was soon awestruck. Jagged mountains, glaciers, and chasms filled with melted ice decorated the entire area—over two hundred lakes, towering cone-shaped pines, countless rivers, streams, and waterfalls—broken only by two-lane roads and walking trails. This was what I wanted to experience in Alaska. Had I focused on a self-imposed deadline and an arbitrary destination, I might have passed through this park and enjoyed a pleasant day, but I probably wouldn't have stayed long enough to live in its grandeur and majesty.

Just outside the park, a resort nestled at the foot of a mountain. It had everything: camping, a view, a clubhouse, a hot tub, a swimming pool, an outdoor restaurant, and great computer facilities. I reserved a campsite for the next few weeks—there was no pressure to move on.

White snowfields atop glaciers gleamed in the July sun, resting on pale silver and dark gray peaks. There was no driving from vista to vista—it was all vista, endlessly changing as I crested a hill or rounded a curve. The road cut into the mountain and was often a few feet from a precipitous drop. Even in a car, I was aware of myself as a part of nature—something impossible in a city of man-made structures. The sky was crisp, a vivid blue contrasting sharply with swollen white clouds and sparkling turquoise water with foamy surf.

While driving, I could have been in a sports car ad, leaning into curves and letting my new haircut blow as the wind entered open windows. But the drive was just an appetizer, a way to taste this banquet. *I could get closer,* I thought, *perhaps on a horse.*

"How long has it been since you've ridden a horse?" a young groom asked me.

"At least twenty years," I said, thinking back to the rare adult forays that followed years of childhood lessons and pleasure riding.

"The horses all have western saddles. That okay with you?"

I nodded, knowing that a western saddle, with its horn in front, would be easier than the English version. Although the horn isn't meant for grabbing, it would be available in case I began to slip.

"Okay. Sadie's a real gentle horse, and she'll be back in a minute. Stand with them," he said, pointing at a few people leaning on a wooden fence.

As I waited, smelling hay and a bit of manure, I thought about the horses at summer camp and riding lessons in Michiana . . .

I'm ten and Donna is eight. Mom and Dad tell us we're going to Camp Zahavo for the summer—two months away from home, living in cabins with counselors and other kids. Jeff is only three and too young for camp. I watch with excitement as Evelyn irons name tags into each piece of clothing. When we drive to camp, Donna and I look out the windows as small towns, and then countryside, replace Chicago's sprawl. I love the sports and new friendships—especially my counselor—but look forward to visiting day when I will get to show my parents my new swimming skills and how I ride a horse around a ring.

Mom takes me aside and tells me she and Daddy are thrilled we're having a good time, but they miss us terribly, adding that sometimes Dad goes into our bedrooms and stares sadly at the neat rooms and empty beds.

During the second month of camp, he tells Mom he can't tolerate another separation from his girls and he purchases a summer home in Michiana, a lakefront town that straddles the line between Michigan and Indiana. "They won't miss camp," he tells her. "There's the lake for swimming and a stable for horseback riding."

In those days, I could easily ride a feisty horse. But not now. The groom brought me a placid nag that stood patiently, occasionally pawing the ground while the boy lowered the stirrup so I could mount. Once seated, legs spread wide across the saddle and reins in hand, I was aware of familiar horse scents—sweat and leather. Within ten minutes, a guide led our group of ten adults and kids on a trail beside Lake Sherburne beneath imposing mountains. Sadie knew exactly what to do. There was nothing for me to control; my only job was to sit, let her take me into this paradise, and occasionally sigh with pleasure at the surroundings.

While camping so near, I returned often to Glacier National Park's scenic buffet, each time taking a different route. I rode in an open-top boat on St. Mary Lake with mountains and glaciers on the banks, breezes against my face, the slight spray cooling my arms. And I drove on Going-to-the-Sun Road, a twisting, bending path hugging the side of a mountain, looking into deep valleys with winding rivers and more mountains beyond. I savored the tastes while knowing I could return again and again.

Stunned into silence, my demons rested, waiting for a more opportune time to appear.

A summer wind under low-hanging clouds greeted me on the morning of my first hike. I wore a long-sleeved flannel shirt and jeans.

My sneakers had decent tread, I thought. The hiker's shuttle—I loved thinking of myself as a hiker—gave me the luxury of gaping continuously, something not safe while driving. The shuttle dropped us at a rustic visitor center where a ranger showed me a map, pointed at the trailhead for what she called a fairly easy three-mile hike and casually mentioned there would be a bit of snow.

I strolled across the first couple hundred yards, enjoying the bracing weather, hardly expecting to find the six inches of semi-packed snow on a hill I had to cross. The tread on my shoes quickly filled with the white powder, and I began a series of slip-sliding falls, eventually taking me to flatter ground on the other side. Soaking wet and freezing, inching forward and able to remain upright most of the time, I was determined to finish this trail; no way would I return to shelter until I had accomplished every step of this first hike. Away from cement and traffic, far from anything built by man, the only sound was the soft thud of my feet hitting snow.

At the summit, two mountain goats watched my approach. When I arrived, they joined me for twenty minutes, stopping to wait for me when I didn't keep up, as if to make sure I remained safe. Hikers didn't feed these animals—few people carry food on a three-mile hike—but these agile creatures had learned to trust people and enjoy their company. They were a delightful substitute for Mazie, not speaking but indicating the way—as she did—whether or not I needed instruction.

It was still cloudy when the circular trail brought me back to the visitor's center to catch the shuttle. Teeth clattering in July, wind rippling my jeans and flannel shirt, I looked for the hiker's shuttle to take me home. Thinking there would be a fire, I went inside to wait. Nope. No fire. No heat of any kind. It seemed that a week passed as I watched for that bus.

That evening, after replacing my snow-drenched pants, shoes, shirt, and underwear with dry clothes, I drove to the town of St. Mary and found a stylish, locally owned sporting goods store. I parked in front of the door and walked in. A tall young man, blond and wiry, greeted me and smiled.

"I'm Barry. How can I help you?"

"I need waterproof hiking boots, pants, and a jacket."

"What size shoes?" he asked, walking toward the racks. When I told him, he took a box from the shelf, removed the top, and told me to have a seat.

"These're really comfortable," he said as I tried them on.

Half an hour and several pairs later, I chose the first ones he'd shown me. We moved on to the pants and jackets.

I didn't let myself think about the expense; I had to have these things.

Several items later, he said, "I know all the trails here. You're gonna want to hike in areas where your feet'll get wet, even with waterproof shoes. I've got some socks that're made like wet suits—socks that'll keep your feet warm, no matter how wet they get."

"That sounds good. Throw them in."

Then he asked if I'd considered hiking poles. "Huh," I said. "What're they?"

He showed me a few, all easily adjustable for my height, and told me, "If you stay here for a while, you'll want to hike some areas that have steep sections. See these metal points at the bottom of the poles? When you're going higher, they dig into the ground and help pull you up—and on the downside, they keep you from falling."

Two hours after entering the store, Barry followed me to the van, tossed the bags and poles on my bed, and said, "You're gonna be a lot happier on your next hike!"

Glacier National Park ⊙ ● Granite Park
Montana   Montana

CHAPTER 8

The Energizer Bunny

After the friendly goats joined me on my first trek, the idea of meeting wildlife on trails became reality. Now I had to consider what to do if I met dangerous animals, especially bears.

The park rangers gave a safety lecture and told a rapt audience: "Carry bear spray. Don't threaten the bear. Make yourself as large as possible, but if attacked, roll into a ball, fall on your face and put your backpack between you and the bear; don't forget your bear spray; ring a bell." And my favorite, "Talk loudly or sing." As I later obeyed this instruction, faster hikers stopped and inquired solicitously about my well-being.

A brochure advertised a seven-mile trail to Granite Park, a lodge, and a night in a charming chalet. Guests would cook their own dinner in a large, communal kitchen. I would have to carry everything I'd want for the evening and next day: food, a change of clothes, pajamas, hair-brush, and tooth stuff. Thus, I needed a backpack. This would be a long hike for me, especially carrying extra weight, but several days of shorter hikes got me sort of ready. Hiking like the Energizer Bunny without a drum—slow but steady—I could go the distance.

Reservation made, dehydrated food purchased, and pack filled, I set out early to complete the trek before dark.

This was a day of sun in a cloudless sky. The entire hike was on the side of a steep mountain, with streams and rivers below, and more mountains on the other side. Water trickling from high above often rose above my boot tops, making the nearly vertical inclines difficult to navigate. But the new set of poles kept me upright, and I gave thanks for the wet-suit socks that kept the water in my shoes at body temperature.

Acutely aware of the warm sun, the aromas of flowers and pine trees, the roar of rushing water, the brown mountain walls, and the steep drops, I was rarely bothered by the unbidden, intrusive thoughts that had been my companions—the noise blocking my senses. Yet even in this setting, I sometimes walked without seeing.

One minute I would be looking into a gorge, appreciating the precipitous drop and the contrast between rocks and the water below; a moment later I would be deep into memories, some happy, some not . . . seeing nothing as I walked. At one of these times, I remembered black-and-white photos of me, taken in front of our home, a serious expression on my face, not smiling yet not unhappy, so little behind me, so much still to come—all shaped by events that happened not far from our street . . .

I am ten, standing beside the synagogue a few blocks from my home with two friends my age and Marge, a thirteen-year-old. She squints as she swears us to secrecy. Pointing at her crotch, she says, "And he puts it in here to make a baby." I'm horrified, hoping she's wrong—but knowing she must be right.

I'm thirteen, in love with my pretty teacher, the youngest I've ever had. All the boys have crushes on her, but she pays more attention to me. I think about her constantly, fantasizing about going to the movies with her, having dinner at a restaurant, or saving her life.

And then, one night before sleep, I imagine kissing her.

I'm fifteen and have a crush on an older girl who hangs out at the beach where my friends swim and sunbathe. When I go to parties with older kids, she's there. I dream about being older and able to drive to her house to see how she lives. My driver's license, only a year away, will free me from my tethered life.

On my sixteenth birthday, my father picks me up at school and drives me to take the test. The man behind the counter hums "Happy Birthday" as he finishes the paper work. Little do they know how I will use this freedom . . .

I stopped walking for a moment, closed my eyes, and thought about those streets, the paths I walked, and the people I left behind. This time, these tender memories brought sadness, but no muscular tightness, no shallow breathing. Perhaps the strenuous walking burned away the adrenaline, or perhaps it was the fresh air and gorgeous environment. Whatever the reason, the tentacles of emotional distress have now untangled themselves from my throat and chest.

Although the views made it worth the effort, the steep climbs and my fifteen-pound backpack made this a difficult hike. I thought it would be easier on the downhill sections, but going down presented its own problems. With each step, my toes banged painfully against the front of my boots. The slower I walked, the more folks stopped and chatted before passing on to check into their chalets.

"You doin' okay?"

"Yeah, I'm fine. Just slow."

"You from around here?"

"No. Atlanta. How 'bout you?"

"Idaho. This's my fifth summer here. Love it!"

"You going to the chalet?"

"Mmhmm."

"See you at supper."

With a quarter of a mile to go, my Energizer Bunny pace slowed to that of a turtle—each step like lifting a cement block. Barely able to lift a leg and move myself forward a few inches at a time, I imagined the charming chalet and the respite it promised, and it kept me going.

A few of the men who had passed me wondered where I was and jogged effortlessly back to find me.

"You look like you're having a hard time. Want some help?" Weariness overcame my need for independence.

They relieved me of my burdensome backpack and sprinted ahead as I increased my speed to a painful stroll. As I staggered to the entrance, they were there to greet me, and they carried my pack to the counter where I checked in with an Amazon, over six feet, unsmiling but not unpleasant. Her thick muscles were apparent as she flipped her blonde ponytail from her shoulder to her back. My thumb and index finger went of their own accord to my earlobe where I touched a sensitive bug bite. She looked down at me with what I interpreted as pity.

"There're a lot of bugs up here," she said.

As she escorted me to my accommodation, I looked forward to a hot shower and a warm meal. But instead of the appealing chalet of Swiss design, I saw plain, flat-topped wooden buildings that resembled army barracks: no slanted roofs, no flowers, and no overhanging eaves— not the appealing structure of my imagination. Worse, there was no electricity, no shower in the cabin, no heat, and no toilet. I would have to trudge outside when I needed relief in the middle of the night.

I put my things on the bed and walked to the bathhouse. Plentiful soap and hot water did more than clean my sweaty body and soothe my aching muscles; it refreshed my spirits. The lounge had a blazing fire, and the communal kitchen, though gray and industrial, had rows of counter space, burners, ovens, and the tantalizing aromas of real food brought by energetic hikers.

Though the only words we exchanged were about the beauty of the trail and the location of silverware, it was fun to see those who had passed me on the trail. While they chopped, stirred, seasoned, and tasted, I slowly unpacked my two-ounce dehydrated package of something-or-other, tossed it in a pot, added water, and put it on a burner. *Voila,* a meal—bland, yet warm and filling. As I repeatedly lifted fork to mouth, I thought about my joy in completing this difficult hike— and getting some food in my empty stomach. Exhausted after dinner,

I went directly to my unheated cabin where, under four heavy blankets, I fell into a deep, dreamless sleep.

In the morning, too sore to return the way I came, I took an easier path—four miles instead of seven—with gentler slopes and more woods. The trail went through a burned-out area where dead trees, black with silver branches, gleamed in the sun—a starkly beautiful reminder of a devastating fire. Later, in startling contrast, I passed vast fields of bright yellow and purple wildflowers. Shortly before the trail's end, water cascaded over enormous boulders and fell to a river far below.

Back at the campground, I pulled on a swimsuit and dragged my exhausted body to the communal whirlpool, set in a polished wooden deck with yet another mountain backdrop, the luxury contrasting with yesterday's "chalet."

As I slipped into the unoccupied bath, turbulent hot water flowed through jets and soon eased my aching muscles.

I did it! I thought, as I leaned back and rested against the pillowed wall, completely serene.

Glacier National Park
Montana

Browning
Montana

CHAPTER 9

Dyke on a Bike

The first evening after my chalet hike, I sat at my campsite, feet up, reading. A motorcyclist arrived at the next site and began to unload his tent. When the rider, dressed in a lumber jacket, turned toward me, I realized this was not a man, but a tall, muscular woman. She finger-combed the short hair framing her square face and returned to her work, taking a hammer and stakes out of a bag on the back of the cycle, pulling each side of the tent tight and pounding in the stakes.

As the sun set, I meandered to the campground restaurant. There were no walls, but there was a light breeze. I was alone with a book, the only other customers a group of eight adults and kids, animated but not rowdy. I took a seat at another of the wooden picnic tables. In a few minutes, the biker walked toward the café with leisurely strides. Her arms swung so far that her shoulders moved with them. Although each table seated six or eight people, she took another empty one.

Now that she was closer to me, I could see her face more clearly, her eyebrows almost joining above the bridge of her nose and the eyes beneath them a deep, warm brown. Thinking I might enjoy some company, I asked her to join me.

"No thanks," she said in a voice like gravel pouring over cement, "but you can come over here if you wanna."

I slid into a seat across from her and introduced myself.

"Marty," she said as she picked up a menu and stared at it.

"Are you on vacation?" I asked, struggling to make conversation while she barely looked at me.

"Yep."

"Are you staying here long?"

"No," she responded, not looking up from her menu. "Just passing through."

I trudged on. "Where are you heading?"

"A motorcycle convention."

"What do you do when you're not on vacation?"

"I'm a pilot. Crop-dusting," she said with the first hint of inflection.

I thought, *what an unusual profession for a woman.* I could feel my face move from the flat, dead look I had been wearing to animated anticipation of more. "I don't know anything about crop-dusting." The waiter came to take our orders. She ordered ribs and I ordered the chicken.

Marty surprised me by continuing. "Crop-dusting has changed a lot. The first dusters had to use flagmen to tell 'em where to dust. Now we use those GPS things."

Given my dependence on an electronic navigator, I fully understood how useful this would be to a crop-duster.

She continued in this vein—telling me her sprays protect the plants from disease and bugs and how she spreads fertilizer and seeds—maintaining my attention until the waiter brought our food. Marty tucked one corner of her napkin under her shirt, draping it across her chest. She tore a rib from the barbequed slab as the sides of her thin lips moved outward into something resembling a smile. "A guy in my neighborhood had his own little plane, and my folks let him give me flying lessons."

"Wow," I said. I cut a tiny piece of meat, my manners improving as Marty's tongue traveled across her upper lip. "I bet that was a thrill."

"It was the most exciting thing I'd ever done," she said, looking directly at me for the first time. "After I graduated high school, I got a job as a receptionist at our little airport. The pilots let me fly a lot."

Marty paused to take a big bite and then used one corner of the napkin still hanging from her neck to mop the dark red sauce on her chin.

Then I blew it. "Are you with Dykes on Bikes?"

Her smile disappeared. "I'm not *that way*," she growled with disdain. "Got no idea why people always think I'm *that way*." My eyes opened wide and my jaw dropped. More shocked than embarrassed, I mumbled something inarticulate. We struggled through the next several minutes until we went to our separate sites.

Her masculine profession and appearance led me to assume she was gay. I was surprised she didn't see why people questioned her sexuality. On the other hand, why had I been so certain?

The next morning while preparing my breakfast, I heard her rev up her bike and mused about my assumptions as she drove past my site. If I was wrong in thinking this woman was gay, how often have my conjectures about others been wrong? When I meet people, I judge everything from their politics to their lifestyles by their clothes, posture, and voice. I haven't always been aware that these are only hypotheses and probably acted on them, just as with Marty. I thought perhaps this experience could teach me to modulate my opinions.

Perhaps she really was gay—just in the closet. Some people live the life only mentally, never coming out to anyone, never meeting other gay people. And still others, I suspect, live a celibate life, never acknowledging their sexual orientation—not even to themselves. Seventeenth-century writer Francois de La Rochefoucauld said, "We are so accustomed to disguise ourselves to others that in the end we become disguised to ourselves."

In my case, I was slow to come out in the open—and I never came out to my parents. From the time I might have done so, their lives were difficult . . .

It's a few days before my sixteenth birthday and my parents have allowed me to invite five friends to my favorite Chicago restaurant—an elegant French dining room. They struggle with the menu, so I mention my father's favorite dish, chicken cordon bleu, and everyone orders it. We are thrilled to participate in a grown-up experience, sans real grown-ups. Next weekend, there will be a hotel luncheon for twenty-five relatives and friends.

My father has always said that a child needs guidance until the age of sixteen. Then, he or she has probably learned all the values a parent can teach. My parents have told me I will no longer have a curfew. Regardless of the hours I keep, I'm expected to fill all obligations and responsibilities.

During this birthday month, I notice occasional mentions of homosexuality in the Chicago Tribune. *"Dear Abby" answers a letter about it. It occurred to me that maybe, just maybe, I could tell them about my secret.*

I'm coming of age . . .

It's a month after my birthday. One of my aunts has invited me for a downtown lunch. She suggests a glass of wine. Now I really feel grown up.

As we sip, she asks me, "Have your parents told you?"

"Huh?"

"Have they told you . . . you know . . . your father . . . he's lost all of his money. Your dad's in court right now—arranging bankruptcy."

I'm numb. Mom and Dad showed no sign of these problems as I celebrated my birthday. She talks for a while; I look at her, but I'm not listening.

Then I hear her say, "Your father's friends are putting up the money for him to buy a hardware store. He was always so good to his friends, lending everyone money while he worked and they were in college, and then later when he was well established and they were just getting started." She pauses then adds, "You may not remember. You were so little then. He started out with a hardware store." She stops again, looking down at her plate. "But people don't think bankruptcy is a nice thing. It's kind of shameful. They are helping your dad financially, but many won't want to see your mom and dad socially." The full meaning hasn't sunk in, but at least Dad won't have to look for a job . . .

Although I was stunned by my aunt's words, I remembered Mom and Dad sitting at the kitchen table, conversing about a problem in the jewelry departments in his stores. I heard him say something about not understanding why sales had fallen off.

When I returned home from the lunch, Mom asked me about it. I told her what was said. Her eyes were moist as she told me it was true. She obviously didn't expect me to learn of it this way.

My mind wandered over the weeks following the lunch with my aunt . . .

I'm looking out the living room window as two men ask my mother for both sets of car keys—two shiny Buick sedans, the green one a year old and the blue one a year older. They each take one set of keys, and I watch as they drive away with our cars. Mom tells me they are called "receivers" or "repo" men.

We can still live in the house, I'm told. It's in my mother's name.

My father comes home with a friend, each driving a used car. One is a faded green, five-year-old Pontiac sedan, not too bad, just not what we're used to. The other is something out of a nightmare. It's a dull black coupe with the front end down and rear end in the air, like a large bird feeding on seeds in the street. These cars look out of place in front of our home.

That evening, Dad tells me what happened. In addition to the furniture, appliances, and televisions, each store had a jewelry section. A few trusted employees had been carrying expensive jewelry out of the store—a box of watches, a diamond ring, a ruby-studded bracelet. My father was borrowing business capital based on inventory shown in the accounting books, but the stolen merchandise was gone and couldn't be sold. Since inventory was reduced, sales declined, and Dad was unable to repay the loans. He says it was like standing on a concrete walkway, feeling safe on solid ground, having no idea that the earth below is eroding until the concrete cracks underfoot, and you drop into the sinkhole.

He tells me most people are honest and loyal, but warns me to watch for exceptions.

Most nights, my parents are together, needing only one car. As promised, they lift the strict curfews of my earlier childhood. I can use the Pontiac every night and most afternoons. Daddy drives the big black bird. No matter how late I come home, their lights are on as I park but go out before I reach the door. They're watching for me, making sure I'm safely home.

They never ask where I've been . . .

My father opens the hardware store. I get an after-school job selling clothes. I'm proud I can help and think I'm making a real contribution as I spend my paycheck on my wardrobe. My friends join me after work and we go out as we always have. And later, I wander the streets in the green sedan, happy to have anything to drive.

One afternoon, I drive to a park to meet my friend Joyce who is playing tennis doubles. As I approach the courts, I see three men sitting at a table watching the game, perhaps keeping score. The game ends and Joyce joins me. She wants to introduce me to her tennis coach.

We walk to the table and she says, "Marilyn, this is Sally, my coach," and I realize one of these "men" is Sally. She stands, wipes her hands on her pants, and extends her right hand to shake.

I can hardly breathe.

During the next few weeks, Joyce and I often end our evening at the park and go out for late-night burgers with Sally, the first woman I'm sure is a lesbian. Joyce is a strict Catholic and seems to have no idea Sally might be gay. I don't dare discuss my speculation with her; she might wonder at my interest and guess my secret. I'm enthralled and want to tell Sally that I like her. But I'm too frightened. What if I'm wrong? She might tell Joyce, and Joyce would surely judge me—and tell others. I've told no one.

I look up Sally's address, listed in the huge Chicago phone book. Now that I can drive, I can cruise past her house and imagine how she lives. Sometimes I do. Other times, after a movie and ice cream with friends, and after driving everyone home, I drive downtown to the area where homosexuals hang out and look for Sally, hoping I'll find her somewhere in these big-city crowds. If not, at least I'll see some of my people, my dark side. Although I want to park the car and mingle, I'm too scared.

My parents are somber, focused on keeping our lives together, devastated over their loss of material resources and the friends who have now abandoned them. I can't understand what they did wrong. Because of major embezzlement, Dad couldn't pay the bills. How could he have avoided bankruptcy court? And so what if they can't afford to give fancy dinner parties? They are still the same people who gave so much to the community. It's great that their old friends are helping them financially, but it would certainly be nice if they had more emotional support, more fun. Nothing is the same.

I can't tell them now . . .

When I finished my morning meal, I returned my focus to the Glacier campground and carried my laptop to the lodge to check my email. There were a couple of posts from people who, though not on my send-list, were responding to my last group email. Friends were forwarding my messages to other people, who then asked to be included on the list. The group had doubled in size. I was thrilled that so many wanted to follow my journey. My letters spoke only of my travels, nothing about my internal journey. Although I was now "out" to everyone I knew, it never occurred to me to discuss my memories in these communications. I lived through difficult years, but they were in the past. The distractions of the road offered me an amazing way to put the memories into history.

A flyer advertised a dance program in the park auditorium—a performance by champion dancers from the Blackfeet Tribe. I had always heard Black*foot,* but the flyer said they call themselves Black*feet* and they also prefer the label "Indian" to the politically correct "Native American."

That evening, I walked into a packed theater and joined the throng— all seats filled, people standing in the side aisles and sitting on the floor. The hall thrummed with excitement as the dancing, singing, and drumming began. I watched flying feet hitting the stage in time to the beat and handmade costumes of bright red, gold, and blue, fringed and beaded, intricate in design, moving as if part of the dance. As the arms of the dancers swung in graceful arcs, fabric feathers made them look like huge birds in flight; a seamless blend of cloth, color, drums, and human voices, feet, and arms, soaring across the stage.

There was nothing but sight and sound.

After the show, I picked up a flyer saying that North American Indian Days, a mega-powwow coupled with an Indian Rodeo, was about to begin on the Blackfeet Reservation in Browning, Montana.

The drive to Browning the next day took less than two hours, and I found a seat high in the bleachers. In this rodeo, the cowboys *were* the Indians, exhibiting expert bronco busting and steer wrestling with drumming and singing at intermission.

When the show was over, the crowd, wearing everything from traditional Indian dress to tank tops and military uniforms, wandered in and out of the vast area of RVs, tents, and elaborately decorated teepees. The aroma of fresh, homemade baked goods drew me to a silent auction supporting the Browning High School traveling rodeo team. I entered ten dollars on a lattice-topped peach pie.

On what seemed like acres of land, I wandered through tourist junk; real art; an array of hot dogs, Indian fry bread, cotton candy, and peach shortcake; and an unexpected variety of religious booths. At a Pentecostal booth, a female clown was not only saving the souls of children by teaching songs for Jesus, but also having them swear allegiance to the Christian flag.

Until that moment, I had no idea there was a Christian flag.

Methodists gave out free lemonade and a pamphlet. I was surprised to discover a booth for the Bahá'í Temple giving out free water, but no sermons and no pamphlets.

I checked the silent auction results. The pie was mine.

Back at the campground, I picked up napkins and a knife, then took the pie to the pool to share. Ten minutes later, only crumbs remained in the tin. I slipped into the pool, stood in the shallow end with my book on the deck, and turned pages with wet fingers. Kids jumped in, splashing more water on the print. Their delight put a smile on my face. I knew the pages would dry.

A dad pushed a floating bassinette containing a six-week-old baby, dad and baby lathered in sunscreen. A five-year-old walked around the deck, carrying his brand new puppy like a porcelain bowl. On a nearby volleyball court, a family—grandma, teenager, and three-year-old—banged a ball over and under the net.

As I savored the memories of the day, I relished the treasures of my nomadic life.

CHAPTER 10

Crossing the Border

Departing from Glacier National Park, heading north to Canada, I gave little thought to the fact I was about to leave the United States. The border was invisible—only a road sign marked the change from one nation to another. But when I joined a line of cars waiting to pass through immigration, border guards spoke with each driver, checked the vehicle contents, and sometimes removed an item or two before allowing it to pass.

At the front of the line, I opened my window. A guard, holding a clipboard, asked a series of programmed questions. "Where are you from? What do you plan to do in Canada? How long will you be staying?"

After answering his first questions, I said, "I'm wandering. Not sure how long I'll be, but probably at least a couple months."

He looked in the back, noting my bed, fridge, dresser drawers, and microwave. He gave me a big smile, saying, "Be sure to camp in safe places." I put my hand on the starter key—but he wasn't finished. "Do you plan to do any hiking?"

"Yes. A lot."

"Do you have bear spray?" he asked. *Everyone is concerned about safety,* I thought, nodding in the affirmative.

"Bear spray is illegal in Canada," he explained as he asked for and then confiscated the canister. *Oh well, I'll just make sure to talk and sing loudly.* "Have a good time," he said, backing up and waving me on into a foreign nation.

Within a few miles, I stopped for lunch at a restaurant in a well-maintained old house with simple interior: a fireplace, wooden walls and hand-hewn beams, cloth napkins, and flowers. A juicy chicken sandwich with homemade bread was served on a small plate with no added frills, just as my mom would have done. Having a fresh meal in this mature home was like sliding my feet into soft slippers.

After lunch, I headed to the tiny town of Banff at the base of Cascade Mountain. No neon, the town was elegant, old-fashioned, and picturesque, inviting me to stroll, allowing me to smell snow-air far from traffic and pollution. Streets were immaculate—trash dropped by tourists was whisked away as if by elves. A coffee house offered cappuccino and rest. Expensive shops provided visual treats, but nothing I wanted to buy.

The next morning, I stood high above Lake Louise and its famed Fairmont Chateau, looking down at sparkling water, a tiny gem at the bottom of a snow-capped glacier and mountain-walled basin.

Cars and people appeared as moving dots on the shore, and it hit me in a way it never had before: I was one of those people, and my problems were equally tiny—dwarfed by the jagged peaks that protected the lake for millennia.

I understood, at least for this moment, that the happenings of my life were specks in the vastness of time.

My next stop was Calgary, host of the 1988 Winter Olympics, population three-fourths of a million, a metropolis compared to towns I recently visited.

After registering at an in-town campground, I went directly to Olympic Park and waited for a tour bus to take me to each competition venue. Families and couples were engrossed in their togetherness—no other singles.

I wasn't lonely, but wondered what it would be like to share this journey. Although I had many friends, Anna was my last partner. Most of the people close to me were couples, and most of my recent travels were alone. Usually, this was not a problem. I enjoyed meeting new people and appreciated the ability to make my own choices—where to eat dinner, what to do with my day. But Anna's enthusiasm and charm added to any activity we shared. And when I had dated women—or boys and men—I was part of that world of couples. When I went anywhere with a partner, we were immediately accepted in any group; alone—often, but not always. When enjoying a painting or a play, we would glance at each other or share a smile. Alone, I smiled to myself—and planned to tell someone. And perhaps most of all, I loved to feel an arm around my shoulders or a hand in mine.

Once seated on the bus, I closed my eyes and went to another time, thousands of miles and a half-century away. I remembered Justin, a boy with a wiry, muscular body. We met and began dating during my fifteenth summer, the last season my family could afford our second home at Lake Michigan . . .

I am sixteen, Justin seventeen. We double-date every weekend with Chloe and Don. If Don drives, Justin and I are comfortable in the back seat. If Justin drives, we're stuck in front with the console between us.

I have long known the dating rules for necking and petting. On first dates, a boy can kiss you, and as the weeks pass, increase the length of time and adding tongue. Then he may feel your breasts, first just over the sweater, then under the sweater. Heavy petting—below the waist—can begin only after several months. In my circles, it can't go farther than this. No boy will try, and no girl need worry.

I like the kissing, don't mind the first stages of petting, and tolerate everything else, allowing me to maintain a veneer of normalcy: a date for weekend nights, proms, high-school sorority and fraternity dances. (In those years in the city of Chicago, gentile boys belonged to Hi-Ys and girls to Tri-Hi-Ys. These clubs were established by the YMCA, and limited to Christian kids. Jewish kids then established sororities and fraternities.) When Justin leaves for college, I miss him a bit, but there are other boys to take his place—not many, but enough.

I continue to live a second life, my secret life. A neighborhood drugstore sells sodas and paperbacks, a few books by and about lesbians. The first one I buy is The Well of Loneliness, *by Radclyffe Hall, a story of an upper-class Englishwoman who meets her female lover while serving as an ambulance driver in World War I. Reading covertly, I meet most of my first gay friends on the pages of books. I read about how they meet and fall in love. They kiss only where no one can see them. They don't tell anyone. Their hidden relationships are exciting for me. As I read a new book, I hide it in the bottom of a sweater drawer then throw it away when finished. Now I'm not so alone.*

Looking out the window, I remembered that first book, so different from ordinary trashy love stories, both gay and straight. This one was well-written with literary language, developed characters, and a stimulating plot. Published in 1928, it was banned for obscenity, yet became an infamous, underground best seller. Now a classic, it's still in print . . .

I work after school at a clothing store and later go out with classmates. Gas is sixteen cents a gallon. We visit Chicago landmarks like the Bahá'í Temple and nice restaurants on Chicago's near-north side. Though I look about fourteen, they serve me liquor. No one checks IDs in Chicago. Still later, after dropping off each friend, I drive around the city; sometimes I look for Sally.

It's often four in the morning when I get home. My instructions are to go to my parents' bedroom and let them know I'm home. Even though they've heard me come in, I tiptoe to where they are supposedly asleep, whisper hello, and then go to bed. Each time, I worry they'll be furious about how late it is. It never happens. My parents believe sixteen-year-olds are able to make their own decisions— and live with the consequences. They show no anger.

When it's hard for me to wake up, my father gently shakes me and stays with me until I'm alert. If necessary, he takes my arm and walks me around the house while my mother makes breakfast. There's no question about my going to school or work. My parents expect me to meet all obligations and accept the consequences of my late-night behavior, but they're willing to help. Most of my friends had curfews, and lateness would not be tolerated kindly. Like my parents, no-spanking-under-any-circumstances position, they seemed to have unique ideas about child-raising.

Now I'm seventeen, and Dad gets his first new car since the bankruptcy. It's not fancy, but it's a shiny Chevy. He takes the other car to work, leaving this one for my mother. One rainy day, she lets me drive it to work. I'm distracted by thoughts of my latest crush, and though not going fast, I approach a bus, brake too late, and slide into it. The bus driver gets out, sees no damage to his bus, and drives on.

The new fender, however, is damaged.

I drive to the body shop. The manager says it will cost fifty dollars and it'll be ready in two days.

I take the bus home.

There is no question about telling my parents—the car is missing. Mom comes home first, and she takes the news calmly, telling me I will be expected to pay for the repair.

A few tense hours later, Dad comes home. As soon as he gets his coat off, I tell him. He is livid. His lips quiver as he tells me a car is never the same after body damage. This is the first time I've ever seen him more than annoyed. Impulsively, I think this is a good time to tell him I smoke; he can't get any angrier. With hands on my hips, I wait for his response.

His face falls and his shoulders slump. This is not anger—it's sadness. He says nothing as he gets up and leaves the room.

If the fact that I smoke makes him look so unhappy, how can he ever tolerate hearing that I'm gay?

My reverie broke when the bus arrived at Olympic Village.

Athletes, coaches, cooks, masseuses, and spectators were but a memory, the area a skeleton—muscle and fat provided by imagination. The tour bus took us to each competition venue, and our guide described the relevant sport. The ski jump was higher and steeper than it looked on television. Standing at the summit, I was dizzy, terrified by the thought of plunging downward on slippery boards.

The next day I took my lunch to Olympic Plaza, a city park, and found a spot to sit. Everyone seemed to be facing the outer wall of a five-story building. Long, thick ropes hung from the top, ending a few feet from earth. A costumed group appeared on the roof and stood for a moment before reaching for the ropes. Launching themselves onto the side of the building, they morphed into horizontal gymnasts. Bodies parallel to the ground, one foot on the wall and one hand holding a rope, they exchanged places as they danced and sprang from the surface. As skillful as *Cirque du Soleil*, but free to all viewers, they seemed to defy gravity while descending in slow motion.

Thousands of hours of training and skill beyond talent found a home in a park.

A few yards from the show, I found bronze sculptures—philosophical tableaux. The first was *The Family of Man*, each figure over twenty feet tall, thin and graceful, extending their hands to each other in gestures of friendship. Thrilled with the art and warmed by this illustration of human harmony, I was comforted by thoughts of ongoing acts of compassion, seen daily in the news—but simultaneously saddened by the horrors of relentless inhumanity.

I remembered a recent news report about a heroic homeless man stabbed as he saved a woman from a knife attack. While he lay dying, a passerby glanced at him and strolled on, assuming he was drunk. Jangled by opposing realities of kindness and indifference, I walked on, appreciating this bronze vision of the world as it could be.

The other sculpture was of Canada's "Famous Five." This group came together in 1927 when Emily Murphy was denied an opportunity to serve in the senate because she was female. Women—not considered persons in the British North America Act (BNA) of 1867—were unable to hold political office. Emily Murphy discovered that five "persons" could petition the Supreme Court of Canada for an interpretation of any portion of the BNA. Emily enlisted four other prominent women to join her in seeking equality by asking the Supreme Court of Canada to declare women persons.

The Canadian Court ruled that persons in the BNA did *not* include female persons. Outraged by this decision, the women continued to sign petitions and appeal to federal authorities. Women all over Canada joined the insurgency in an effort to enlist support from men.

When any group is successful in passing laws to subjugate others, only members of that privileged class can change these discriminatory laws. The oppressed must cajole, rebel, and otherwise persuade those in power of the legitimacy of their cause. In this case, Canadian Prime Minister Mackenzie King was convinced and helped the women appeal to the highest Canadian court, the British Judicial Committee. This court then declared that women *were* persons, equal to men. Known as the Persons Case of 1929, it was not only important for furthering women's rights, but also originated the Living Tree Doctrine, which proclaims that a constitution should adapt to changing times to avoid falling into disuse.

Rarely had I thought about the sacrifices of our great-grandmothers, jailed and humiliated to give me freedoms I've enjoyed all my life. This vivid bronze scene reminded me that I am accepted as a person only because of their efforts.

I cannot imagine my life a hundred years ago, but it certainly would have been more restricted. My journeys are possible because of these daring women.

CHAPTER 11
The Reluctant Warrior

A young woman outside Calgary's park, perhaps a day-camp counselor, herded a group of preschoolers across the road. A sudden ache below my rib cage accompanied an unbidden memory of my mother's lifelong love of children. Nothing gave her more pleasure than a child—relative or stranger.

Mom would have loved to be a child-herder, but during the summer after high school graduation, her dream of becoming a teacher ended with her father's death.

Dad also gave up higher education. The oldest son of a depression-era family, he elected to work in his father's hardware store instead of accepting either of his hard-won scholarships in pharmacy and physics. But my parents loved learning. Bookshelves lined one wall of our living room, and each evening, they sat in comfortable chairs, facing one another, each reading a book.

Mom and Dad assumed I would go to college and get an advanced degree. Since I always hated uncertainty, I couldn't stand the idea of waiting until my senior year to apply, then waiting again to know where I'd be going. In my junior year, at the earliest possible time, I selected one school—the University of Michigan. Dad went to the local library to check college rankings. Satisfied, he agreed with my choice, and I applied. The positive response came in just three weeks. I could relax until time to go.

Though it wasn't necessary to select a major, my decision was already a *fait accompli*. Two abiding interests dictated my choice. First, fascinated by the study of conflict resolution, negotiation, and compromise, I read every installment of "Can This Marriage Be Saved?" in Mom's *Ladies Home Journal*. And second, I was a neophyte actor and orator who wanted to grow up to help people who had difficulty speaking.

I already knew I would have a double major—psychology and speech-language pathology—and get a doctorate in one of these fields, both helping professions. No annoying uncertainty for me.

At seventeen, I packed my bags and said a final good-bye to childhood . . .

Counseling is free for all U of M students and is especially enticing for psych majors. I want to become a functioning heterosexual and begin to see a psychotherapist. She listens. And listens. And listens. I tell her I haven't told my secret to anyone in the dorm, but I look for lesbians everywhere I go on campus. This distracts me from my studies. She says little about my sexuality, but she does remind me I'm here to get an education while exploring my newly independent life.

I meet Holly, a straight woman in her mid-twenties. I no longer get crushes on straight teachers and friends, but enjoy close friendships—still dating men while simultaneously continuing my desperate search for gay women.

Freshman year ends. Holly invites me to dinner. When I knock at her door, a man answers. He's almost a foot taller than I, but well under six feet, slim, and well-muscled with fair skin, and steady blue eyes under thick brows.

"I'm Kevin," he says. "You must be Marilyn."

I nod, realizing this must be Holly's boyfriend as he opens the door wider for me to enter. My first thought was, What an attractive man.

As we eat and talk, I learn he served in the Army, played baseball in college, is an amateur actor, and dabbles in carpentry. Holly, resting her hand on his shoulder, adds that he's working on a master's degree in physics with a minor in engineering. I tell him about the dorm, friends, and classes.

Kevin sometimes sweeps back strands of thick, dark blond hair that have fallen on his forehead. He's a great conversationalist, always smiling and looking Holly or me in the eyes. He's handsome and talented—different from the boys and men I've dated. I can't help but wonder if I could love even a man like this. I'm not sure.

A few days later, I'm in the Michigan Union, where I hang out. Between classes and after dinner, my friends and I drink coffee nonstop, socialize, and study together. At this moment, I'm alone at a table working on a statistics problem and sense someone standing behind me. I look up to see Kevin.

"Hmmm. Probability theory," he says as he sits opposite me.

"Yeah, it's hard, but I can't stop doing these brainteasers. I'm obsessed."

"Want some advanced problems? I could help you."

How could I turn down an offer like that? We meet, day after day, working on math problems and sharing stories about our lives. Kevin and I become friends— the kind who can't remember when we were not friends.

He helps me with other kinds of problems. My dorm room is a single across from the showers and beside the stairwell, a noisy area. I tell Kevin I've tried earplugs, but I'm still often awakened throughout the night. No solution occurs to me. He suggests a soundproof box that would go over my bed. I love the idea. I realize it will seem weird to most people, so I decide to tell no one except those who might see it. And then only those who see it. Four or five afternoons a week, he works in the basement of my dorm, building what we call the bedbox. No one comes to his work room until, one day, while I'm watching him work, we hear loud footsteps coming down the stairs. I look up to see Betty Ann, the house manager, heavy arms akimbo, angrily asking what we think we are doing. After I explain, she says, "Ha, you must think I'm a fool. I know what you plan to do under that box! And you will not get away with it! This project stops right now." And she stomped up the stairs.

Kevin watches her exit and turns to me, a puzzled look on his face, and says, "How does she think the bedbox would add to the privacy of a closed, locked door?"

And then I meet Lynne. On the first day of a sociology class, she sits in front of me, and I notice her immediately. She's a slim New Yorker with dark brown eyes and short wavy hair. When she speaks in class, her comments are insightful. I want to get to know her. In the second week of class, I ask her if she'd like to study with me. She agrees. We become close friends.

Lynne moves into an apartment with three other women. They throw parties regularly and invite men and women they've met in classes and in the Michigan Union. We sit in a circle on the living room floor, chatting and listening to Lynne play the guitar and sing folk songs. She is the life of every party. These friends meet in the Union to study, the groupings unplanned—we just show up and join whoever is around that day. I'm happy to belong to this smart and trendy group.

One afternoon, Kevin arrives and joins us. Holly has moved to Oregon, but Kevin is never without women. I introduce him to Lynne. When she mentions her father is an actor, Kevin tells her he also is an actor. He has frequent roles in the community theater. He gets her number, and they begin to date. Lynne is smart, attractive, talented, and popular . . . perfect for Kevin. I've never seen either of them so happy. He asks her to marry him. She accepts. But late at night, after their dates, Kevin still finds other women. He cannot resist. Even I did not know.

When Lynne discovers his secret life, she breaks the engagement. They're both devastated. He tells me he still loves her, and I ask him why he continues casual affairs. He says he's always been attracted to more than one woman at a time—he can't help himself. He knows it won't stop, but he loves Lynne too much to lie to her, believing he'll always be unfaithful.

She tells him she'll leave Ann Arbor after graduation and go to Berkeley for graduate school. Like magnets, they continue to see each other, but it's often tense.

She is too depressed to eat, managing just two pieces of toast every morning. That's all she eats for the day. Having had a nice figure and normal appetite until now, it's a shock to see her rapid weight loss. I hold her when she cries at night. When it's time for him to take her to the airport for the last time, he cries as if his arm is being amputated without anesthetic. Yet, he cannot commit to one person.

I ache for them and miss her deeply . . .

I shook myself from memories. Calgary demanded my attention: Stephen Avenue, a historic, pedestrian-only section of downtown is lined with shops, galleries and restaurants, many in restored sandstone buildings from the late 1800s and early 1900s. Along wide sidewalks were live performers—magicians, artists, musicians, mimes—each with its own spellbound audience.

I pondered a statue as another observer tucked some money into its pocket. This "cement" figure slowly raised one arm—and froze again in this new position—remaining motionless for many minutes, until paid to move. An inebriated heckler used a feather to tickle his face. At first, the actor didn't move, but the man continued his efforts to irritate. Suddenly, the mime broke his pose and shook his finger close to the startled man's nose while saying, "Get. The. Hell. Away. From. Me." As the embarrassed drunk slinked away, the "statue" returned.

What makes one person study to learn a craft, while another takes pleasure in destroying the work?

A few yards away, a magician with several inches of ribbon protruding from his ear got down on his knees and asked a toddler his name.

"Freddy," mumbled the child.

"Well, Freddy, could you help me get this ribbon out of my ear?"

The child took hold of the free end and pulled, slowly backing up as more and more ribbon appeared. As he tugged, his mouth formed a circle, opening wider as he continued his efforts. When Freddy was several feet from the magician, he succeeded in freeing the ribbon and promptly plopped down on his behind, still holding his end and looking as though he was about to cry.

I wanted to take him in my arms and comfort him. His mom did just that, and while she held him, loud applause brought a big smile to his little face.

I looked at my watch and smiled, realizing this was now a superfluous habit.

One day later, I visited Calgary's Glenbow Museum, one of Canada's largest and most comprehensive. Temporary exhibits from all across the world supplement its vast collection of art, artifacts, and historical documents from Western Canada. Though I was unaware of the movement of my feet, they nonetheless took me through the Asian exhibit: intricately carved Hindu and Buddhist sculptures from the second to the eighteenth century.

Art occurs in communities of people, and with communities comes war. At the entrance to the military exhibit, I stood beneath a memorable quote, from Golda Meir—the Milwaukee-raised grandmother who became Israel's fourth Prime Minister. In huge lettering, it read: "I am sure someday children . . . will study the history of men who made war as you study an absurdity. They'll be astonished; they'll be shocked, just as today we are shocked by cannibalism."

Moving from destruction to creation, I returned to art: landscapes and wildlife paintings, Inuit clothing, masks, and sculpture, art in the inhospitable Arctic—some contemporary, some ancient.

I left Calgary with swirling thoughts: incomprehensible human differences, the fight for women's rights, creativity in freezing climates, skillful mimes and magicians, world history, my history. And Golda Meir, the reluctant warrior.

Edmonton
Alberta

Ukrainian Cultural Heritage Village
Alberta

Calgary
Alberta

Saskatoon
Saskatchewan

Moose Jaw
Saskatchewan

CHAPTER 12

Conflict and Kindness

West Edmonton Mall is forty-eight city blocks—the largest indoor shopping complex in the world. I wandered by a twenty-five-lane bowling alley, the sound of balls striking pins reaching the mall corridor; a roller coaster and water park both full of screaming kids; families sitting in bleachers watching a dolphin show and more standing in line for submarine rides in a lake; and couples holding hands, all while gliding on a full-size ice skating rink.

Every time I thought, *Now I've seen everything,* something startling showed up. Turning a corner, I found myself on a European street. Another turn and I was in an Asian grocery market. Restaurants of all kinds and two hotels rounded out the picture. I had wandered into an indoor city pretending to be a mall.

One could live a full life here and never want for anything—except sunshine and rain and wind.

That night, exhausted from the day of touring, I was about to slap some peanut butter on bread and call it dinner when a knock at my van door startled me. It was a woman from a nearby RV I'd greeted in passing. These neighbors were a family of three: mom, dad, and a small boy. The adults spoke with foreign accents I thought might be Middle Eastern.

"This is a traditional Afghani dinner," she said, looking down and speaking softly as she handed me a covered plate of food. "This is comfort food for us. We're so far from home. And I made too much."

She looked up and continued, "My husband and I had a bet about what you're doing alone in a campground. I said you were on vacation. He thinks you're a botanist researching Canadian plants."

"A botanist, huh," I said with a grin. "*Your* guess is right. I'm just on vacation . . . and thanks so much for this delightful supper. It smells wonderful! I was too tired to go out. Toured the West Edmonton Mall all day. Fabulous."

She paused, and then said, "We went to the Muttart Conservatory this afternoon and enjoyed it so much. We both thought you'd like it. If you have more time in Edmonton, it's something special."

I wanted to give her something in return but went blank for a moment. Then, remembering an unopened package of rich black tea, I reached into a drawer, handed her the box, and thanked her, hoping she would understand how much I appreciated her visit.

After she left, I uncovered the dish and tasted it. Rice, chicken, and almonds, baked until lightly browned. Delicious!

Though we had been at war against the Taliban in Afghanistan since 2001, my neighbors went out of their way to offer a kindness to me. Many Afghanis made it clear they hated America, and many Americans extended their anger at Islamic extremists to hostility toward all Muslims.

As a Jewish child born in the time of Hitler, I understood that large numbers of people were able to despise and abuse every member of some group other than their own, but I have never understood why . . .

It's 1960, a time of racial discrimination, a time of "white" and "colored" drinking fountains, a time of nonviolent resistance. Kresge, the largest national dime store chain, enforces segregation at its lunch counters, meaning blacks may not sit with whites. University of Michigan students are outraged and organize a march to protest this humiliating discrimination. I'm close to the sidewalk, the throng moving en masse, inch by inch, down State Street, past the dime store. I'm thinking about kids who can't sit down to eat—I'm imagining the sad, puzzled expressions on their small faces—when something hard hits my arm. Before I can even turn to look, I feel wetness joining the pain. It's a raw egg. I continue to walk, happy to pay the price of a physical bruise that will soon heal . . .

My sociology classes taught me about scapegoating, but I couldn't then—and still cannot—grasp how someone could revile people because of race, nationality, sexual orientation, or a different belief system. How is it that there are those who can cause pain and feel nothing? They look like other humans, but perhaps they have a genetic mutation. They cannot be of the same species as the men and women who create art, build churches, compose music, and design botanical gardens.

The Muttart Conservatory, recommended by my Afghani neighbors, is enclosed in four glass pyramids, three of which contain florae from different climates; the fourth, seasonal exhibits. As in nature, several varieties of birds and small animals live among these plants and flowers—a riot of color, as if from Van Gogh's palette—a garden to escape the concrete of daily lives. Recommending this conservatory was yet another kindness, especially for this hypothesized botanist seeking such wondrous natural spectacle.

The population of greater Edmonton, Alberta's capital, is just over a million people, but it has more museums, art, and culture than any US city of similar size.

In the Provincial Museum of Art and History, I found Japanese cloisonné, hand-painted porcelain urns and bowls, Victorian realist paintings, and dazzling geological stones. In the local Indian history section, I was awestruck by the displays of practical items—gracefully draped leather garments with elegant stitching and perfectly matched beads. Beyond providing sustenance, clothing, and lodging, the native population had the interest, time, and talent to add exquisite art to functional objects.

During a visit to the Edmonton Art Gallery, while admiring a collection of Post-Impressionist paintings by Canadian artist James Wilson Morrice, I thought back to my art appreciation course in Ann Arbor—and art I hadn't appreciated. I remembered examining slides of the world's most famous art and studying my textbook while a large part of my brain was elsewhere. The only time I concentrated on my work was while scribbling class notes and during exam-cramming hours. Fantasies of women invaded every other activity.

A well-built, salt-and-pepper-haired man walked past me, examining the art.

He looks like Kevin. Is it possible? I last saw him when I left Ann Arbor thirty-five years ago. A year later, he toured the northern states with a friend and didn't return with his friend. Though I didn't expect to find him, I found myself looking for him in areas he might have traveled. *Would I recognize him now?* I walked toward him to get a better look. He was not Kevin.

Kevin. How I missed him. If only I could see him again. If only I could tell him of this journey. Like a big brother, he followed my parents in giving me confidence in my abilities. And how I wish I could share these adventures with Mom and Dad, the first to encourage independence and exploration. I ache to be with them again—give them more as they aged—do things differently, better.

Past days: how I'd love to re-live some, and excise a few others . . .

I'm in my junior year, walking through the Michigan Union looking for Kevin when I see Shelley, a cute, freckled, red-haired classmate. She's sitting with a woman—curly light brown hair, a serious expression, and deep brown eyes a bit too close together. She wears a tailored shirt—handsome, but not mannish. Somehow I sense they're a couple. Shelley introduces Chris as her roommate.

Although Shelley and I are both psychology undergraduates, Chris, a doctoral candidate in clinical psych, speaks to us as equals. We set up a study date here at the Union.

Studying and socializing with my other friends, I do so with only half of my attention. The other half is on Chris. I'm in turmoil. She already has a partner, but I'm obsessed . . .

I don't want to love a woman. I want a traditional life, and I try.

Justin is with me at the University of Michigan. We haven't been a couple since high school, but we date from time to time. One night, we return to Lynne's apartment after a movie. I hang out here as if I'm one of the roommates.

After checking to see that no one is home, he grabs my shoulders, laughing as he pulls me down to the sofa. Here we go again, I think, as he kisses me and begins the routine. Sweater and bra hit the floor, and my jeans are unzipped. I dislike this part, but it's expected, and I wait for it to be over.

I wonder if one of the girls will walk in on us. I remain motionless, not resisting as he tugs on my underpants, forcing them past my knees and then off one foot. And this time he also removes his clothes—all but his shirt. Uh oh, high school is over. The rules have changed. He's waited a long time for this. I don't participate, nor do I stop him. The sensation is not pleasant, but it's bearable.

In a few moments, I'm no longer a virgin . . .

I remembered every detail of that evening with Justin, but only a little about the men who followed. I allowed each current boyfriend to go as far as he wanted. Some initiated kissing and clothed petting, but waited for me to respond before continuing. I didn't—so they didn't. Others assumed an evening automatically ended with intercourse. On those occasions, I stared at the ceiling and endured it, hoping to find a man I might want, a man whose touch would delight me. On reflection, my sexual passivity with men seems odd to me. In all other things, I was in control of my choices, my actions. But this—sex without love—this was something I thought I should try, not something I wanted.

On my way to Saskatchewan, a sign to a restored Ukrainian village brought me out of my trance. The steering wheel turned, seemingly without my help.

In the early twentieth century, a large influx of Ukrainians created villages in Canada much like those they had left behind. Structures originally built many miles apart had been moved to this one location to replicate a full village. Costumed actors ran each enterprise, their roles appropriate to proprietor of church, hotel, restaurant, or shop.

When I arrived at the schoolhouse, the schoolmaster, white shirt sleeves rolled up and chalk dust on his black vest, was straightening bookshelves. The room was immaculate.

"The children here must be very neat," I commented.

"Of course," he said, deadpan, remaining in character. "They know I would thrash the hand of any child who dared to deface a desk."

In a village bakery, an old woman with a bit of flour on her face kneaded dough. She smiled, tapped her fingers on the counter, reached for a muffin, and said in a Jewish-mother's voice, "You look too thin, dear. Have one. You'll love it."

For a few hours, I again lived in a world not my own—far from my memories.

I headed east, through vast empty spaces broken only by the road to Saskatoon, a city of two hundred fifty thousand. Seven bridges over the Saskatchewan River connected the two sides of this town. On each bank, a thick border of trees shaded walking paths, and the Gothic revival Delta Bessborough Hotel, the city's most notable landmark, dominated the river view.

I walked for hours on the river before driving to town for dinner. Since most streets were closed for the annual French Festival, I parked as close as possible and continued on foot, walking on sidewalks of smooth bricks in shades of gray and magenta, laid in geometric patterns and decorated with large flowerpots. *Canadians take advantage of every warm moment to enjoy colorful flowers,* I thought.

A maître d' stood under hanging baskets in front of a restaurant and invited me in. Hoping to find a good steak or fresh grilled fish,

I didn't imagine citrus-flavored table water, peach soup with a touch of anise, and portobello mushrooms sautéed with grapes.

After dinner, performers of every variety occupied each side of the street, and more on the median, interspersed with art displays, food, and huge toys. I stopped frequently to look at pottery—my favorite art form. There were items I would have bought if I were at home, but there was no room in the van. And food smells were enticing, rich, and pungent. I couldn't resist a bowl of chili. A blow-up dog, the size of a small garage, sported a trampoline across its back. When kids jumped, the giant dog wagged its tail and bobbed its head, causing lots of giggling and falling. Noise often bothers me, especially when in a nice restaurant, but the sounds of children laughing, even screaming with delight, make me smile.

Fringe Theater, part of the festival, had six venues presenting thirty different plays during afternoon and evening—each production pushing the edge, not of the mainstream. I selected a one-woman drama about Carry Nation's life. When her first husband died young of alcohol abuse, Carry became obsessed with ridding the world of "evil" drink. The play illustrated how her early life led to powerful efforts to end alcohol use for all time. The final scene was a Prohibition-era saloon—with jarring sounds of machine-gunfire offstage. Her passion successfully led to a ban on liquor, but also to terrifying, unforeseen consequences.

With Prohibition came speakeasies and the mobs needed to supply them. As with drugs and abortion, any attempt to make illegal that which people want leads to a criminal element willing to supply the contraband or service needed, no matter the risk.

I left the theater pondering moral dilemmas and slid back again to memories of days with Kevin—and with Chris . . .

Drinking beer at the Pretzel Bell is what one does on one's twenty-first birthday. Kevin picks me up to take me to the P-Bell, as we call it. To celebrate my special day, he wears a single button tuxedo, tailor-made in Europe when he was in the army. I'm in new jeans. I'm delighted to be out with my handsome best friend, one who took the trouble to dress up for me.

A few friends join us in the noisy, smoky bar. We drink just one pitcher between all of us. Kevin doesn't like to be drunk or high. He says he has enough trouble holding on to reality. And I fall asleep with too much alcohol.

For this birthday, my father, middle-class since bankruptcy, buys me a new car: a white Ford Falcon with blue interior. I drive it to Chris and Shelley's, ostensibly to borrow a book, but really to see Chris again . . .

West of Regina, the famed Murals of Moose Jaw drew me in. These were not any old murals: over forty of them, huge museum-quality artworks depicted historical places or events and covered entire sides of buildings. This town, the size of an Atlanta neighborhood, has managed to create and maintain a living art museum.

Moose Jaw's other attraction is a set of tunnels constructed in the early 1900s to allow boiler-maintenance men to remain warm while going from one building to another.

Not long after these first tunnels were completed, a wave of Chinese immigrants arrived. As in Havre, Montana, prejudice made it dangerous for Asians to appear in public, especially at night. They had little choice but to accept poor wages and live and work in the expanding tunnels.

A few years later, Prohibition demanded surreptitious alcohol transport. The passageways were perfect. Secret underground passages, hiding everything from daylight and the authorities, were also used for gambling and prostitution.

A century later, residents re-invented the tunnels—now an elaborate tourist venue where live actors, robots, and animatronics showed the Chinese living underground, Prohibition-era bars, game tables, and "loose" women.

I went first to the immigrant tunnels, where an actor portrayed a despicable foreman, and we, the tourists, were newly arrived Chinese laborers learning about our upcoming lives as indentured servants. It would take many years, the foreman told us, to pay off our passage and head tax. When we "went to work" in the laundry, an animated robot played the owner, instructing us about our tasks and expected behavior.

On the second tour, we joined a group of "bootleggers" who, we were told, came to Moose Jaw to buy liquor. A bootlegger escorted us into a speakeasy where we saw a realistically simulated pianist playing a ragtime tune. He stopped as another animatronics character, the bartender, welcomed us to town and told us to keep a low profile. He warned about who to avoid and how to stay safe while in this notorious town of illegal activities.

Climbing the stairs, to return to the streets of Moose Jaw, I blinked in bright sunlight and came back to the twenty-first century. Although I love going back in time during travel adventures, I sometimes reflect on what it must have been like to be gay in those days. One never sees gay people in period movies or town reconstructions, yet we know they were there—hidden as I was in my youth. I'm sure most lesbians married and endured sex. A few probably managed to have "roommates" or live life as spinsters. But many probably attached themselves to obviously masculine women. Some were accepted, but several lived as outcasts. So much of our happiness depends on the attitudes of those around us.

CHAPTER 13

Courage

By the time I reached Winnipeg, at the intersection of the Red River and the Assiniboine, I realized I no longer thought of this voyage as a vacation, but rather as my life. The van was home, and roaming these roads my mission. Towns and wilderness, history and art, culture and food—each has moved me further from petty concerns and useless anxieties. This insight made me wonder about my future. Should I buy a larger traveling home and join the folks who live on the road? This would allow me to continue this life indefinitely . . . wandering wherever the mood took me. None of the stress or anxiety connected to close friendships. Make continual the pleasure of new sights and sounds and people. *No*, I thought. *Probably not*. As much as I love this, I also crave deep relationships, the intimacy of long-time friends. But for now, I could continue to enjoy this traveling life with Winnipeg, another new place to explore. The city's heart—a confluence of two rivers now called "The Forks"—the place to begin.

Six thousand years ago, Aboriginals thought—correctly—this area would be a great place to settle, a perfect place for trade. Business thrives in Forks Market, a marriage of modern mall and old-fashioned bazaar begun in the early 1900s as a pair of adjacent stables. Unlike a bazaar planned from inception for shopping, Winnipeg's version originated when bridges joined these neighboring horse stalls, soon providing an area for fur trading. Now this market had a multitude of shops offering everything from cigars to baked goods, gourmet cheeses to aboriginal art. But unlike a modern mall, it had the atmosphere of an old marketplace, the complete opposite of the West Edmonton Mall fourteen hours behind me.

The aromas of freshly cooked food reminded me I was hungry. Unlike any Atlanta food court, a wide variety of edibles was displayed on counters—no neon anywhere, no fast food, no golden arches. I was tempted by noodle dishes, curries, skewered meats, fresh baked pies, souvlaki . . . a seemingly endless array of choices.

I chose stuffed grape leaves then strolled halls lined on both sides with crafts and artworks: silver jewelry, ceramic dinnerware, framed photographs, watercolors and oils, handmade totes, batik cloth, and silk scarves.

The tranquil waterfront outside readied me for the quiet of the next drive. Leaving Winnipeg, I noticed many car dealerships—more than one might expect. At a gas stop, I asked the cashier about this curious phenomenon.

"Well, they're all owned by Mennonites from Steinbach—that's a town a few miles down the road. See, everyone knows you get a fair deal from Mennonites. All of Winnipeg buys cars here."

"What's that about?"

"They're very honest. And with cars, you gotta bargain. When you bargain, you gotta know the seller's not gonna cheat you."

With a population of fewer than ten thousand, Steinbach had twenty-two churches. It was clear that a place of worship was the heart of each small community. Here I found Mennonite Heritage Village, preserving traditional sixteenth-century life, a manner of living that has all but disappeared.

An interpreter at the church explained Mennonite values. "A really important issue for us is peace," he said. "But even though we're exempted from military duty, we struggle with the moral issues of war. For some of us, there's a time to make exceptions. During World War Two, for example, some folks bought war bonds, and a few even chose to serve in the military. This stuff isn't simple. Honest hard work, a simple life, contributions to society, and help for the less fortunate. The reason we go to church is to learn to live virtuously."

I left the church with a gut-wrenching memory of my own battles with morality and my efforts to find answers in religion . . .

Several days a week, after dinner with Kevin, I go to Chris and Shelley's to study.

When I look up from my book, I often see Chris's deep brown eyes fixed on my face. She returns my feelings, but remains committed to Shelley. We finish our evenings with conversation and Scotch or bourbon. We usually drink too much. Sometimes Shelley falls asleep. Then Chris and I talk, but rarely about our feelings for each other. Sometimes while sitting beside me, she lightly touches my hand. Once, late at night and very drunk, she tells me she loves me.

My problem isn't only that I love a woman; it's also that she already has a partner.

I make an appointment with the rabbi at the University's Hillel House. I'm not a member, but he'll see me anyway. I talk to him freely, assuming correctly that he won't judge my sexuality. He understands that the main problem is Chris's involvement in another relationship. He advises me—kindly, gently— to find someone else.

I'm unable to do this. I have never found it possible to deliberately end a love, even those that have come to fruition only in my imagination. And to make it even harder, there is nowhere to go to find lesbians. It happens by accident . . . or not at all.

I want to talk with my sister Donna—like most sisters do. But how will she even begin to understand my life? Like me, she went to college, but after three months of struggle, she phoned to tell Mom and Dad she wanted to come home. They weren't happy, but they knew she tried to fulfill their wishes. She returned to Chicago to study hairstyling, and to Chuck, her handsome boyfriend since early high school. She married him a few years later.

She's four feet nine inches and weighs less than one hundred pounds. When my friends first meet her, they must think, What a tiny woman. *But they tell me they're impressed with how straight she stands and the authority in her voice. She wants to be close to me, but she might tell Mom and Dad. She's close to both of them. Their lives are still too difficult, too stressful. Dad still works twelve-hour days. They have never recovered a social life due to the ongoing stigma of bankruptcy. This news would be like someone handing them an ice cube during a blizzard.*

I can't talk with her . . .

She tells me now that she cried when I left for college. I had no idea. She wrote every week, and I responded only with letters to the entire family. And my letters said nothing of feelings—only the daily facts. I missed them all, but they were in the background. My focus was on trying to find a man I might love—while simultaneously looking for lesbians—and going to classes and passing exams.

After Steinbach, the next stop was Eagle Canyon and Canada's longest suspension footbridge—six hundred feet across. Though I am bridge-phobic while driving, there was no way I would miss the excitement of walking across this deep chasm.

Starting across the bridge, I faced a ragged rock wall, four hundred feet high. Massive trees clung to the opposite bank. Rocks and trees sheltered a slim, calm, serpentine river. I looked across, down, left, and right, thrilled to see from a bird's vantage. The structure rocked and swayed as people moved, but its wooden slats were solid under my feet, and the mesh side-walls preempted any fear of falling.

I stare down from the edge into a twisting, craggy riverbed, a feature of this glacier-carved landscape—the most beautiful place I've ever seen—transfixed by its slow yet unexpected turns. I'm twenty-three, Chris thirty. We're in Watkins Glen State Park with Shelley and another friend. Chris and I walk together on the side of the rock wall, lagging behind the other two. Between my romantic thrall, the curved craggy rocks, the long waterfalls, the steep drop, and her hand in mine—I'm in an agonizing ecstasy. After a sharp turn, we're suddenly, momentarily alone. She puts both hands on my face, gently pulls me to her, and we kiss for the first time.

Then, just as quickly, we part, not speaking, walking on in this magical place . . .

I left the swinging bridge at Eagle Canyon, savoring my exploit and wishing Chris had shared it. I returned to the van and continued to Thunder Bay, the home of Old Fort William, an early-nineteenth-century construction, the largest fur trading center in the world. A young "colonial" welcomed me to the fort, conversing in his early-nineteenth-century British dialect, helping me feel at home in this time and place. Leaving him, I wandered in and out of structures, meeting other "inhabitants" dressed in period clothing. Scottish managers evaluated profits and inventory, clerks kept records with quill pens, and Canadian laborers paddled canoes and delivered furs carried by Frenchmen while Ojibwa canoe builders worked on lightweight boats.

I encountered an argument between a craftsman and the fort's manager and, in another area, a council meeting to discuss trading confrontations between the North West Company and the "treacherous" Hudson Bay Company. Allowed to eavesdrop, I felt invisible and omniscient.

After leaving the fort, the far eastern edge of Thunder Bay offered a poignant moment: a nine-foot bronze memorial to Terry Fox, a man who lost one leg to cancer when he was only eighteen and had a recurrence a few years later. The suffering he witnessed in cancer wards inspired him to work for cancer research.

Terry raised close to twenty-five million dollars and won several awards, some posthumously, for his achievement. Others, stirred by his courage, follow in his path and continue his work.

In 1980, Terry began a fund-raising run across Canada, starting in Newfoundland and expecting to finish four thousand miles away in Victoria, British Columbia. Reporters followed him as he ran to

Thunder Bay, three thousand miles through snow, rain, and intense heat, stopping only when cancer resurfaced in his lungs.

He ran for one hundred forty-three days. He was twenty-two when he died.

I stood by his statue, awed by his willingness to give the last days of his young life to benefit others. At twenty-two, focused on my career and accomplishments—and women—I was considerably less aware of the plights of others . . .

I am a graduate student, studying communication disorders and clinical psychology. I intern in the Speech and Hearing Clinic, working with patients under supervision, and I also work as a research assistant. I spend a lot of time thinking of Chris. My patients are, to me, experimental subjects. I distance myself from their pain.

I'm excited about a model I've developed for post-stroke patients who have trouble remembering words. I call it "self-cueing," and I'm writing about it, hopefully for publication. I invite a fellow student to co-author. The paper is accepted, and we're pleased with the response. It was the first effort, at least in print, to develop coping strategies in addition to reducing the problem itself.

My research assignment is to analyze data for an experiment conducted by my professor. He adds my name as second author. He teaches me research methodology, but he also gently reminds me that the work we do is ultimately to benefit patients. I need the reminder. I am still preoccupied with Chris while simultaneously hoping to find a man. This conflict is driving me nuts.

He introduces me to Dr. Wilson P. Tanner, a well-known professor of experimental psychology and the director of the Sensory Intelligence Laboratory. Dr. Tanner says, "Call me Spike."

His model, known as Signal Detection Theory, analyzes decision making in the presence of uncertainty. His research indicates that subjects draw conclusions based on probabilities. This interests me because it may explain how listeners make a decision about slurred or distorted speech. I enroll in his seminar, and after finals, he invites me to work in his lab.

He tells me I'll be an assistant on one of the established grants while I write my dissertation proposal. After an agency agrees to fund my idea, he'll expect me to pay one of the new students. This lets me know he believes my research will be funded.

My proposal describes a new way of examining how listeners understand distorted speech. In current tests, a subject listens to a list of unclear words and attempts to identify each one. The score is based on how many words are correctly identified. In my research, instead of looking at the percent of correct responses, I'll use a mathematical model to measure the degree to which the listener is uncertain. My thinking is that this is a more accurate representation of the degree of distortion in the speech and that the listener selects a word based on probabilities, just as Spike has demonstrated in the detection of signals.

My proposal is accepted by the Navy. As I work with data, I often forget the admonition that all this is done for patients, real people.

I'm proud of my accomplishments . . .

Before returning to my van, I looked again at Terry's statue and thought about the value of his short life. I had been nothing like Terry Fox. I remembered my early grad school days as a student clinician. When in a therapy session, my focus was totally on the patient, on his struggles, and what I might do to help. But when doing research, I concentrated intently on the numbers, never thinking about how they might be used for human benefit. It was many years before I matured to Terry's level of empathy for others, enabling me, at last, to add compassion to my clinical work.

It was good to get back on the quiet road between tiny communities on the north shore of Lake Superior. There was nothing unnatural: no billboards, no shacks, no shops, and no cappuccino. Instead, thick forest, dark pink-and-gray rock, and water—all changing colors with the sun's movement—flanked the curving road blasted out of the mountainside.

Late in the afternoon, I found Rossport Inn, built in 1884 to house railway travelers.

Simple antiques, bookshelves, and handmade quilts decorated my cabin. Bright pink and purple flowers filled the window box overlooking Rossport Harbor. The silence was broken only by the sounds of waterfowl.

In a small dining room facing the lake, I ate broiled whitefish and corn on the cob so sweet it would have been an insult to add butter. Alone, I relished bird songs, the drone of hushed conversation from neighboring tables, and the gentle lapping of waves sliding on the shore.

I didn't feel the passage of time. There was no destination propelling me forward, no past and no future. Each glorious moment was replaced by the next.

Eagle Canyon
Ontario

Agawa Bay
Ontario

Sault Ste. Marie
Ontario

Manitoulin Island
Ontario

CHAPTER 14

The Soo

I left the Rossport Inn, heading across Lake Superior's north edge toward Sault Ste. Marie . . . another set of gifts waiting to be discovered and unwrapped.

The first was the drive itself, skirting the stunning blue water, again with almost no traffic. About thirty miles north of my destination, I saw large, lifelike wooden sculptures displayed on the side of the road and a sign saying "The Canadian Carver." I screeched to a stop and turned in to get a closer look at an elderly couple sitting in rocking chairs, a man smoking a pipe, a woman working on a piece of embroidery, and a woodsman with a mustache, cap, and rifle. Each piece was museum-quality art, notable for their natural postures, expressive faces, and detail in the wooden clothing.

Thirty miles further down the road was the boat ride I'd been wanting since first setting eyes on Lake Superior. This one was a tour of the Sault Ste. Marie Locks, the "Soo Locks," an immense waterway traffic system: an elevator allowing boats to navigate the twenty-foot height difference between lakes Superior and Huron.

A total of five locks raised boats and ships the seven meters between Lake Huron and Lake Superior, the largest ones for the huge Great Lakes freighters.

I climbed into the boat, excitedly anticipating the experience of going through the lock. As we approached, an opening appeared, allowing us to enter a walled area not much larger than our vessel, and then a gate closed behind us. As water was released, the boat descended to the level of Lake Huron. As we sank, the walls seemed to rise. Dwarfed in a channel between twenty-foot barriers, I marveled at the magnitude of this engineering accomplishment and wondered aloud about its birth.

I was told that on the way from Superior to Huron, there is a section of rapids where the water falls twenty feet, a drop that made ship passage impossible. Prior to the locks, it was necessary to unload the boats, haul the cargoes by land, and reload onto other boats, adding immensely to the effort and cost of transport. The US Army Corps of Engineers tackled the problem and came up with this inventive solution.

After a night of camping, I took an afternoon train ride to Agawa Canyon. I chose to sit in an upper-level car, a dome with immaculate wide windows arching into the ceiling. We departed from an ugly, industrial part of town, but dirty concrete quickly gave way to gasp-inducing scenery. Sometimes we rode so high that we looked down at treetops, rocks, and rivers. At other times, the tracks were carved into the mountainside, with the rocks and trees close enough to touch. At one point, the train crossed the Montreal River on a curved, six-hundred-foot trestle—one side perched over clear water; the other, a steep, forested drop. I could pay full attention to my surroundings—something not possible when I had to navigate.

With the sparkling windows and a bit of imagination, I could imagine floating through this remarkable landscape.

Disembarking at the canyon, I saw a narrow band of manicured lawn, landscaped flowers, and a walking path.

With some of the other passengers, I walked along the canyon's ridge to two waterfalls, each a thousand feet high, one straight down a stair-stepped rock face and the other with many streams flowing over the irregular stone surface, both exuding a fine spray.

Several yards in front of me, a small boy walked behind his parents. His mother shivered in the cool mist. The dad took his jacket off, put it over her shoulders, and pulled her close—a display of affection and intimacy appearing like muscle memory.

It's the day after Thanksgiving and warm for the season. Slacks and a sweater seem perfect for our movie date. But, as we wait in line for our tickets, the temperature drops. Raymond removes his jacket, places it around my shoulders, and leaves his arm around me. I wonder if a woman would do this for me.

Raymond was one class ahead of me in high school. Now we're both in graduate school. I'm still in Ann Arbor, and he's in Massachusetts studying physics. We date when we're in Chicago for holiday breaks. The following month, we're home for winter vacation. It's Christmas Eve and we're going to a party with other couples from our old crowd. On the way home, we stop to make out. He calls me "darling" as we kiss in the back seat.

At the end of the evening, I'm puzzled that he doesn't ask me out for New Year's Eve, and I wait all week for his call . . . a call that never comes. Someone tells me he has a date with his campus girlfriend who's come to visit him in Chicago.

A week later, his mother tells me he's engaged. She says he agonized over his decision—which girlfriend to marry. I don't tell her he made the right choice. What, I wonder, would I have done had he asked me?

After Agawa, the road led to Manitoulin Island, a respite where museums were unlike those in cities. Throughout the history of the island, residents collected family relics, items once commonly used but long ago replaced and saved as a memory. Each museum was tiny, with its own purpose and personality. The "Post Office Museum," originally built in 1890, had been a general store and post office.

I was impressed by ice-harvesting tools, a milk-processing machine, and butter-making equipment, all relocated from pioneer farms. A wicker wheelchair was something I never imagined. In lieu of an electric dryer, they used a flat, sock-shaped board with quarter-size holes to shorten sock-drying time. The town doctor recorded his notes on a 1925 Dictaphone's wax cylinder. An 1890s phone booth contained a large black device with separate ear and mouth pieces and a hand-crank. I couldn't help but compare it to the cell phone in my pocket.

All of these items were in common use during the time of my grandparents. What will we use in another hundred years?

I'd rarely considered the engineers and scientists who created my everyday miracles: ice dropping out of a hole in my freezer and light appearing when I flick a switch, a video entering my living room, a voice floating from my phone to Japan—much less a navigation system that knows exactly where I am and where I'm going.

My campsite on Manitoulin Island was on the bay and I awoke each morning while it was still dark. The first day, as I sipped morning tea, black sky lightened over the lake while gold and lavender decorated the horizon. No anxiety, nothing but this view.

The second day was gloomy. Sunrise consisted of two narrow strips of white between thick clouds and murky water. Darkness gave way to grays behind thin black branches waving in the wind of an oncoming storm.

Everything I needed was in the van: more tea, a couple of hard-boiled eggs, a fresh roll heated in the microwave. I slid under the electric blanket and read, listening to fat drops crashing on my metal car.

Since my decision, many weeks ago, to forego Alaska in favor of the freedom to choose to stop—and stay—in every appealing place, I have honored my impulses, rarely planning beyond the next day.

No rush. What a feeling. Stratford, the next stop, would be there no matter when I arrived.

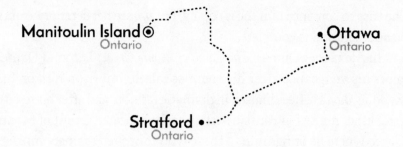

CHAPTER 15

Illusions

Though Stratford is home to just thirty thousand residents, it hosts a half-million guests each summer for the annual Shakespearean Festival. I drove into town and went immediately to the ticket office. Four theaters were presenting fourteen plays. I selected three, none by Shakespeare: *The Elephant Song*, a tense psychological drama; *The Human Voice*, a one-woman monologue about a love affair's end; and *The Count of Monte Cristo*.

In *The Elephant Song,* by Nicolas Billon, a prominent psychiatrist disappears. Michael, a patient obsessed with elephants and opera, is the last person to have seen him. Insanity and hospital politics complicate the investigation. My muscles stiffened as I remembered hospital politics at my VA Medical Center, but I was abruptly transported back to the play when Barbara Dunn-Prosser began to sing, exquisitely and hauntingly.

Jean Cocteau's *The Human Voice* unfolds in a monologue: a woman conversing with her ex-lover. Talking on a mid-twentieth-century phone equipped with a party-line and operators, she recalls events from their time together and tells him of her heartbreak. Desperate, she tries to convince him she is coping, but we see her deteriorate until her devastation is complete.

In Alexander Dumas' *The Count of Monte Cristo,* Edmond Dantes plots his vengeance after his enemies falsely imprison him on his wedding day. He frees himself in dramatic fashion, and after his rescue, establishes himself in Parisian society as the educated Count of Monte Cristo where he brings ruin to those who conspired against him. Sets and lighting effects allow split-second shifts, moving the action instantly from a jail to a storm at sea to a bar with no curtain-closings or stage hands.

Injustice and the triumph of good over evil—the theater was a complete diversion. While fully absorbed, I had no sexual preference, I forgot the hell of my parents' last years, and Chris did not exist.

Years ago, I had been to Stratford with Chris and Shelley and loved everything about it: theaters, rivers, parks, and food. This time, between theater events, I hiked, picnicked, and kayaked on the Avon River, just as we had done before . . .

Chris and Shelley and I have driven north from Ann Arbor to Stratford. We see plays, listen to folk songs, and wander on the river. As we sit on the bank, eating sandwiches bought at a gourmet wine and take-out shop, I think about how to answer recent letters—one from my sister and one from my dad. I'll tell them about this trip to Stratford but will not tell them about my companions.

My letters home are superficial: weather, my exams, a new guy. My sister would like to know more about my life, and I want to tell her—but I don't. She'd probably tell Mom.

My parents have moved from our four-bedroom home to a small apartment. Dad works long hours, and Mom has a part-time job; they smile at weddings and bar mitzvahs. We're all pretending.

Home for a holiday, I see my dad in his easy chair, feet up, wearing pajamas and slippers, reading my psychology textbook from last year—his way of trying to share my life. I want a real relationship with my family, but with a significant part of my life a secret, a censor sits on my shoulder during every communication.

No conversation flows easily . . .

How I wished I had found a way to come out to my family in those difficult college days. I needed them. But forty years have passed, and there's nothing I can do to correct the past.

One afternoon, I was walking in the Shakespearean Garden, enjoying every flower and fragrant herb he mentioned, when it began to rain—quarter-sized globules, with almost no space between the drops. Far from my car, I walked fast, head down, as if I could get less wet that way. At a crossroad, I looked up and saw a tea shop. Hoping to dry off and drink a hot "cuppa," I rushed in, bedraggled and dripping on the floor. There was one other customer, a well-dressed man, browsing the selection.

I walked to the counter while trying to dry my hands on my wet shirt. "A hot cup of whatever you recommend," I said to a man in an apron.

"We don't serve tea. We just sell it," he said kindly. "We're planning to get set up so we can give out samples, but we're not there yet." He waved his arm toward display shelves, and added, "We sell bulk tea and spices from all over the world—nothing you can drink here. But you can rest inside 'til the rain stops."

So I settled for shaking myself in an effort to dry off, inhaling aromas while waiting for a reprieve, and chatting with the manager.

"I love tea but don't know much about it. Why do connoisseurs laugh at tea bags?"

He smiled and said, "Good leaves are used only for bulk tea—usually it's leftover shavings in the bags."

"And what's the story with green tea? Why's it supposed to be so healthy? Is that a myth?" I shivered, still damp and chilled.

"Nope. And do you know about white tea?" I shook my head. "Well, white tea comes from very young leaves, low in caffeine and high in antioxidants. Green tea is between white and black. So white and green teas are very smooth—and healthy too."

Another man appeared at the door, shaking water from his umbrella before entering. He approached the other customer, kissed him on the cheek, dripped some water, and said, "Sorry dear." The first man pulled a handkerchief from his pocket, wiped the wet forehead of the new arrival, and said, "Not important, sweetheart. What matters is you're here."

They do nothing to hide their affection. How different this was from relationships during my college days. In public, gay couples looked like pals, never holding hands on the street, never sitting in a movie with an arm over a loved one's shoulder. We were able to find each other through gossip, guessing, and the few who were out to the world.

It's a stormy day, and I'm sitting in the Union at a circular table with several friends and acquaintances, including Tom, an openly gay man, and Jennifer, a straight woman.

Hugh arrives, dries himself with some table napkins, and joins us. He is a slim, perfectly-groomed Canadian, clean-shaven with neatly trimmed hair. He's about to complete his PhD in clinical psychology. Tom has told me Hugh is gay. Jennifer knows about both men, but not about me. In this group, only Tom knows I'm one of them. Jennifer has told me about her concern that Hugh will try to get homosexuals to accept their "condition." She pretends to be open-minded about gays, and perhaps she thinks she is. But like so many in these days, she believes we are sick and should be cured. And that can only be accomplished by a heterosexual therapist.

Hugh puts his briefcase on the table, hangs his wet jacket on the back of the chair, and then goes through the line for a cup of coffee. When he returns, Jennifer makes an attempt to influence Hugh. She opens a conversation about the fact that the American Psychiatric Association considers homosexuality a disease. She adds that homosexual therapists might be okay for some patients, but they shouldn't try to treat homosexuals.

Hugh doesn't realize Jennifer knows about him. He's unaware of her motives. He looks down and says nothing.

Tom and I are both in therapy—hoping to find our buried heterosexual selves. Our therapists share this goal and work diligently to "cure" us. Since

I believe the goal of treatment is to heal this "disease," I silently wonder if Jennifer is right.

I like Hugh too much to say anything . . .

In the Stratford tea shop, in the rain, I thought about my two selves—ripped apart in childhood—living in one skin. When I sat with friends in the Union so long ago, I believed the only way to repair the cleft was to learn to live a heterosexual life.

I shook myself again, this time to shed thoughts.

The rain stopped, but I didn't want to leave this shop with its wonderful aromas and the openly affectionate men. I savored a few more minutes before moving on.

My next stop was Ottawa, Canada's capital. In addition to traditional urban offerings, fifty thousand acres of green space distinguish this city: flower gardens, vast lawns, and tall trees. New York City's Central Park is less than a thousand acres.

The Ottawa River divides the land into Ontario's Ottawa and Quebec's French Gatineau. The architecture is a stunning mix of sleek modern and elegant neo-gothic, with copper roofs and steeples of various shades of green and brown, especially stunning when sunlight brightens the metal.

The roof of the Canadian Museum of Civilization consists of over one hundred thousand square feet of copper, more than any other building in the world. Built of pale tan stone, the exterior is a graceful sculpture.

There are probably many reasons to visit museums, but the best one was posted at the entrance of this museum. "Our elders say that the old people are speaking to us through the stones and bones they left behind long ago. It is time to listen and hear their story."

The bottom floor is fifty feet high with fountains and floor-to-ceiling windows along one long, curved wall. Twenty-five totem poles, carved of red cedar, range from ten to forty-five feet high with bases as wide as four feet. I imagined the carvers watching as the finished poles rose to stand vertically for the first time and wondered how they felt standing at the base of their amazing finished creations.

One exhibit of small Canadian villages, each from a different time period, has a one-hundred-foot-high ceiling that—with tricks of lighting, color, and fabric—successfully mimics sky. Although I was inside, it seemed as though I was outdoors strolling through real villages.

The next day, inside the National Gallery of Art, I saw a full-size restoration of the nineteenth-century Rideau Convent Chapel, originally a part of the Convent of Our Lady of the Sacred Heart on Rideau Street, one of Ottawa's major streets.

When the convent was demolished in 1972, the chapel was salvaged and put on permanent display in the National Gallery. I thought about how humankind creates, enjoys, and then destroys—and that this beautiful structure was one we managed to save.

The chapel, completely enclosed, has no access to outdoor light, but artificial illumination behind stained-glass windows spread a soft glow across the interior—making me feel I was bathed in sunshine. As it was in the Museum of Civilization's Canadian villages, creative lighting transported me outdoors while my corporeal body remained under a solid roof.

What is it about illusion that is so satisfying?

CHAPTER 16

Antonio and Danny

Before leaving Ottawa, I sat at my picnic table with a guidebook and a glass of wine, reading about the seventeenth-century founding of Montreal. Situated at the intersection of two major waterways, it was ideal for fur trading. The French Catholic founders established a varied society with large colonies of Italians, British, Chinese, and Irish, alongside the natives already thriving in the area, each playing a role in the development of this eclectic Canadian city.

Book knowledge aside, I heard that French Canada has outstanding restaurants, stunning architecture, and an old section that would give me a taste of history.

After arriving in Montreal, but before finding a campsite, I parked on a side street and walked the oldest part of town. It was easy to find my way—it was a square mile on the river. Nearby, a newer section occupied another square mile. Unlike cities where sound comes from machines and the décor is concrete, the predominant sound of Montreal is music from cafés and street performers, and concrete is rendered nearly invisible by brilliantly colored flowers, green copper roofs, fountains, and cobblestone streets.

As archeologists uncovered wooden furniture, cooking implements, and pottery from every period in the city's past, they left them where they were found. The Museum of Archeology and History, a triangular structure on a sharp corner, was built on top of them, leaving the artifacts for display in the exact spot where they had last been in use.

In this unique museum, I walked underground between partially destroyed stone walls of the early city. Projected onto these walls were films of actors participating in eighteenth-century life. The effect was so real that I felt I had joined them, clinking mugs of ale across a wooden table, browsing in the market, and buying meat for my family supper.

In another section, under glass panels in the floor, miniature replicas of the town showed how the city changed over four centuries. The segments—each approximately twenty by thirty inches—contained models of buildings and streets as they were in a particular time period. In a neighboring section, the same area was duplicated as it was some years later. It was thrilling to see the changes as historic Montreal developed into the international city it is today.

Leaving the museum on foot, I was soon startled by a full city block of glass-paneled windows: red, yellow, green, and blue, the colors dramatically cast onto the gray stone floor inside. *Is this a hotel? An art center?* I wandered inside, bathed in iridescent hues, searching for answers.

It was Montreal's popular convention center, *Palais des congrès,* as bold and unique as the city—a city in which beauty accompanies function.

The next day I visited the early nineteenth-century Notre Dame Basilica. The ornate and elegant interior is encircled by elaborate scenes in stained glass depicting Montreal's history. Carved wood trimmed with gold leaf, a seven-thousand-pipe organ, bronze sculptures, and corkscrew staircases only begin to describe the sumptuous space.

I drove three hours from Montreal to the town of Levis, where I found a good campground. A brief ferry ride across the St. Lawrence

River took me to Old Town Quebec, where a huge castlelike building dominated the shoreline: the Château Frontenac, the city's most celebrated structure—where the price of a suite *started* at two thousand dollars *per night!* Massive chandeliers hung from the ballroom ceiling. My entire eighteen-month trip, van included, would cost less than one of those chandeliers.

With its medieval architecture, sharply pitched and patinaed copper roofs, stone shops and houses, curving cobblestone streets, and views of river and mountains, Quebec City, capital of the province, was one of the most enchanting cities I'd seen anywhere.

Old Town was a small village including an upper and lower section. Two routes, both difficult, led from one to the other. One was a steep, winding street called *Côte de la Montagne,* the other a stairway built into the nearly vertical cliff. I flipped a coin and took the stairs.

Winding through narrow streets, I passed shops and chic cafés with French and English menus posted near the sidewalk. Drifting aromas were tantalizing. Famished after my climb, I stopped for a *tourtière québecois*—a sizzling hot meat pie with pork, potatoes, and onions inside a flaky pastry, with gravy leaking onto the plate. Calories be damned!

Feet and legs weary, I returned to the ferry and watched rippling water while anticipating my return the next day.

On the second morning, I moved slowly, exploring more streets and shops. I stopped to look in a clothing store window with colorful Mexican serapes covering the side walls. In French Canada. *How funny!* And I remembered Antonio, the only Mexican I met in college. He was as unusual in Ann Arbor as a serape here . . .

I'm in my mid-twenties. The phone rings in my one-room efficiency graduate-student apartment. A man introduces himself as Antonio Friedman, a Mexican-Jewish astronomer who wants to meet a female Jewish graduate student. He's been looking for Jewish names in the graduate student directory, and early in his alphabetical search, he found Berman.

Was I interested in meeting him?

Sure, I say, still hoping some man will make me fall in love, and arrange a date for the following night. The next evening, I go as usual to Kevin's house for dinner. One of us cooks and the other does dishes. Tonight, Kevin has invited his girlfriend, Caroline, and Danny, a friend from his undergraduate days who has recently moved to Ann Arbor.

Danny is an Air Force captain studying for a master's degree in physics. He's as handsome as Kevin, also as muscular, but broader. His short brown hair contrasts with Kevin's longer locks.

During dinner, I tell them the story about the Mexican-Jewish astronomer and that we'll be meeting immediately after dinner. Danny asks if I mind if he does something humorous during my date. I tell him I don't mind and give it no more thought.

Shortly after I return to my apartment, there's a knock. I open it to see Antonio, a dark, slim man with regular features and a serious expression. Oh, I think, this won't be too bad. We sit, drinking wine as he speaks about astronomy—in a monotone. Then he speaks about his home in Mexico. No inflection whatsoever.

I look at my watch and hope he'll go soon, but he asks for another glass of wine.

When I get up to pour, there's another knock on the door. Puzzled, I open it to see Danny dressed in full flying gear, goggles on his head, holding a pair of shoes in one hand and pants and a sweater on a hanger in the other. I'm speechless.

"Hi," he says, grinning as he enters and opens the freestanding closet. He throws his boots inside, hangs the clothes, slaps his hands together, and says to my guest, "I don't care what she does when I'm gone, but I'm back. She wasn't expecting me."

Danny turns to me. "I need to change. Do you mind?" I shake my head dumbly and he begins to unzip his one-piece flying suit, pulls it off, and exposes his muscled physique covered only by his white long johns with a drop seat. Antonio says nothing and sits motionless.

Danny pulls jeans over his underwear and then puts on his sweater. He sits in the small space between me and Antonio, looking directly at him. "Would you like to have us help you find a date?" Antonio apologizes for intruding, stands, and puts on his coat. "It was nice to meet you," he says as he opens the door and disappears.

"This is great," Danny says, looking at his watch. "We've got twenty minutes before we're supposed to meet Kevin and Caroline."

I smiled, remembering Danny and the fun we had that year, returning to the present only when a delicatessen window displaying cheeses, breads, and fresh fruit interrupted my thoughts. I splurged again, this time on berries with a large wedge of locally made brie. This sensuous city encouraged indulgence.

The next day delivered truly nasty weather—strong winds and a driving storm. But I had no intention of sitting in the van or the campground clubhouse. The ferry was running, so I boarded, sat near a window, and watched rain pounding the waves.

Disembarking couples previously holding hands grasped umbrella handles, working to prevent the ribs and canopy from turning inside out.

It was an easy decision to take a guided bus tour instead of relying on my feet and wet maps. The option I chose was *Île d'Orléans*, not far from Quebec City. The bus would take me from site to site, let me out to explore, and tell me what time to return—an effortless day.

Though the bus leaked over every seat, and each site was several yards from the bus door, nothing dampened the spirits of these hearty tourists.

The most enchanting stop was another church, the Basilica of *Sainte-Anne-de-Beaupré*. Its two towering spires and six-sided entrance, lit night and day, dominated the pastoral setting on the Saint Lawrence River.

Once through the doors, the first thing I saw was a huge pyramid filled with discarded crutches and canes, giving credence to its reputation as a place of healing. I thought about people who didn't have full use of their legs, or any other significant body part. How trivial my problems were in comparison—how hard this is to remember. My life, my difficulties, me, my, mine.

Entering the nave, I stopped. Though visitors had been conversing as we walked, there was now only silence. I was stunned again by craftsmanship and artistry.

This church was larger than most, and less ornate, but elegant in other ways. Frescos decorated vaulted ceilings highlighted with gold leaf and painted simply in cream and tan.

Mosaics filled round skylights and covered the aisles. Columns displayed more mosaics, capturing light and causing pillars to appear as though they were made of stained glass. This was a place of prayer—spiritual and transcendent.

Montreal and Quebec had exceeded every expectation.

I left Quebec and headed south. Passing a river, I saw a couple canoeing, gazing at each other as they meandered through the narrow waterway. I thought again about my romantic interlude with Danny . . .

Danny and I continue to date. He doesn't initiate sex unless the woman does—I never do. He tells me he finds our relationship unusual in that he really doesn't know what to do with a woman with whom he isn't intimate. But, he says, he finds himself thinking about me often. He adds, carelessly, that I'm not really his type—cute but too short—yet he still wants to spend time with me.

Spring is over. He completes his degrees and is transferred to Boston. I'm a counselor at a summer camp near his new home. When he picks me up for an evening out, my campers tell me they think he's gorgeous. On our last date before my return to Ann Arbor, he takes me canoeing on the Concord River. We stop at an isolated site, a historic cabin with a trapdoor covering a place to hide during Indian raids.

Back in the canoe, soft breezes, a deep blue sky, and feathery clouds escort us on our last date . . .

It was mid-September, and I'd been living on the road for almost five months. While most others go south from November through April, I wanted to experience winter drama on the New England coast. I have dreamed of a winter like this for many years, but even if I could find campgrounds open, I didn't think the van would be comfortable at night.

It would be an odd move after months on the road, just Mazie and me; it certainly appeared more stagnant. And yet, I thought, it won't be my old familiar house. I won't have to worry about the lawn and broken appliances and plumbing repairs. These things would be the owner's problem. I would still be far from home, exploring new territory at my leisure and joy. Being in a static home would not end my travels; it offered a new type of living, different from two-lane traveling, but also the homunculus life I was living before. And I had the freedom to stay for the entire winter, not just a two-month vacation, allowing ample time for whatever adventures arrived. I had decided months back that my journey would cease focusing on destinations and expectations—I would embrace what was in front of me. As with the abandoned frontier of Medora or the staggering allure of Glacier National Park, I was not going to pass it by.

My first job was to find a home for the next six months. After I knew where I would be staying during the cold months, I would fly to several social events around the country—sufficiently important to interrupt my trip and fortunately all in the month of October.

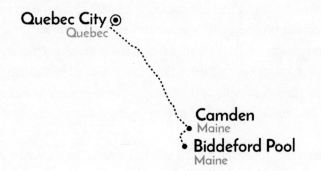

Quebec City ⊙
Quebec

Camden
Maine
Biddeford Pool
Maine

CHAPTER 17

Winter Is Coming

Maps lay unopened on the seat beside me as Mazie led the way from Quebec to Maine. At the border, a guard approached and first asked for my passport, and then what I'd been doing in Canada. After hearing I'd been touring, he peered into the back of the van, turned toward me, smiled, and said, "So, you lived in the van! Hope you enjoyed your visit. Have a nice trip home."

And then he waved me on.

Driving across the invisible boundary, there was no change in either the landscape or the people. *Borders*, I thought, as I often thought during international travel, *are imaginary lines arbitrarily separating peoples*. A psychologist friend has told me Homo sapiens are hard-wired to distrust anyone outside our group, whoever that might be. And it's so easy to recognize an outsider by language, skin color, or shape of eyes. Perhaps that's the problem heterosexuals have with gays. They don't know who we are unless—by word or action—we tell them.

The road wound through mountains and alongside an unspoiled river, treetops brushed with the subtle touch of early autumn. Author Anne Perry expressed my feelings when she said, "A deep calm lay over everything, so sweet and unbroken it seemed to be within the very nature of the land itself, as if in time it could resolve all ugliness and sorrow and melt grief as the spring melts snow to feed the birth of flowers."

When gently curving Route 1 was not embracing the ocean, it hugged forests, lakes, and rivers. Further south, it passed quiet harbor towns, with colorful sails and fishing boats reminding me of the yellow-slickered fishermen on seafood packages. Although there was an occasional chain store or fast-food restaurant, most businesses were locally owned.

Fresh fish, crab, and lobster were sold everywhere.

Route 1 became Main Street with no warning, cutting directly through the heart of affluent Camden—a town on one of the best-places-to-retire lists. Old buildings had been reborn as restaurants and shops, including galleries featuring watercolors, woodworks, sculpture, glass, and pottery.

Before browsing, I stopped for lunch on the deck of a café where the Megunticook River ran under its foundations on its way to join the waters in the harbor.

How about this gorgeous place for the winter, I thought.

Just outside of town, I found a campground with luxurious amenities: free wireless, a clubhouse, a hot tub, and the morning paper delivered to my van as I drank my tea—perfect for the several-week stay before my flight to the first October event. Glacier National Park was the last place I had stayed for several weeks. Like Glacier, Camden offered a wealth of activities for entertainment during the hours I wouldn't be house hunting. Daytime weather was ideal for hiking and water activities, but finding a house was the first priority.

I engaged Margaret, a local realtor, to help me look for a waterfront site. She showed me a few on the harbor—pretty, but lacking the drama of open ocean. Other options were on the water, but far out of town and isolated.

The next day she said she'd like to show me Rockport, six miles from Camden, adding that her brother Harry was in the hospital there, being treated for a painful skin disease. Perhaps I wouldn't mind, she asked, if we stopped to visit him.

In Atlanta, business would be separate from the personal. It's different here, I noted, and accepted her offer.

As soon as I saw Harry's red scaly patches, my mind wandered to the time when Uncle Izzy, a close family friend, came to University Hospital in Ann Arbor for his excruciating psoriasis . . .

I walk into Uncle Izzy's room. He gives me a big smile, extends both hands, and tells me, sounding surprised, that I've grown into a lovely young woman. With the renowned hospitals in Chicago, I wonder aloud why he has come so far for treatment. He explains that this hospital has a new method of treating his disorder and he's optimistic that here he will get some relief.

He asks if I'll finish my PhD soon, and when I tell him another year, he mentions this would be a good time to consider marriage. I say my life is good and I'm able to support myself. A man would have to add something special to my satisfying life—a new idea for his generation, but then again, so is my getting an advanced degree.

I know he will spread the word . . .

I was twenty-eight at the time of that visit, near an age when I would soon be considered a spinster. My parents never pressed me to marry, but brought up the subject of boyfriends. I responded with a brief description of whoever I was seeing at the time. They occasionally asked if there was a special man. There never was.

I sometimes wondered what they thought. Did either of them guess the truth? Did they discuss it between themselves?

After completing the house tour, I told Margaret I would think about it. None of the choices felt quite right. While considering options, I phoned Beth and Ada, a couple I had known in Atlanta before they moved to Biddeford Pool, an ocean community two hours south of Camden. I invited them to meet me for dinner. I also asked if they knew of an available ocean-view house in their area. They said they owned one—usually rented only in summer, but they would be willing to rent it to me for the winter. Would I be interested? *Why yes, I would.* We made an appointment to see their house.

Biddeford Pool was close to Portland and Kennebunkport, towns that would offer more than Camden. I fed Mazie the address, and off we went, finally crossing the ground-level bridge to the town. The house was on a quiet street the width of a large driveway, with a clear view of the rocky shore and open sea.

Beth and Ada, both tall and striking, met me at the door and brought me inside to the fully windowed front porch where I would be able to watch waves hitting the rocky cliff while eating meals or sitting by my fireplace.

I signed on the spot—house hunting complete—and returned to Camden to continue exploring. Not only was it terrific to know I had a place to stay when all northern campgrounds were closed, but I would now fulfill my long-held dream of living with winter storms on an ocean outside my window.

I headed back to my campsite in Camden and stopped at a local deli. Shelves were loaded: fresh breads, unusual cheeses, gourmet meats, and several varieties of teas. At one stop, I found a sign saying "SALE" above a barrel filled with small bottles of wine. I turned a bottle upside down and saw a sticker. Ten cents.

How can a bottle of wine—even a small one—cost ten cents? They wouldn't be selling them if they had gone bad. Were they samples?

I asked at the counter. Everyone in earshot smiled as the clerk patiently explained that, in Maine, returned empty bottles yield ten cents each. The sale price, $4.25, was still a bargain, $4.15 plus the ten-cent refund.

In the campground office, I found brochures telling me about kayaking and boat tours. Impatient to be on the Atlantic, I went to the dock for my first expedition: a lobster boat.

The captain, an ecologist, talked about the lobster industry and Maine's conservation efforts. As we moved through the water—rocking slightly, feeling the breeze, and smelling salt—I learned that fisheries have long been in crisis. But one of the best managed was Maine's lobster industry, partly due to innovative regulations designed to maintain the health of the population.

If a lobster is too small or too large, it must be thrown back; if it's an egg-bearing female, a tail flipper is notched with a V and then returned to the sea. This notch takes two or three years to fill in, during which time she cannot be harvested, thus free to produce more eggs. Since lobstering is one of the most important industries in the state, maintaining the lobster population is crucial to the economy.

Our captain took us to a seal-covered island, where a seven-foot bald eagle's nest looked down on sleek mammals basking on rocks. I had never seen a bird's nest larger than ten inches, nor had I seen an eagle close-up. It never occurred to me that they might be a yard long and have a wingspan of eight feet! The bald eagle, an endangered species until 2007, now has a stable population—another result of conservation.

The next day, I took a four-hour kayaking trip from Rockland to Camden Harbor with a guide and five tourists, traveling together in separate kayaks. Fortunately, my young companions had no interest in speed and meandered down the coast. Nonetheless, it was still difficult for me to keep up. Though I had to concentrate just to stay with them, I was able to see the spectacular mansions on the shore and brightly colored sails decorating the sky—all invisible from the street.

After climbing out of the kayak, aching and exhausted, I treated myself to a boiled lobster dinner in a dockside restaurant overlooking the boat-filled harbor. Wearing the traditional bib to protect my clothing from the rich juices, I cracked the shells with the tools provided and licked melted butter off my fingers. Pure joy!

While enjoying Camden, I was also gathering supplies I would need in my house when I returned from the October trips. An Ace Hardware provided a toaster oven, light bulbs, and a tool set. Walking in the aisles with signs indicating tools, plumbing, garden supplies, light bulbs, and nails brought back poignant memories of the hardware store my father owned after his bankruptcy. Working seven days a week, never complaining, he continued to give steep discounts to any family friend, a practice he had observed all of his business life.

Standing in an aisle, small appliances on one side and storage containers on the other, I floated back to a time when he offered his help . . .

I've moved into an old house. My landlord has given Kevin permission to make numerous repairs and upgrades. He puts up new plaster board and paints the space. I live amidst the chaos like a typical graduate student. I have a shower, heat, and a kitchen, albeit with ancient appliances. Mom and Dad visit. They are horrified at my lack of furniture and the "hippy" way I'm living. When they meet Kevin, they express gratitude for his efforts on my behalf. Dad tells him that he will give him whatever he needs at no cost.

When they return to Chicago, Dad ships a basic Danish Modern sofa and a window air conditioner to make me more comfortable.

I take the train home for a long weekend. The second day, without telling me, Kevin rents a truck and drives the five hours to Chicago to accept Dad's offer of free stuff. I wake up, and he's sleeping on the living room sofa. My parents don't know if he is a friend or a boyfriend, but they don't ask. I sense their ambivalence.

On the one hand, Kevin's a bright, capable young man. On the other, he's Methodist. They would prefer I marry a Jewish boy, but they would also like me to get married, even to a gentile.

I ride back to Ann Arbor with Kevin—in the fully loaded truck . . .

I returned to the campground with my purchases. The next day, preparations complete, I drove to the Portland airport and hopped on a plane for the first of three trips—all special events, all in October.

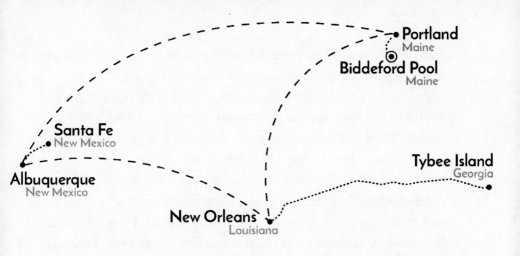

CHAPTER 18

Intermission

Who were the people and what were the events important enough to interrupt my adventure?

First Carol, whom I met when she was the associate director of my VA hospital and is now a dear friend, invited me to Albuquerque for the balloon festival, an annual gathering of balloonists from all over the world. While she was in Atlanta, she made my job a pleasure and has continued to enrich my life through the years since she moved from state to state as she advanced in the system.

Then Anna, the woman I loved and lost—and then loved as a friend for the many years since our separation. Susan, her partner of many years, was throwing a birthday bash at an ocean hotel on Tybee Island, Georgia. I wouldn't have dreamed of missing it.

The last invitation was for a not-to-be-missed commitment ceremony—for Carol's daughter Ashleigh and her female partner—to be held in New Orleans.

Since Carol and her husband, Bill, were both members of the Federal Senior Executive Service, their assignments rarely allowed them to live in the same city, but he was in Albuquerque for the festival and would also attend the upcoming commitment ceremony in New Orleans. Daughter Meredith and her husband, Tim, came from Texas. And I flew in from my new temporary home in Maine.

On the first day, we were in the car, long before daybreak, driving on congested roads open only to festival traffic, and finally herded to a spot in the parking lot to view the "dawn patrol." Then a walk to a dark, crowded field and a short wait before flames appeared, illuminating balloons as they rose, one at a time, to decorate the still-night sky.

With the slow approach of dawn, more massive, multicolored shapes materialized: a cottage, a witch, cartoon characters, animals, birds, a stagecoach . . . any object imaginable, floating high above earth while we craned our necks in awe.

I stayed for a few days after the festival, and Carol entertained me in Albuquerque. She habitually wakes early in the morning and goes nonstop until time to drop into bed, instantly asleep. I am the Energizer Bunny; she is Road Runner. Thus, when we hiked in Cibola National Forest, I worked to keep up while Road Runner paused frequently to wait for little Bunny. The hike ended at a mountain-top restaurant overlooking a precipitous, tree-covered drop to Albuquerque. Blues of sky faded near an invisible horizon, blending with blue-gray mountains, which then seamlessly merged with the sandy soil and tans of the city.

We couldn't be in Albuquerque without a trip to Santa Fe, driving between beige-and-black mountains dotted with green cedar, gray sage balls, and tumbleweed. Golden cottonwoods and neon yellow aspens shone against the tawny ground.

We had lunch in the Terrace Room at the renowned La Fonda Hotel, at the end of the Santa Fe Trail. This was no ordinary hotel and no mundane dining room. Prominent persons such as Zsa Zsa Gabor and Salvador Dali, Ulysses Grant, and Rutherford B. Hayes once sat beside the same wall of hand-painted glass that we now admired.

Santa Fe is a magical city, colorful and diverse: art galleries in striking adobes, the museums—including the Georgia O'Keefe art museum—Mexican influenced architecture, and amazing people. Native American, Hispanic, and Anglo influences are apparent in the gourmet restaurants, performing arts, shops, and markets. Differences here come together to contribute to the whole. I knew I would return.

Next, a plane to New Orleans where I rented a car to drive to Tybee Island. I would return to New Orleans for the commitment ceremony. The birthday celebration was a laid-back time: long walks on the beach, fresh seafood dinners, table-games, and conversation. The party itself was special mainly because Anna was surrounded by close friends—people who cared—and that included me. It had been fifteen years since we separated, and I was now happily a part of her group of friends. After the first difficult year of being alone, I was happy that Anna had found someone to love. It eventually became easy for me to care for her in this new way.

Several of the guests were looking for rental properties. I joined them on this quest. Together we signed papers for a four-story, five-bedroom home with an elevator and a private pool. The year was 2004. We believed the property would double in value in the next few years. None of us had a clue that this would be the top of the real estate market. To celebrate our purchase, the realtor took us for a fast ride in his high-powered speedboat.

I drove my rental car to New Orleans a few days before the commitment ceremony and settled in to appreciate the city.

Enjoying old architecture with intricately wrought iron balconies and hanging plants in the French Quarter, I turned onto Decatur Street, where the rich smells of dark coffee and sweet beignets drew me to Café du Monde. I was wearing just a cotton shirt, but it was warm enough to sit outside, alternating sips of milky coffee with bites of hot, flaky pastry—savoring the flavors before leaving for a walk to the outdoor market. Tables overflowed with bargains: T-shirts, art, jewelry, and antiques from all over the globe. And the bags of shoppers overflowed with souvenirs.

Like the downward spiral of the housing market, no one predicted that Katrina would soon bring destruction to this city.

The next morning, I walked beneath a canopy of five-hundred-year-old live oaks in Audubon Park near Tulane. Here, in the middle of a bustling city, was a natural setting that rivaled my travel destinations. When I returned to Atlanta, I would need to remember that my city also provided such escapes.

That afternoon, a three-mile walk took me to the Besthoff Sculpture Garden. Though drenched from New Orleans heat and humidity, I forgot my discomfort as I walked beside a tranquil pond and elegant gardens, contemplating sleek bronze and stone sculptures. My favorites were *Ruth and Naomi*, subtly portraying the two women as if they were lovers, and *Grand Val de Grace,* a stunning bronze depiction of a well-muscled man with a withered left side. The latter reminded me of the statue of Terry Fox, the young man who lost one leg to cancer and then, with an artificial limb, ran across Canada to raise money for research.

Then, the ceremony, my reason for stopping in New Orleans.

A hundred guests converged in Napoleon House, where lit candles and red-and-white roses decorated the room. Straight and gay, young and old—all dressed in traditional wedding fashion—but not everyone who came was pleased. And not every invited guest came. Bill, Carol's husband and Ashleigh's stepfather, gently chided a dissenter, saying, "It may not be your kind of deal, but if it makes them happy, I wish them well."

We witnessed the union of Ashleigh and her partner, unthinkable when I was their age.

After the ceremony, Bill took a group to Pat O'Brien's. Waiters served wine as we waited for table space in the jazzy piano bar. The service, wine, and music made standing in line part of the entertainment. Inside, beer steins hung from exposed ceiling beams above brick walls. Two musicians, known as dueling pianists, sat at back-to-back pianos, singing, banging, and jiving. Slanted mirrors behind the musicians reflected the sheet music littering the piano tops and the rocking, swaying audience.

Later, Eldridge Gabriel played "trays," using metal thimbles under the tray to make music. Bill told us how Gabriel walked into Pat O'Brien's bar in 1938 and, without being hired, began to wait on tables. Soon he was onstage, tapping his aluminum tray with coins, thimbles, and lively fingers, entertaining audiences for the next sixty-seven years.

Eldridge Gabriel died in 2006. I was among the last to see him onstage.

The next day, celebrations complete, I flew back to Maine. Life had been full of people and activities—nonstop for an entire month. Now I would take up residence in a tiny town, where I knew only Beth and Ada.

I landed in Portland and picked up my van, needing Mazie to travel these unfamiliar roads to my new home. The van was not to be my home for a few months. Now, it was simply transportation. But I was delighted to see Mazie, my old friend and guide.

As I climbed the stairs for my first night in Biddeford Pool, the sun slid below a distant watery horizon as waves crashed against the rocks. A full moon, low in the sky, cast its light over my ocean.

I live in a house! was my first thought as consciousness returned, eyes still closed. My bedroom window, on the second floor, faced the ocean and was open just enough for the sound of waves and the smell of salt water to slide in. I opened my eyes, turned my head toward the window and didn't move for several minutes—not until the urge for a hot drink propelled me out of bed.

Wrapping myself in a fleece robe and pulling on warm socks, I went downstairs to boil water and stood by the front window, arms crossed in the slight morning chill.

After daydreaming by the fire, I moved the meager contents of my van fridge into the full-sized version in the kitchen. Beth had stocked the refrigerator with eggs, cheese, and a fresh loaf of bread. Soon I was sipping strong breakfast tea and making toast. Ada had stacked firewood on the porch and laid matches, kindling, and newspaper by the fireplace. I planned to make a fire and then do absolutely nothing.

I crumpled a few pages of newspaper, slipped them under the grate, and laid the kindling and then three logs. I lit the paper and sat back to watch it light the kindling, the flames licking the logs until they also caught. Maintaining a thriving blaze required only an occasional new log and a few taps with the poker.

We had a fireplace in my childhood home, but my parents never learned to use it. We had no wood, the tools were for decoration, and the hearth remained spotlessly clean. Kevin's house had a fireplace— not the elegant, unused fireplace of my parents' home, but a brick-lined hole meant to supplement the furnace. He taught me how to set up a fire, placing logs so the spaces between them were just right—not too close, not too far apart.

I remembered a winter night in Ann Arbor. Kevin and I had dinner in his kitchen, a fire blazing in the next room . . .

We talk about his next play and my language-impaired patients. I'm wearing a blue sweater. He says it's a great color for me. I clean the kitchen while he sits by the fire watching the news. Then I join him and fall asleep on the floor.

I wake up, feeling him pressed against my spine, moving gently. He turns me onto my back. I remain motionless, waiting for it to end and asking myself why I'm not involved. When it ends, he lies still for a moment—and then gets up.

Neither of us speaks.

This man I admire more than any other, this man who needs many women— and wants me for this moment—is not a man to love.

I wish, at least, to enjoy sex with him, and then, perhaps, love a different man, one like Raymond, a man who would put a warm jacket over my shoulders on a cold night. But it isn't going to happen—not with Raymond, or Danny, or Kevin.

I get it. It won't be a man . . .

CHAPTER 19

Biddeford Pool

When it was time for lunch I examined the options, made a cheese sandwich, and began to think about dinner. Another sandwich? A restaurant?

Uh-uh. I decided to go food shopping.

Logs separated in the fireplace, I climbed into the van and drove from Biddeford Pool to the larger town of Biddeford, across the bridge and twenty minutes on a two-lane rural highway. Chicken, ground beef, vegetables, cans of tuna and soup—just enough to get started—and back home again.

I set up my laptop, opened email, looked at the ocean . . . and realized I wanted the phone to ring. *How strange*, I thought. *I've been alone for five months, never lonely, but now, in a house, I want human contact. Why now?*

Although I enjoyed the extra space, the compactness of the van never bothered me. Nor had the fact that I was alone. Living in the van, almost everyone I met was transient. If my phone rang, it was an Atlanta friend, or a family member, just checking on me or sharing news. When I had a permanent address—it seemed like years ago—the phone rang with invitations to the movies, a play, or dinner. I assumed, since at least some people lived here year-round, there must be activities during the winter. How would I even know what was going on? How would I be invited? In the van, I would just find my location in the guidebook and it would tell me what was nearby, and I didn't care at all that I was alone.

I needed a distraction from these disturbing thoughts. It was time to find an activity, perhaps explore my new surroundings. The afternoon was chilly, but sunny—bright and inviting—a wonderful day to walk the half-mile to town, and I could check with the post office about the sweaters I'd bought in New Orleans and mailed to my Biddeford Pool address.

In addition to my destination, the village consisted of Union Church, the community center, Eve McPheeter's gift store, Peter McPheeter's realty office, a general store, Beth and Ada's Lobster Company, a bed-and-breakfast, and the yacht club. I entered the post office, a wooden structure behind a four- to five-car parking lot, and saw one small counter and three walls of PO boxes. Soft classical music came from behind the work station; a large, well-tended philodendron rested in the window. A sign over a neat trash bin read RECYCLE YOUR JUNK MAIL HERE.

A slim man, fortyish, stopped his work to greet me. He was serious, but pleasant, and waited attentively. When I told him my name, he reached for a box and said, "Ah, I almost returned this. Had no idea who you were. We don't usually get new folks this time of year."

"Thanks. How come it didn't just come to the house?"

"There's no mail delivery in the 'Pool.' You'll need a box. I'm Greg . . . I'm the postmaster. We'll be seeing lots of each other."

I rented a box and then walked the few yards to the remaining town.

At the end of this short street was the Lobster Company, owned by Beth, Ada, and Beth's sister, Cathy. Like all the other shops, it was closed for the winter. But I wanted to see it anyway.

Beth and Ada were pleasant acquaintances in Atlanta, where Beth had co-owned the trendy restaurant, Agnes and Muriel's, named after the owners' mothers, and Ada was a respected mortgage broker. Looking at the streets of this tiny town, I realized the answer to my earlier question—why I needed human contact. While on the road, everyone was a migrant, passing through. This was a permanent community; people *stayed* here. I wanted to belong.

I returned to the house and a few minutes later heard a knock at the door. Beth stood on the porch and said, "I came by to see if you needed anything."

"Well, not really," I said, "but have a seat. I'd love to hear about the town. I'll build a fire while you tell me what people do here in the winter."

Beth sat, facing the fire-to-be. "About a hundred stay year-round. The others go south for the winter. Actually, some just live here in July and August. And then they come for a few weekends in the spring and fall. But there's a lot to do—even in winter. The community center . . . have you seen it yet?"

"Yeah . . . I passed it this morning on my way to the post office."

She told me about a bulletin board outside the center with flyers announcing upcoming events. "There's a catered cocktail party this weekend. You really should come. Everyone'll be there."

I *hate* big cocktail parties, but conscious of my wish to make friends, I nodded, indicating I would come.

She went on to say that some parties, like this one, were held in the center. But bigger events took place in the fire station. Then she mentioned her nondenominational Christian church and wondered if, as a Jew, I might be interested.

I told her I enjoy sermons and ethics, adding that I've never cared which god is the right one.

"Do they have a problem with Jews?"

"No. And they don't have a problem with gays either. When they were interviewing Jan—she's the minister now—a gay couple wanted a commitment ceremony at the church. Not all the trustees agreed, but Jan said that'd be a deal breaker for her . . . wouldn't take the job if they vetoed it. And Ada and I are very active. No one cares that we're gay. There're other gay couples around. We're all 'out' . . . listed in the Church directory as couples."

I certainly landed in the right town, I thought, just before remembering to ask about Maine winters. "About the weather . . . how bad does it get? Does power go out a lot? How're the roads?"

"Winter's gorgeous, and snow's not a problem. When it snows, the city of Biddeford clears the roads immediately. And, no, power doesn't go out often."

"When can I get a key or some way to open the garage?"

"Oh," she said, pausing briefly. "I thought Ada told you. We keep our stuff in the garage. Summer guests don't need it. We have a guy who'll plow your driveway. He'll be out at five in the morning if it snows overnight. You'll just have to clean your car off."

Oh, shit, I thought. "Okay," I said.

When Saturday came, I dreaded the community center party. At age seven I had been shy and quiet around people, but my sister Donna, two years younger, was already outgoing and friendly. I watched her success and began to imitate her, continuing this pattern all my life. So, in spite of my anxiety, I went. I walked in, glanced at folding chairs against the wooden walls, and tables laden with trays of stylishly arranged appetizers, heard the din of small talk, saw no one standing alone, and almost turned around.

Instead, I stayed and participated in the stranger-at-a-cocktail-party routine, moving from group to group, determining if the conversation was open and, if so, joining, usually just long enough for superficial introductions.

There were a few people who seemed interested in the lone woman who was living in their beach community for the winter, Carol Basset among them. She joined me as I was getting a glass of wine, introducing herself and husband, Jerry, and as the caterers circulated with elegant hot and cold hors d'oeuvres, she told me a bit more about the community center.

"There's a small library, right over there," she said pointing at one side of the room. "I volunteer one morning a week—it's a good way to meet people. And another thing you might like—the book club meets here, too."

At home that night, armed with mental notes of the people I'd met, I booted up the computer and downloaded the information from my brain to a Word document. I would review these notes before the next event so I could recognize at least a few people.

In the morning, my cell phone rang as I was finishing a breakfast bagel. It was Ada. "We changed our minds. Is this a good time for me to empty the garage?"

"Oh, how great! Sure. Come on over." I couldn't believe my luck.

She arrived, boyishly dressed for action, and sat briefly for a cup of tea before beginning her task.

I watched as she struggled with the garage-door opener. "Hell. This thing isn't working right. It's going to go soon. I'll have to get a new one for you—well, not just for you. We need a new one anyway."

I was ecstatic to have a garage for the winter, not having to worry about cleaning snow off the car and scraping ice off the windows— I needed my kitchen ladder to reach the ice in the middle. I hated winters in Ann Arbor for just these reasons.

While Ada worked, I sat by my fireplace. I remembered Kevin and my poor attempt to make love with him. Soon after that memorable event, Kevin fell in love and promised to remain faithful. They married and had bright, gorgeous children. I spent a lot of time with the family and fell in love with those kids.

A few years after realizing I would never marry a man, I had my first affair with a woman I loved . . .

It's a spring evening. Chris and I come to my office to pick up some papers. I unlock the door. Chris walks in behind me. Once inside, she puts both hands on my shoulders and turns me around. We come together like two magnets, released by our twin captors: integrity and fidelity. She slides her arms down my back and pulls me to her.

We break apart, and she says, "Can we meet tomorrow? Lunchtime? Your apartment?"

I nod in agreement.

The next day, I arrive first and watch for her car. The door is open when she reaches it. Her hands are in my hair as we kiss.

We've waited six years.

Our movements are slow. There's no rush now. When we slide under the sheets, I am aware of the strangeness of smooth, soft skin—no hair on chest or arms or legs, no abrasive beard.

Later, alone in my apartment, conscience overwhelms me. Shelley knows nothing about this affair. She is sweet-natured and trusting. She would not doubt Chris's love or my friendship. I turn off the remorse and bury it in an inaccessible part of my brain.

Chris and I meet again every day that first week. Every night she goes home to Shelley; some evenings I join them. I am numb, guilty, ecstatic, and sad. I tell Chris we cannot continue.

She agrees.

A few weeks later, the three of us go away for a weekend, sharing a cabin. After dinner on the first night, we sit and talk. No one wants to be first to end the evening. After hours of sipping bourbon, Shelley falls asleep. Chris gets up, takes me by the hand, and pulls me out of my chair. Still holding hands, we go outside to a clear, starlit spring night and sit under a tree. It begins again.

Through the hot and humid summer, we meet most days at noon. When I ask Chris if Shelley knows, she says no. One day, as I am about to get out of her car, she stops me, reaches into her purse, removes a small jewelry box, and gives it to me. When I open it, I find a gold wedding band. "My grandmother's," she says, brow furrowed and with a slight smile. "I want you to have it."

I go to the office but only pretend to work on my dissertation. On weekends, I join Chris and Shelley and other friends at their home on a nearby lake. We water ski all day, barbeque dinner, and sip bourbon through the evenings. My eyes often drift to Chris, and I find her looking back at me. With a furrowed forehead, her deep brown eyes hold an expression of concentration and love. We're both waiting until Monday, when we will be alone again.

As the months go by, I don't think at all. I just feel . . .

CHAPTER 20

Life in Maine

On a cold Sunday morning in November, frost licked the edges of the bedroom window. Open curtains allowed me to see the peach horizon as the sun began its upward glide. Biddeford Pool: my home for the winter.

I stretched and enjoyed the water rolling over rocks below, then cracked the door to the deck—just enough to hear the surf while I lay still for a few moments, listening, until the urge for a cup of hot tea prompted me down the old wooden stairs.

Then back up to sip and read before my first visit to Union Church.

No one cared that the visitor sitting on the back bench was Jewish—or gay. Union Church and its pastor, Jan Hryniewicz, cared only that a new person was in town, not for the tourist summer but, remarkably, for the cold winter.

I sat behind a couple who, at the end of the service, turned around and introduced themselves as Heather and Erv Davis. The first thing

I noticed was the softness and welcoming warmth in Heather's eyes. As we left the pews and joined the line for cookies and coffee, Erv asked me how I happened to be in Maine for the winter and how I handled banking chores while away from home. Before we left church that day, I had two new friends.

With a commanding presence and thoughtful intellect, Jan fostered acceptance of differing points of view about God. She also promoted equality of all residents, gay or straight. Beyond tolerance, beyond acceptance—complete parity.

In a tiny community, everyone is crucial; no one can be considered less than any other.

During the service, I thought about the contrast between this town's attitude about sexual preference and a dreadful memory of another town in another time . . .

Mitch is an acquaintance at the University of Michigan. He's a handsome boy, always well groomed, never wearing the graduate student uniform of jeans and rumpled shirt. He's beginning his doctoral work in physics and hangs out, as I do, in the Michigan Union. I see his name in the Ann Arbor paper, and curious, I read the article. He's been arrested for "indecent behavior," caught in a campus men's room sting by a cop posing as someone interested in picking up a gay guy for sex.

Mitch is released from jail but expelled from school. I wonder what will happen to Mitch. Will another university accept him?

Women don't participate in bathroom sex, so no police are looking for me . . .

I remembered worrying that if my secret were exposed, I too could be expelled. My thoughts were interrupted by the donation plate as it passed down the row to me. Though I rarely attended a church, I did attend various synagogues throughout my childhood. Sitting in church was the same to me as sitting in a synagogue—I was interested in the sermon, the music, and the companionship of people who cared about the planet. At the age of ten, I chose a reform synagogue near Lake Michigan where the emphasis was on ethics and charity—the only temple in town offering Sunday worship instead of the traditional

Friday night and Saturday Sabbath services. More conservative Jews called it "the church on the lake." From the time I learned there were different religions, I thought it odd that most people firmly believed in the God of their parents. For me, the true nature of God was unknowable; humankind alleviated fear and uncertainty by picturing their gods with specific characteristics.

So it was not a search for God that brought me to a house of worship, but rather the emphasis on a moral code. Although I certainly did not always live up to my values, I never forgot *tikkun olam*—repairing the world or performing good deeds—a basic tenet of Judaism. Union Church exemplified the same values. And along with a moral code, members of the Biddeford Pool Union Church also believed in fun—like most Jews. Exhibits by local artists or photographers, fireside chats, and parties, every activity accompanied by lovingly prepared appetizers, entrees, and desserts—just like the synagogues.

After the service, I saw a flyer in a local gas station advertising a lecture on human rights in Muslim societies at a nearby branch of the University of New England. I wanted to see the campus and the topic was enticing. Dr. Azizah al-Hibri, a professor of law and philosophy at the University of Richmond, spoke on Islamic law and how jihadists have distorted religious texts. Not only does the Koran specifically disallow terrorism, she said, but it also abhors inequality for women and people of other beliefs.

As I listened, I thought with anger, as I had so many times before, how extremists of any religion assault the books of faith. I remembered the Orthodox Jews who chased me through an Israeli neighborhood . . .

I'm visiting Zivah and Yoni, Israeli friends living in Jerusalem. On a Sabbath morning, I walk with a very pregnant Zivah in an Orthodox Jewish neighborhood. She's wearing a sleeveless dress, and I'm in summer slacks. A group of men appears, and they begin to throw stones, shouting in Hebrew. We run. When we reach a safe spot out of their range, we stop to rest. She speaks the language and tells me they said we were whores. How dare we expose ourselves this way?

On our way back to the hotel, I tell her about a classmate's bar mitzvah where girls and women sat in the balcony. When I asked about this, I was told that women pollute the atmosphere for praying men . . .

Zivah and I spoke of the male dominated hierarchy in Orthodox Jewry and the busses where men retain their seats and stare straight ahead as handicapped or elderly women look for a place to sit. I reminded her of so-called Christians who conduct anti-gay protests at military funerals or the ones who burn synagogues and mosques. The Jews and Christians who blame all Muslims for the acts of Islamic terrorists are ignoring their own extremists.

In Biddeford Pool, our little church community offered a spiritual reflections group where issues like this were discussed. We also had a volunteer library, a book club, and a bridge club. I joined them all. Heather D graciously hosted the reflections group, and Heather L, the bridge club. It was in the home of the latter that I saw the photo of her son and his partner. Heather spoke of them proudly, as she would have discussed a son and daughter-in-law.

The book club was held at the community center and managed by Heather L with low-keyed, effective leadership. Year-round inhabitants approached me to express interest in my travels and appreciation of my desire to spend the winter on this northern Atlantic shore. But when summer residents visited for a weekend, their eyebrows would lift in surprise upon learning I was a cold-season resident. They seemed to think I had my calendar backwards.

Thanksgiving was approaching, my first holiday in Biddeford Pool. It's always been my favorite holiday, and I was excited by an invitation from Anita and Brad Coupe, my nearest year-round neighbors, to join a group of their friends, including Beth and Ada. Anita and Brad were retired—successful attorneys who designed and built their elegant ocean home. Both leaders in Union Church, Brad was a skilled painter, and Anita was prominent in the National Humane Society.

On Wednesday, I made my "killer" mashed potatoes. While the spuds boiled, I assembled sour cream, chives, heavy whipping cream, and cream cheese in the largest bowl in the house. When the potatoes were cooked and peeled, I stood on a kitchen stool to get enough leverage to mash and mix, and as usual, I got splatter on my hands, arms, and the front of my shirt, and even in my hair and on the walls. Butter and shredded cheddar completed the hot and creamy offering.

I carried my Thanksgiving dish past the three unoccupied houses between mine and the Coupes'. I was proud of my contribution—and this invitation. But I also had a dry mouth and sweaty palms, the result of some anxiety, different from the dread I felt going to the cocktail party, where I encountered a large group of strangers and made small talk. This was to be only a few people. There was no way for me to hide. Conversation would be deeper, and my options were to speak and expose my thoughts or to remain silent, staring intently as others spoke.

I imagined each guest would be attractive, sophisticated, wealthy, talented, intelligent, and thoroughly informed about politics and the world.

Who was I to be with these people?

The last time I had this question, I was participating in sorority rush . . .

I'm dressed expensively, but am terrified that I've chosen the wrong outfit. I'm short and ten pounds overweight. Will they like me? Will they ask me back? I enter the first house and find myself talking to a member about how the dorms only have showers and how I miss a bathtub. I'm blabbering as I watch her eyes glaze over.

In spite of my clumsy conversations, I'm asked back to several houses. Though being in a sorority was "the thing to do," I don't return for the next set of parties. I realize it would be hard to hide my sexuality in the closeness of a sorority. The privacy possible in the dorm or an apartment is better for me . . .

Although I had taught at two major universities and was a department head at a VA Medical Center, I felt dull and inferior as I walked past the fine, weathered houses on the ocean road. Still, I dared to hope some of these paragons might befriend me. I swore that bathing habits would not be part of my conversation.

We sat at a well-designed table, arranged by Anita with apparent ease and laden with favorite traditional recipes. I was tempted to pinch a bite off the browned turkey, but I restrained myself. It was all I could do to wait, salivating in anticipation of the first bites of rich casseroles, hot rolls, and a moist bird. Pecan and pumpkin pies waited in the kitchen, but I guessed no one would save room. We would instead loosen our belts and make a space in already full bellies.

As we passed dishes, served ourselves, and began to dine, conversation ranged over a variety of topics: church, the war in Iraq, the supposed weapons of mass destruction, and the danger of global warming.

As topics shifted, we continued to eat, commenting on the weight we would gain. My mashed potatoes were a hit, not in spite of the artery-clogging ingredients, but because of them.

Among the guests were Judy and Bob MacGillivray, also newly retired. I asked questions about how people spent their time. Bob had been a nuclear engineer and, when remodeling their home, the couple did most of the work themselves. Judy, small and slender with short gray hair, worked part time at Lovell Designs, a jewelry store in nearby Kennebunkport.

Beth and Ada worked in their town business during the tourist season. Almost everyone, even those not yet retired, held a leadership position in the Union Church. Ada was the moderator and active in the choir, Beth the clerk and a deacon, Brad the treasurer, and Judy another deacon. The only exception was Bob, who walked his dog while everyone else was at church.

Oh, I thought, *these are people—special people, but pleasant and approachable, not the fantasy characters I concocted.*

Judy told me she passed my house every morning as she walked Max, a large, rambunctious dog, and she would show me the East Point Sanctuary, an Audubon Park that was a few minutes away.

"I thought Audubon Park was in New Orleans," I said, leaning forward.

"They're all over the country . . . all support environmental issues and have sanctuaries for local wildlife. Ours is one of the premier birding spots on the northeast coast."

The next morning, Judy stopped by my house as promised, her feet planted firmly as Max panted and pulled on his leash. A golf course sat at the tip of Biddeford Pool, a short distance beyond Brad and Anita's and, just a bit further, the East Point Sanctuary. After strolling on a winding trail beside the ocean, Judy took me past my house to a path leading to miles of beachfront walking, a path I would use almost every day during the coming months.

Later, I walked to town to pick up my mail. Greg, on the other side of the PO boxes, recognized my *hand* reaching into my box and greeted me. I was elated to be recognized.

Next door to the post office was the home of Carol and Jerry Bassett, where energetic carpenters and painters were remodeling in preparation for a family wedding. I smiled at a large Christmas wreath hanging on the outdoor porta-potty. Enjoying the humor, I was delighted to know Carol and Jerry.

Gradually, my friendship with Beth and Ada blossomed. December was a month of house parties, including the McPheeters' chic catered affair for the entire community. I dressed for the Arctic Circle, wearing heavy sweaters over long underwear, but each time I entered another brightly decorated home, a warm fire blazed and beads of sweat dotted my forehead. I soon learned to dress appropriately.

I mixed socializing with solitude: reading and hiking to town or beside the ocean, times of reflection and memories. Alone and serene, I compared this joy with other days alone, turbulent, and painful . . .

As summer heat fades, autumn comes to Ann Arbor and leaves begin to fall. Chris tells me she can't leave Shelley. I absorb her words, my forehead crinkled as I grasp the struggle she's been facing.

Chris and I have kept our love a secret from Shelley, just as I continue to hide my sexuality from my family. My life is full of pretense. Chris cannot continue the deceit.

Our tears communicate overwhelming grief.

That night, the searing pain of loss keeps me awake. Grit lines my inner eyelids. My chest aches, and my breathing is shallow. I doze only minutes at a time.

In the morning, I sip coffee, but the idea of eating makes my stomach churn. As the minute hand on the clock moves slowly toward the time I should be dressing, I don't move. I skip my eight o'clock lecture.

There's a blanket of white in my head—all thought blocked, pain the only sensation.

At ten past nine, the phone rings. It's Chris, calling from a phone booth on the sidewalk outside my class. She tells me she was waiting for me to come out of the building and worried because I wasn't there. The next night I see her drive slowly past my house. A few days later, I drive by hers.

Knowing our affair is over, I go to parties, work, and even smile and laugh a bit, but like a robot. My hands move, I speak, write, and use a calculator— automatically, numbly. I never get enough air without consciously filling my lungs. Forcing down a few bites of food, bile rises beneath my breasts. Night after night, my brief periods of sleep are tormented by dreams of wandering around campus looking for Chris, of catching a glimpse of her just before she turns a corner and disappears.

I've never known such emptiness.

I'm twenty-seven. If I'd just broken up with a man, I could lean on my parents or my sister or my brother. But I fear my siblings might leak the information to Mom and Dad. Since the bankruptcy, my parents have focused on providing for their basic needs. Even the friends who helped financially either consider their situation shameful, or are at least embarrassed for them and find conversation difficult. So Mom and Dad remain depressed about their difficult days, absent social life, and substantially reduced income. I cannot cause them any more grief. This is not the time to share my secrets.

How I wish for the support of family, their words of comfort, their loving arms around me . . .

If I were looking for a new boyfriend, socials and blind dates would have provided another guy. But how would I find a woman to date? It was the sixties. There were no lesbian bars in Ann Arbor, no gay social groups. Other than Chris and Shelley, I had one gay friend with whom I could share my pain. I had to function as though nothing had happened.

Shaking off the sadness of my daydream, I felt again the joy of this moment in Maine, the freedom from anxiety and pain. Released from libido and no longer buffeted by sexual needs, I didn't need a partner, but wanted a sense of belonging and warm companionship.

I found both in Biddeford Pool on the rocky coast of Maine, a tiny town in which the exciting events were a church supper, a walk on the ocean, or carrying a bowl of killer potatoes down the road.

CHAPTER 21

Eleanor

Eleanor, petite and white-haired, had recently celebrated her ninetieth birthday, but you'd never guess it from her activities and mannerisms. She had two homes, one in Maine, the other in New Hampshire. Not wanting to give up either, she spent winters in Maine and summers in New Hampshire, often driving between the two on weekends.

She had shared these homes with Helen, her lifelong companion who died five years earlier. It wasn't enough for Eleanor to house-hop across two states, entertain friends and sit by her huge, ocean-view window. She also volunteered with "Elder Elves" and transported patients to their medical appointments.

I first met Eleanor when, one afternoon before Christmas, she invited Beth and Ada for holiday cocktails, and they asked if I could come along.

She greeted us at the door with a welcoming smile. The first thing I noticed was the floor-to-ceiling, wall-to-wall windows facing the water. The living room, elegant and simple, was furnished with two sofas separated by a coffee table, every seat offering an ocean view.

Conversation drifted to our various travels, and from time to time, Eleanor would indicate an object and say something like, "When Helen and I went to Italy, we picked up that stunning vase. I've always loved the way it sparkles in sunlight."

A warm but formal Bostonian, she was a retired math teacher. Helen had taught civics in the same school. Eleanor never discussed the nature of her relationship, even with close, openly gay friends like Beth and Ada. What did this reserve cost her? I guessed she and Helen must have met at school and wondered what their colleagues thought about their living situation.

Eleanor lives a somewhat private life. In addition to Beth and Ada, she is close to one other couple and members of her family. One Sunday, after a new friend saw me talking with Eleanor in church, she said with some surprise, "You even know *Eleanor*?"

Although Eleanor and I would become friends, I never asked— and wasn't told—about her relationship with Helen. Having lived a secret life, I knew its cost. I was eighteen when I first spoke the scandalous words to my Ann Arbor therapist. Homosexuality was against the law and considered a mental illness . . .

Twice a week I talk and talk and talk to her about my anxieties, my loves, my double life, and my efforts to love a man while looking for a woman, rambling about minutiae and how I feel about each detail. What a relief. The words, long trapped between the bones of my skull, are released.

Our stated goal is to cure me of the disease listed in the psychiatrists' bible: The Diagnostic and Statistical Manual of Mental Disorders, *known by clinicians as the DSM . . .*

As I sat in the office of an Ann Arbor psychologist in 1957, Eleanor and Helen would have been in their forties, living with their shared "disease." It wasn't until December of 1973, eight months after *my* thirty-fourth birthday—Eleanor and Helen approaching sixty—that the American Psychiatric Association would declare, ". . . by itself, homosexuality does not meet the criteria for being a psychiatric disorder . . . We will no longer insist on a label of sickness for individuals who (say) that they are well and demonstrate no generalized impairment in social effectiveness." This resolution paved the way for the still-to-come anti-discrimination laws and the repeal of criminal statutes penalizing sex between consenting adults. The last of these laws would stay on the books for another thirty years.

No wonder Eleanor didn't speak of the relationship. What a price they paid. But the only other option was a celibate and lonely life.

Beth and Ada invited me for Christmas day at their home, Eleanor to be the only other guest.

To shop for gifts, I drove thirty-five miles to the town of Freeport, which was founded in 1789 and now consisted of more than two hundred upscale, freestanding factory outlets and the flagship store of L.L.Bean. The original town buildings—homes, library, courthouse, bank—are still standing, but they now sport simple signs designating them as Cole Hahn, Freeport Woodworking, Talbots, and Samsonite—even McDonald's.

L.L.Bean is open twenty-four hours a day, three-hundred-sixty-five days a year. Since they never close, there are no locks on the doors.

This was the week that ice sculptors performed their magic behind L.L.Bean's building. The artists, wielding electric saws, stood on ladders to reach six-to-ten-foot blocks of ice. As I watched, the ice came alive as a horse or child or cabin, sculptures that could grace any museum, but each would melt and disappear. Perhaps these artists share the philosophy of monks who create Tibetan sand art: carefully constructed—and then destroyed—to symbolize the impermanence of life.

In the L.L.Bean lobby—smartly decorated with multi-colored plastic water bottles and tiny lights—I stood dwarfed beneath an eighteen-foot Christmas tree and remembered the chairs that held my childhood Christmases . . .

I'm almost five years old, and Donna is three. My parents light some candles and then give us presents. They tell us it's Chanukah. As we rip open the packages, they say it will soon be Christmas, and Santa will come and give us more gifts.

On Christmas Eve, I try to stay awake to hear Santa arriving, but I fall asleep. In the morning, I awake and shake Donna from her slumber. She doesn't quite get the idea yet, but she follows me downstairs where we find two armchairs in the living room, each loaded with presents. I can read my name, so I know one chair is mine and the other must belong to Donna. My father hears us and comes downstairs before we can open our gifts and says we need to wait for Mom. He makes us some scrambled eggs, and we make extra noise so Mom will wake up.

After we open presents and play, I ask Dad why we don't have a Christmas tree. He explains that we're Jewish, but Christmas is a big holiday in our country, a day to show love with thoughtful presents, and we will share that tradition . . .

On Christmas day, 2004, I joined Beth, Ada, and Eleanor for gift exchanges, gourmet food, and a card game before a roaring fire. I had been here just two months, and I had people I could call friends.

I was recognized and greeted wherever I went. In this town, within hours of any activity, everyone knew who went where and with whom. I regularly heard such comments as "Eleanor said she had a lovely time with you and Beth and Ada" and "Judy told me she took you to Marden's Discount Store." It was just two months since I had moved into my house on the ocean and wondered if I would find friends here.

The ever-changing colors of sky, clouds, and ocean were the new backdrop of my life. Sometimes the palette consisted of contrasting shades of blue, sometimes silver and gray, but always punctuated with black and brown rocks against which the waves crashed, even on a calm day. When the sun shone on the water, it produced wide strips of white or gold.

Each day, I woke at sunrise. Sometimes morning sun slid above the horizon, shining against pale morning sky. At other times it hid behind bleak clouds. Most often the sea was calm, but occasionally rain hammered against my windows with wind roaring and waves smashing against rocks, foam shooting in every direction. But watching nature rage outside, I felt the safety of my warm shelter.

Then, the day after Christmas, the news of the Indian Ocean tsunami stunned the world.

The splendor of the sea before me collided with a vision of the destructive violence of hundred-foot waves in an ocean, waters connected to this one. Beyond my ability to imagine, beyond the television coverage of this vast suffering, the reality of waves crashing a few yards away brought home this deadly disaster in a way the media could not.

I understood—again—that my personal dramas are but pale ashes in contrast to the inferno of great tragedies. I joined the world community in *tikkun olam* and contributed my small share of the seven billion dollars in humanitarian aid, knowing there was nothing more I could do.

Biddeford Pool
Maine

CHAPTER 22

I Once Was Lost

Still half asleep, I listened to crashing waves and a morning weather report: ". . . wake-up temperatures are moderate this morning, mid-teens and low twenties with heavy snow."

The official snow total was twenty-one inches, but winds blew with such force that accumulation varied from a few inches to six feet. Tree limbs sagged, no match for wet snow. Road plows deposited fat piles on the shoulders, sun reflecting off their icy surfaces. I stayed inside all morning, watching the flakes—tiny diamonds under a bright sun—blend into roiling ocean waves.

When I roused myself to leave the warmth of the house to check on the state of my driveway, I discovered the fellow charged with this duty had plowed in the wee hours. But he couldn't reach the mound directly in front of the garage door, a pile that would foil any attempt to enter or exit the garage. My job was to remove the four foot high drift—a daunting pile almost as tall as I was.

I began energetically, filling the shovel and flinging its contents to the nearby lawn, but I felt the first signs of fatigue two shovelfuls later, leading to less snow with each stab. It wasn't hard to get the snow on the blade; the difficulty was in throwing it. An exhausting hour later, the garage door was free of unwanted snow, and I could go shopping for skates.

When Donna and I were children, Dad would take us to a field on the University of Chicago campus—a field flooded every Thanksgiving and left to freeze for skating. Since Dad never learned to skate, he sipped coffee on the sidelines while an instructor initiated us to the sport. As I entered my early teens, Dad worked more hours and these adventures stopped. I had not skated since.

Here in frozen Maine, it was time to try again.

In a Biddeford sports store I bought thick-bladed hockey skates, and then went to the outdoor rink. Before venturing on ice, I stood for a while watching nimble skaters and remembering childhood skills. Finally, I got up enough nerve to walk into a wooden hut where a grizzled manager collected fees. He closed the cash drawer and asked, "Are ya new to this sport?"

"No, but it's been a really long time."

He pursed his lips, saying, "Hmmm. You need something to keep you from falling 'til you're steady on the ice. I've got just the thing." From behind the counter he walked to the back of the hut toward a wooden contraption resembling a medical walker. Putting both hands on the bar, he slid his feet forward, showing how it glided across the floor. "Five bucks an hour . . . well worth it."

For the first half hour I gripped the handles like a nursing home patient on slippery tile. Then, when I had my balance, I returned the trainer and skated off on my own, flailing a bit, yet managing to stay upright. An adolescent boy approached and paused before asking, "Is this your first time?"

I told him I hadn't skated since I was thirteen. With no embarrassment or guile, he asked, "How old are you now?"

"Sixty-five," I admitted. He nodded sagely and skated on.

A few minutes later, a young girl came by and asked if this was my first time on ice. Before I could answer, her female companion said, "She skated when she was thirteen . . . now she's sixty-five."

Realizing the word had spread among the teens, I laughed—and promptly fell. The two kids graciously helped me up, each pulling on one arm.

Children can't imagine that someday they too will be sixty-five.

During the first months of my journey, summer and fall in the Rocky Mountains and across Canada's Great Plains, I was most often invisible and anonymous. But during winter in "The Pool" I quickly became known everywhere, by everyone, absorbed into this loving town like a snowflake joining an ocean wave, each water molecule essential for the whole. I loved every minute.

I have always cherished time alone. Reading of course, but there are other activities I enjoy either alone or with companions—movies, museums, theater, shopping, and even restaurant dining can be delightful with just a book. But I am also a highly social being, needing intimate friendships as I need water and food.

As holidays passed and the year turned, friends, singly or in pairs, came from Atlanta, Albuquerque, Seattle, and Mexico to join me for a few days. The people who traveled from warmer climates to wintery Maine were people I had loved for a long time—for their loyalty, humor, courage, and new ideas.

I have known most of them since we began our adult lives, when no lines marred our faces. We've shared enormous and repeated fun, and sometimes pain, over many years. Our relationships survived debates and disagreements. We know and appreciate the challenges in each other's lives.

But the Biddeford Pool companions reminded me of the pleasure of new beginnings, of fresh starts: looking at the face of a new friend, learning the unique qualities of this special person, knowing only the rudiments and surface, knowing there is a deep history, but not yet knowing what it is.

I see myself as a filter through which each person and each event passes, leaving me changed in some way, large or small.

Each friend represents a world in us, a world possibly not born
    until they arrive,
and it is only by this meeting that a new world is born.

                           —ANAÏS NIN

Lesley, an attractive and plump, gray-haired clinical psychologist, was the first to brave the Maine winter. Over the years, Lesley's intelligent humor regularly enhanced my good days—and reduced tension in life's more difficult hours.

Liz was next. A cute blonde, droll and fun, she delivered her witty lines deadpan; you had to be attentive to realize she was joking. When I met her, she was dating my friend, Carol O, but wouldn't commit to the relationship. Liz, a dedicated physical therapist, cared deeply about her patients and, wanting a bit of whimsy at the end of her usually poignant workdays, found Carol somber. So Carol asked me to join her on Halloween night, going to Liz's home to trick or treat—wearing giant bird outfits! Those costumes, on that long-ago night, did the trick. Liz moved in with Carol O a few weeks later, and they've been together ever since.

I didn't always remember the lesson of the bird suit. While working at the VA, I approached my job and its problems with a single-minded seriousness—my friends put up with many melancholic interludes. Like any large corporation, the politics could dominate, overwhelming patient-care efforts. They tell me now that they kept me around for the occasional bird suit.

Carol Fillman, the hospital's associate director in the '90s, who also visited me in Maine, looked—as always—younger than her years: tight skin, coiffed hair, full makeup, always stylish whether on the job or off. Serious and focused in her leadership role, she was equally riotous and fun over drinks and dinner. I soon found myself in her newly formed, instantly influential "old-girl" network, balancing my gay life with this different social group.

A skilled golfer and artist—even a pilot—Carol rarely spoke of her talents and, when she did, never boasted. Over time I learned she was the kind of friend who could always be counted on to provide any desired help, no matter how inconvenient. I will never emulate her skill as a golfer, or an artist, or a pilot, but I can and will provide help to those who want it.

Audrey came too. She was one of the people who, thirty years earlier, interviewed me for my job in Atlanta. Some years later, during a picnic lunch, I told her about my sexuality. She was stunned. Although she never rejected me, our frequent conversations revealed that she had a more difficult time accepting a gay woman than a man. But accept me she did. She proved repeatedly that she could embrace new ideas and unfamiliar values. Somewhat rigid in my own opinions, I worked to adopt Audrey's flexibility. As Lao Tzu, the father of the Tao, said, "When I let go of what I am, I become what I might be."

In Maine, on a silent cold morning, as a pale sun peeked from between thick clouds, Audrey walked beside me on the beach road. She stopped, put an index finger to her lips, and whispered, "Shhh. Listen." I did. Waves rolled over pebbles and then receded, carrying clinking, clattering musical stones as they returned to the sea. I had heard crashing whitecaps, but not until Audrey's visit did I notice these delicious, soothing sounds.

Andie Grater and Nancy Gray came next—from spring-like Mexico. They arrived in Atlanta in 1980, shortly after pulling up established New York roots. Both were trained artists and established business-women, each using her creative talents in the business world. In 2001, they again left home and all that was familiar, this time in a move to Mexico. They learned Spanish, started a bed-and-breakfast in Cuerna-vaca, developed Mexican friendships, and continued to use artistic skills in their varied business ventures. I continued to be impressed by their abilities and bravery, their willingness to start a new life.

And Toni, a tall, blue-eyed brunette who chopped wood and smiled warmly and cared little about her appearance—the only friend to drive to Maine—arrived with her friend Thorian from West Virginia. Toni lives in a tin-roofed, A-frame cabin she built at the foot of the Blue

Ridge Mountains. I don't mean "built" in the usual sense of hiring a contractor and standing by until it's time to decorate. Not this gal. She built it, hiring help and mentors as needed. When I face a daunting, yet-to-be-learned task, I think of Toni and the enthusiasm with which she faces any new enterprise.

Bridgton •········ Portland
Maine   • Maine

◉ Biddeford Pool
   Maine

CHAPTER 23
Weatherbeaten

When it snowed, as it often did, the driveway was plowed before first light. My various guests and I slept soundly, protected from storms and wind, never hearing the plow beneath our windows. Soon after breakfast, we would be on the road to some inviting spot in Maine.

I took almost everyone to Freeport, with its famed L.L.Bean store and several other well-known outlets. While on the street, we walked in what appeared to be a long-standing New England village. Inside the shops, we could have been at any upscale mall. The consummate shoppers were ecstatic, but even the browsers appreciated this unique concept in a historical town—with a break at Starbucks.

From there, we would go to Yarmouth and "Eartha," the world's largest rotating globe. Established in 1998 in its home at the DeLorme map company, it tilts on its axis, has a waistline of one hundred forty feet, stands eight times my height . . . and weighs almost three tons.

As we stood dwarfed beneath Eartha, I imagined the gentle rotations of planet earth, a giant to us, occupying its minute place in the universe.

And for all my guests, a trip to Portland, a large city by Maine standards but with less than a tenth of Atlanta's six million: fresh seafood, art, and antiques all on tree-lined commercial streets, stop signs in place of traffic lights—"traffic" a word with new meaning. I sometimes would wait for a stop sign to turn green!

Shivering even in warm jackets, ravenous after a morning of browsing, we often chose Becky's Diner on Hobson Wharf, a perfect spot to warm up and eat something delicious.

The only sign that this modest building was a special place was the packed parking lot. The sound of gulls and smell of salt water invited us to look at the harbor, but our empty stomachs and the enticing aromas from Becky's lured us inside. Among the choices were omelets, juicy burgers on homemade buns, lobster rolls, and an array of desserts that made you want one, even if you already had more than enough. My favorite top-off was Becky's famous whoopie pie: two discs of chocolate cake with a sweet, creamy filling. Sinfully satisfying!

Lesley and Carol, visiting at different times, had told me they were anticipating a trip to the slopes. So I went to Walmart and bought a simple one-piece ski suit before driving to Shawnee Peak, less than two hours from Biddeford Pool—five lifts and hills for every ability level. We checked in at Noble House, a bed-and-breakfast in Bridgton, eight minutes from the mountain, changed clothes, and headed out to ski.

My skiing friends had skills superior to mine. I controlled my speed and managed my turns with simple snow-plow maneuvers, skiing carefully but usually remaining upright and dry. To warm up, my guests began with me on the beginner's slope, but after a couple of runs moved on to more challenging trails.

Riding the lift, sun glinting off snow, planting skis firmly at the summit, and wandering downward in full control was thrill enough for me.

Near sunset, we changed into warm jeans and sweaters and took our tired and hungry bodies to dinner at a New England tavern to feast on prime rib and Yorkshire pudding.

Back at Noble House, we crawled into our beds, motionless until sunlight drenched the room. After breakfast—a feast of hot muffins, homemade preserves, thick omelets, skillet-browned cottage fries, and fresh fruit—we walked outside and gaped at icicles hanging from rooftop and gutters.

On the second day of Lesley's visit, it snowed in Biddeford Pool, snowed again that night, and continued the next afternoon. It was a day to stay home, but I wanted Lesley, originally a music major, to meet Eleanor, another music lover. I phoned to ask Eleanor if she'd like visitors, and she enthusiastically invited us to come for tea. With fat flakes rendering visibility near zero, we drove the few miles down the ocean road and breathed a sigh of relief as we parked in her driveway.

Eleanor suggested we have a seat by the fire while she brewed a fresh pot of tea.

We had just gotten settled when she returned with three glasses and a bottle of wine, saying with a sly smile, "I couldn't find the tea."

Driving from Biddeford Pool to Portland, Liz commented with astonishment about Mazie Grace. "How does she know where we are? She talks to us! She said left, but we ignored her and turned right. All she says is 'recalculating.' How does she *do* that?" I had become so accustomed to Mazie that I no longer wondered about her skills and achievements. I stopped questioning how she accomplished her difficult tasks—just as we no longer ask how our voices travel instantly across thousands of miles of phone wires or how light fills a room after we flip a switch.

One of my favorite haunts in Portland was Stonewall Kitchen. After seeing it, Andie and Nancy suggested we visit the flagship store in York, only forty-five minutes from Biddeford Pool and a grander experience than the quaint store in Portland.

Just thirteen years earlier, two men began this thriving business with a card table at the local farmers' market and, as they say now, "displaying proudly the few dozen vinegars and jams" that they hand-labeled a few hours earlier. Although the founders say the company was named for the "graceful stone walls that surrounded the original farm," we wondered aloud if the true origin might be the famed gay Stonewall uprising in New York.

Predictably, my two artist guests wanted to see the Portland Museum of Art, one of the oldest art museums in the country. As the collection grew, a mansion was donated to add much-needed display space. When the museum outgrew even these two structures, a wealthy donator contributed seventeen Winslow Homer paintings and eight million dollars for a new building to house these and the beloved Maine Collection.

Designed by the renowned architectural firm of I. M. Pei, the exterior presents enormous, semicircular windows. From the inside, through mesh-covered openings, street views looked like softly muted paintings. The architecture, interior design, and lighting are an integral part of the exhibits. Sunlight enters from the upper part of the wall, flooding the space as it illuminates the works of art.

Influenced by living with whitecaps across the small street, my favorite was Homer's *Weatherbeaten*. He lived with the Atlantic Ocean at his doorstep, as I was now. *Weatherbeaten* is based on close observation of this immense body of water culminating at his home. Winslow captures an instant in time—waves crashing viciously against the rocks. Yet we know that the violence of the sea will alternate with episodes of peace, water gently licking the same boulders it had beaten just moments before.

We left the museum in a cold rain. Wind blew water onto the backs of our legs, and we pulled on our hoods to cover a portion of faces, and yet my artist friends declared it was well worth the trip. "A *lovely* exhibit," they said.

I've visited so many incredible museums in towns of a half million, or even less. It's hard to understand how so few people can gather such magnificent collections and build glorious structures to show, and even enhance, their brilliance.

With Toni and Thorian, who visited near the end of my stay in Maine, I shopped for a jade plant, a gift for Heather and Erv, who had announced they were hosting a going-away party for me. Thorian, with bright red hair and a punk look, volunteered to pretend to be the nursery's delivery person. Toni and I parked down the road and watched from a distance as Heather answered the door with great surprise, saying something like, "This must be a mistake . . . it isn't our anniversary."

Molecules of each friend firmly implanted in my brain, I was able to plan this adventure—this wandering alone, this new life. Author Alexander McCall Smith said, "That we have the people we have in this life, rather than others, is miraculous . . . a miraculous gift." Even here in Maine, some people were drawn to me—and me to them— but not others. It is as though we unconsciously recognize those who have potential to connect with, and understand, our deepest feelings. This bond cannot be rushed; it happens with the passage of time and shared experience. And some pairings will fall away as both parties learn that the fit is imperfect. But those who stay give us gifts that can be achieved by nothing else in life. And when they are taken from us, they leave a permanent particle of themselves in our brain. The intimacy of my long-time companions inevitably led me to remember those who, though once close, were left behind . . .

It's been two years since my relationship with Chris ended. My dissertation now complete, I've been invited to join the faculty at Indiana University. The day before I am to leave, I rent a U-Haul and pack the lighter items. Kevin and his wife take me out for a celebratory dinner.

The next day, Kevin brings the family to be with me as he loads the heavier things. And finally I'm ready to take off. Kevin has been my best friend for a dozen years; I've watched the kids grow from infants to toddlers to school-age children, and we have become close. As I watch them slowly shrink in the rear view mirror, there is something in my throat I can't swallow.

I drive directly to the airport in Indianapolis. Jeff is flying in to help me unload . . . but there is a blizzard, and his plane is delayed. I'm stuck in the airport until morning. Although weary from the trip, I let my elders have the chairs; I join my generation, still limber enough to sleep on the airport floor.

Jeff arrives in the morning and stays a few days—his visit a bridge from past to present . . .

Back in Biddeford Pool, Toni, Thorian, and I visited Ada as she prepared to open the lobster pound. Elegant when not working in the pound, Ada was also fetching in her orange, waterproof jumpsuit. She showed us the electrically powered equipment generating a steady flow of ocean water to the tanks. Power failures, Ada said, necessitate emergency action to keep the enormous numbers of lobsters alive. She showed us the special room for "picking"—staffers spend the day doing this tedious work to provide us with lobster meat, free of shells.

The lobster business, she adds, is exhausting, but the season is short. And it is far less stressful than the business world in a chaotic city. As an Atlanta mortgage broker, Ada never dreamed she would make a living in Maine schlepping lobsters. And Beth, an executive in a notable restaurant chain and then owner of her own fine Atlanta restaurant, had also donned a noticeably different hat.

On Oscar night in Biddeford Pool, Beth and Ada hosted a lobster dinner in my ocean house. Before popping lobsters into the cooking pot, Ada noticed a female with exposed eggs on the underside—a seeder. She made a V-shaped cut in her tail, identifying her as a breeder and then, carrying a flashlight and the live lobster, walked across the street onto the slippery rocks. Ada dropped the hen back into her ocean home, knowing she would find new friends. Both believed in conservation, believed in leaving the world intact for future generations. Saving one lobster was a little piece of their efforts.

I remembered the going-away party held for them in Atlanta, and remembered thinking of their bravery in leaving metropolitan Atlanta, buying a house in a tiny town on the ocean in Maine, and starting a totally new life. I would have liked to imitate such a move. But my career choice didn't lend itself to such a shift.

While Beth and Ada chose their entrepreneurial careers as adults, I decided my future as a child on a drive home from the skating rink. Dad pointed vaguely at the University of Chicago campus and said, "That's where people go after high school. They get a bachelor's, then a master's . . . and some go on for a doctorate."

"What do they do then?" I asked. He said, "Some teach at universities. Some do research. They're the experts." I knew from the respect in his tone that I wanted to be one of those experts. But I didn't know what I would study until a high school teacher told me, "You know, you speak very well. And you care about helping others. Why don't you consider being a speech pathologist, or maybe a psychologist?" I went off to university life with a predetermined path for the future.

After completing my degrees, I began my professional career as an assistant professor at Indiana University, leaving my Ann Arbor life behind. I now focused on my students and developing courses that would give them useful tools for their future careers. I knew from my many years as a student that it was also important for me to be enthusiastic and, when appropriate, even entertaining. The people I met and loved in Ann Arbor were no longer in the forefront, but they were not forgotten. Especially Kevin . . .

I'm starting my job on the faculty of Indiana University. I live with Mandy, a colleague and divorced woman with a deep, sexy voice. It was her voice that first attracted me. She is of medium height, with perfect posture. Her short straight gray hair makes me think she might be gay. She's not, and although we are not in love, she is open to a temporary lesbian relationship. We get along well, and we each have a partner—for now.

The phone rings. I answer in the kitchen. It's an old friend calling from Ann Arbor. His tone is somber. I know something is wrong as soon as he speaks. He confirms my suspicion as he continues so softly I can barely hear him. "Kevin has been shot . . . on vacation with a friend . . . robbery in a gas station . . . dead before he got to the hospital . . . closed casket."

I hang up the phone and stare at Mandy. I can't move, can't speak . . .

CHAPTER 24

Good-Bye

As I prepared to leave Maine in the spring of 2005, I reflected on my mindset since leaving home a year ago. Even though I retired from the VA, I continued to work in responsible positions, teaching part time and managing a nonprofit organization. Both jobs came with supervisors, both with deadlines and judgments. Although the stress was nowhere near as intense as my corporate career, my life was certainly not relaxing. Ever since I began school, someone expected something from me—parents, teachers, peers. And then there were the years of hiding, living one life in the real world, the other nagging me from crevices of my mind. Now, with no one watching over my activities, I was truly free. I'd never known such peace, such calm. What a contrast to other times, other places . . .

It's spring in 1970; I still live with Mandy in Bloomington. I have one other close friend, Mary Ann Carpenter, known by all as Mac. She hosts a party for students and faculty every Friday—I never miss it. Talking with students while drinking Scotch is quite different than talking at them from behind a desk.

Many are passionate about ending the Vietnam War.

Richard Nixon, who had promised to end the conflict, allows an invasion of Cambodia, inciting protesters across the country. In Ohio, students at Kent State University organize a demonstration early in May. They are joined by a few looters, arsonists, and drunks relishing an opportunity to add commotion to this already edgy event.

In Bloomington, we follow the news, absorbing every detail of the war in Southeast Asia and the turmoil at home.

Ohio Governor James Rhodes holds a press conference, pounds on his desk, and declares these students are "the worst people in America . . . the strongest, (most) well-trained, militant, revolutionary group that has ever assembled in America." He promises to use every available law enforcement agency to eradicate the problem.

On Monday, May 4, 1970, with tensions at a peak, students gather on campus. The public and media take sides while the well-armed National Guard orders the protesters to disband or face arrest. Enraged activists hurl expletives, rocks, and stones. The crowd increases. The police launch tear gas. Tension turns to terror—students and police fear for their lives.

Panicked, a few guardsmen fire into the crowd, killing four, all of whom are students in good standing . . . two of whom are just walking from one class to the next.

As news of the Ohio killings reaches us in Bloomington, students here plan an immediate protest against both the Cambodia incursion and the recent Kent State deaths. School administrators rapidly call for university, town, and state police. They are asked to come in full riot gear.

It's the night before the scheduled event. A chain call begins: faculty leaders ask junior members to mediate between protesters and university administrators—the goal is not to cancel the event, but rather to dampen rage on all sides.

I hang up the phone, change into an outfit suitable for a professor, and head for a campus auditorium where about a hundred professors are receiving all-night assignments and instructions. I'm sent to a sorority house and then a fraternity; they're expecting me. In both houses, I warn, "Under these conditions, *someone could start shooting. Please stay peaceful, I beg you. The cops are very tense."*

It's not difficult to convince them . . . everyone is frightened.

When the faculty regroups to share results, we're told the stress was too much for one of the top administrators. He's drunk. Senior faculty members are holding him under the shower until he sobers up.

After a sleepless night of meetings, still wearing my teaching costume, I join my colleagues in a thin line on a wide street, separating an estimated five thousand protesters from armed police. As the speeches begin, red paint drops from a rooftop and splatters onto the pavement . . . and on my new beige shoes.

That afternoon, with no time to change clothes, I teach, still wearing the new beige shoes now dotted with symbolic blood.

Cambodia and Vietnam weren't our only wars. The nation was at war with itself. Many well-meaning administrators resigned: their role had become that of sandwich-meat in a triple-decker made up of students, trustees, and legislators. Few faculty members wanted those newly vacated positions. It seemed to me that the new administrators were loyal only to the trustees and state politicians. Students and faculty be damned.

I began to hate university life.

When I moved into my ocean house, thirty-five years had passed since the volatile spring of 1970. Peaceful Biddeford Pool was a town that had known no violence for two and a half centuries . . . not since the French and Indian Wars ended in 1763. Politics was discussed here, sometimes debated, but never heatedly.

Most residents moved here for the ocean, the woods, and river. They find, sometimes to their surprise, the treasure that is the people, the others who moved here for the ocean, the woods, and the river. Self-sufficient and independent, they nevertheless appreciate community. Although no one spends time discussing the weaknesses and foibles of neighbors, any needs are quickly learned, as if by magic, and help offered by those who can. Though gossip was rare, spiritual philosophy was a common topic, or party planning or repairing something.

Heather D held the regular spiritual reflections group in her lovely home in the woods by the river. I spent a few days with Polly, a lovely new friend, shopping for materials to repair her mildewed bathtub caulk, followed by the dirty—but fun—renovation. When the tub looked like new, we celebrated with dinner at an Indian restaurant in Saco. Anita hosted a feast for friends who wanted to lose or maintain weight. We called it the "CHEAP" dinner, which stood for something like Casual Healthy Eating—A Party. A high tea at Heather L's with several members of the bridge club featured finger sandwiches and rich chocolate cookies in shapes of aces, hearts, diamonds, and spades. Christmas caroling brought us to the convent, where we sang to the nuns as they enjoyed a pizza-and-beer supper.

Though it was winter, outdoor activities were also plentiful. One afternoon, Heather D taught me to walk on snowshoes in her white woods. While playing bridge at Heather L's, I mentioned the skating rink and told my table that the park was open and lighted in the evening. After my first venture onto the ice, I'd skated often and was planning to go that evening with Heather D. Heather L broke into a wide smile and said she and her husband Randy would join us. The four of us skated that night under a star-filled sky, kept warm by motion and friendship. Heather and Randy glided with arms crossed in front, holding hands.

Days sped by, and new friends became dear to me. To show my appreciation for their warmth and hospitality, I invited seventy-five people to a bash at my house in March.

I planned a full buffet and bar. Only one issue concerned me: limited parking. Because the street in front of my ocean home was the width of a large driveway, I needed a solution for cars. So a few days prior to the event, I headed to the police station to discuss the problem. On the way, I saw a local police car and stopped. As luck would have it, this policeman was scheduled to be on duty the night of my party. He followed me back to my house and identified acceptable parking places on nearby side streets. He also suggested I buy a banner informing visitors where to park.

"If I see a car parked illegally, I won't ticket 'em. I'll just knock on your door and letcha know if someone has to move," the officer said. I promptly asked him to join the party and get a plate of supper on his break. I couldn't imagine this in Atlanta.

After acquiring and hanging the ten-foot parking banner, it was time to prepare the table. Wanting a tasteful setting, I asked a few friends to help. And help they did! A pewter chafing dish kept mini-meatballs hot, a colorful fruit tray lay at a slight angle in a wicker bowl, a divided dish held an assortment of cheeses, and a three-tiered, glass-footed platter displayed desserts. Parsley and roasted red pepper slices decorated serving plates.

Four college kids were ready to take coats, serve hors d'oeuvres, replenish the buffet, and prepare drinks. My job was to circulate and enjoy my company.

Guests arrived in ones and twos and, within what seemed like minutes, my house was full: people at the fireplace, at the bar, the buffet, and mingling in ever-rotating conversational groups. It reminded me of that first party, the one held at the community center soon after my arrival. But now, instead of introducing myself to strangers, I actually introduced a few of my guests to each other.

The policeman knocked on my door and told me everyone was legally parked. Before leaving, he accepted my offer to fill a plate for his supper.

Though winter blizzards were coming to an end, a different kind of storm assaulted us. A few weeks before Beth's April birthday, Ada phoned with the news that Beth had breast cancer. Surgery . . . chemo . . . hiring someone to fill in for Beth . . . many problems still ahead.

How did I absorb this news? At first with fear . . . then anger . . . and some time later, I reconnected with my favorite Buddhist philosophy: there are things we can remedy, but some things we cannot influence. We can control only our attitude. Modern medicine and Beth's positive attitude, mental fortitude, and physical strength might well pull her through this.

Meanwhile, I vowed to help as much as possible before time for me to leave my now beloved Biddeford Pool.

On May 1, 2005, the date I was to vacate my ocean home, even Maine was warming to spring. Heather and Erv hosted a bon voyage party in their beautiful home with their customary elegance. Ada and Beth, now out of the hospital, joined the friends who came to share a superb meal and winter stories. Their generosity and warmth were, and still are, incomparable. I wrote a thank you ditty to entertain the guests.

> As last summer was about to end
> I wanted shelter on which to depend.
> A home by the ocean, winter on the sea.
> So I hunted for one just perfect for me.
> Drove into the Pool to see Ada and Beth
> And saw the house. It took away my breath.
>
> "But, there's nothing to do," said the summer folk,
> As they left for destinations south.
> "If you try to speak," they added,
> "You'll probably freeze your mouth."
>
> How wrong they were; activities abound.
> Quiet we say? Not this town.
> Leaving one event and heading out
> People can be heard to shout,
> "You don't have time to take a shower.
> The next party's in half an hour."
>
> And now, preparing to again be alone,
> I will end this poem with a different tone
> To thank you for the warmth you've shown,
> As I spent the winter by the sea
> With all of you so kind to me.

As author Alexander McCall Smith said, "(It was an) . . . unequivocal pleasure—pleasure at hearing what all of us wanted to hear, at least occasionally: that there was somebody who liked us, whatever our faults, and liked us sufficiently to say so."

Now it was May 1, 2005, and it was one year ago that I left my Atlanta home. I had been wandering alone for half a year when I settled in Maine for the winter, hoping to meet a few people and enjoy hours of reading and ocean viewing. I met far more than a few: I found many friends, a warm and welcoming community, and a place of intellectual and spiritual stimulation. And yet, it was time to get back on the road and experience again the joy of solitude in new places. Carol B surprised me with homemade chocolate chip cookies to take on the road, providing me not only with a tummy treat, but also a transition—I brought something of Biddeford Pool with me as I re-entered the world with Mazie.

CHAPTER 25

Transitions

When I left "my" home in Biddeford Pool, chocolate chip cookies in easy reach, I headed to Canada on curving two-lane roads to reach the strangely named "Downeast." Since I was heading north—up on any map—the name Downeast seemed odd. I learned that this New England term usually applies to the coast of Maine from Penobscot Bay to the Canadian border, and it has been in use for two centuries and originated with sailors. When they sailed with the wind to their back, they were sailing down wind, and since the most frequent prevailing wind came from the southwest, they were sailing to the east—down wind and to the east. Thus the area became known as "Downeast."

I continued north on the two-lane through tiny towns, passing old stone-and-wooden churches, a profusion of galleries and antique stores on otherwise untouched roadsides. Coming around a curve or reaching the crest of a hill, a panoramic view often appeared—land or sea—more awesome for its unexpectedness. In the hectic packing and good-bye parties, I hadn't given a thought to this next part of my adventure nor to the anticipated pleasures of Nova Scotia and Newfoundland. But now that I was back on the road, the familiar feeling of excitement returned. Bar Harbor and Acadia National Park share an irregularly shaped, mountainous island in northeast Maine. A highlight of Acadia was Thunder Hole, now a spectacular cleavage in the natural granite seawall created by the power of waves against what was originally a slight flaw in the rock. Waves rushed into the cavity, thunderous against its walls, and produced a massive spray. Once again I was reminded of the power and drama of the ocean, so easy to forget when gentle waves softly visit a quiet shore.

Acadia is also home to one of Maine's eight remaining covered bridges. With a façade of stunning local pink granite, it has three magnificent arches for boat passage. The same pink granite was cut to create safety barriers on roads. Individual stones—like fat, wide teeth—are strung out along the roadside to prevent cars wandering off as curves meet cliffs.

Most of the campgrounds were not yet open. When unable to find a suitable one, motels were the less desirable alternative. Late one afternoon, I drove into a campground and found the owner raking a site. He said they wouldn't be open for another few days, but looking at his watch and the slowly setting sun, he asked if I would like a not-quite-ready space near staffers already living on the property. When I gratefully accepted, he directed me to a scenic spot and turned on the power. He refused to take any money because "I'm still closed."

Preparing to leave the next morning, I noticed my magnetic spare car key holder had fallen off the fender's inner wall. Wanting a replacement, I stopped at a home-based locksmith shop. For insurance reasons, he doesn't usually work on cars, but he made an exception for me, a small woman traveling alone, "for that odd moment when you might be locked out of the car." He not only made a new key, but he spent an hour making a container and attaching it under the car. His fee was five dollars.

Almost a year earlier, I had driven from Montana to Canada across the invisible line dividing one country from another. This time I made the transition three thousand miles east, crossing the international border shared by Calais (Maine, USA) and St. Stephen (New Brunswick, Canada) and then drove to St. John, where a ferry took me to Digby, Nova Scotia. The blue sky was so pale it was almost white. Puffy clouds were underlined with wide strokes of gray, and in stark contrast, the ocean was a dark cerulean blue.

Digby was founded about four hundred years ago by British loyalists. It still points its antique cannons at the serene Bay of Fundy to remind visitors (they say with a wink and a smile) of how this town defended itself from the American rebels.

Digby described itself as the "world capital of scallops." Eager for an opportunity to sample them, I stopped at a restaurant on the Bay of Fundy, a place with both awesome scallops and the world's greatest tide differential.

These towns thrilled me with the passion of a new love. *Had I lived here*, I thought, *I would wake each day eager to join in the excitement.* But as I watched people casually going about their business, looking straight ahead while thinking about plans for the day, indifferent to their surroundings, I grasped that intense passion is in the freshness, and as with a lover—if the relationship lasts—it would settle into profound affection . . .

It's January 1973, the night before my first day of work at the Atlanta Veterans Administration Medical Center. Clothes are neatly folded in drawers and hanging in closets, dishes are in the cabinets, and sheets and blankets are on the bed. I go out to explore the city, stop at a drugstore, and pick up a free newspaper—Creative Loafing. *I turn the pages, looking for a gay venue. In the personals I find a one-inch notice about a meeting for "feminists"—code, I think, for lesbians. I plan to attend.*

Bloomington, my last home, had fifty thousand people, invisible gays, and one good restaurant on its solitary main street. Over a million people live in Atlanta! I'm in a city with gay venues. Will I find gay friends here? Will I belong in a "crowd"?

An expressway takes me downtown to busses and taxis and high rises outlined in neon. My breath is shallow with excitement. After fitfully dozing—nervous about my first day—I shower, dress carefully, find matching heels, apply makeup, and check the mirror before leaving for work. I arrive early to find a few colleagues already gathered around our clinic's coffee pot, sitting on stools, elbows on a counter. Lee, a handsome man with straight black hair and mustache, is dressed in suit and tie with a perfectly pressed, gleaming white shirt. He pours a cup for me. Even with my underdeveloped gaydar, I sense he is a brother.

Later that week, I begin a search for a therapist who will help me accept being gay in a nonaccepting world. Knowing that anything I say is confidential, I interview a psychiatrist who teaches at Emory. He recommends a psychologist who is a lesbian and gives me her contact information. But he adds that most therapists, gay and straight, now see acceptance as an appropriate outcome. I meet the woman he has endorsed, and I like her.

I'm in therapy again—but it's quite different now. She's a successful woman, a lesbian, and she's not trying to change me. I am slowly accepting myself, slowly understanding that being gay is okay.

Nova Scotia

Digby ◉
Nova Scotia

CHAPTER 26

Evangeline

Nova Scotia added a bit of the World Wide Web to a lifestyle of the 1940s. In a country farmers' market, a computer with public Internet access rested near the front door while gourmet deli meats and international gifts flanked bulk foods. The general store carried furniture, food staples, and cell phones. Although the gas stations took credit cards, few accepted payments at the pump.

The first time I stopped for gas, I went inside to pre-pay and the fellow behind the counter said, "Oh no. You don't pay now. Come on in when you're finished pumping."

On the road heading northeast from Digby, the towns were so tiny they had to count their pets as residents to reach a four-figure population. Numerous art galleries dotted the streets, many in artist's homes. Parking lots led to backdoor entrances, often opening into disheveled workshops leading to neatly arranged pottery, paintings, woodcarvings, and burl-turnings.

Though the sparse populations of small-town Canada could not afford the luxury of big museums, they tended to honor the history of ancestors with collections displayed in their homes and shops. British mystery writer P. D. James wrote that a museum is about "the individual life, how it was lived . . . men and women organizing their societies. It's about the continuing life of the species." I thought of how these towns contrasted with Atlanta's sprawl and varied cultures. My life would have been so different here . . .

It's a Tuesday afternoon in May of 1973, I'm sitting at my desk, handwriting an evaluation report. Lee, whose office is down the hall in Medical Administration, knocks lightly as he walks through my open office door. He pulls a chair up next to me, sits down and crosses his legs. He pauses then says, "I may be wrong. If I am, please forgive me."

Another pause: "Doc-tor Berman," he says, accenting and elongating "Doc," using my title to be funny. "Have you figured out I'm gay?"

He pauses briefly, not long enough for me to respond. "I get the feeling you are too. True?"

I nod, speechless.

"Wanna meet some people? I'm going to the bars tonight. I'd be glad to take you and introduce you around." When I agree, he tells me he'll pick me up at ten. "You'll want to take a nap before we go out."

He takes me first to Sweet Gum Head on Cheshire Bridge Road. We're greeted by disco sounds as soon as we open the car doors. Inside, the dance floor is packed with same-sex couples and a few straight ones. Lee tells me it's the liveliest bar in town. We order drinks and find a table to watch.

"Wanna dance?"

The only fast dance I know is the Twist, popular more than a decade ago. I tell him this. He says, "It's okay. Start with that and you'll pick it up fast."

We dance. Then another drink while we watch men in drag lip-syncing to popular music. Some of the boys make gorgeous women—others not. The latter group exaggerated their homeliness and performed finely-honed comedy routines.

"This is the best drag show east of San Francisco," he tells me as a smiling woman joins us at our table. Lee introduces me to Sally. He tells her I'm new to this world.

She says, "Oh, then we need to take you to Garbo's, a lesbian bar just down the block. Lee knows where it is. You have to be a member . . . that's to protect the regulars from being outed. There are some straight members, but like everyone else, they have to be sponsored by a known lesbian. I'll get you in."

The three of us go to Garbo's. At the door a broad-shouldered female greeter-bouncer stands behind a podium, recognizing most of the customers and stamping their hands to indicate that they've paid the entrance fee. She reviews the names of the others on a membership list, as a maître d' checks a reservation.

Sally leads the way for the three of us and vouches for me. In the time it takes to light a match, I'm added to the membership list. Now it's documented. I'm a real lesbian. I don't have to roam the streets looking for gay bars. I now belong. But, of course, I'm still living a double life. Lee is the only colleague who knows about my secret.

Although it's one o'clock, the gay world is dancing and drinking. We speak only to order drinks and have to shout to be heard. No wonder Lee holds his head in his hand each morning until he finishes his first coffee.

Several women ask me to dance. I'm beginning to pick up some disco steps and feel less awkward. While taking a break from the dance floor, I see a woman coming straight toward me, swimming through the crowd until she reaches my bar seat. With a pronounced New York accent, she says to me, "I heard a big-city Jewish voice."

She pulls a business card from her pocket and adds, "I'm Doris. Bagels and lox, our house, mine and Wendy's. Address on the card. Sunday. Noon." And she was gone.

Sally introduces me to Barb. I'm aware I'm meeting my first Atlanta gay people. And this is the first time ever that I might have the opportunity to hang out in gay venues, to have a group of gay friends. A few hours later, the crowds thin and Lee, Sally, Barb, and I cross the street to have breakfast in a diner, the late-night thing . . .

A stationary sailboat on the side of the road jarred me out of my reverie. I slowed and saw eight tall mesh screens situated to look like a set of sails, but only when viewed from a particular vantage point. As I drove, the panels transformed from sails to paintings.

On this gray day, the mesh was the color of sky, and from the right place, the faux boat seemed ready to travel down the road. I parked nearby and walked back and forth, stopping each time at the spot where the illusion was perfect.

I drove past gently sloping, emerald-green meadows giving way to manicured, cultivated fields, often with the sparkling blue coast in the background. Amoeba-shaped lakes, narrow churning creeks, and wide calm rivers, a limitless variety of shapes and sizes flanked the road, endlessly different, always thrilling.

And then, in the midst of my idyllic vacation, an unsettling visit into history took me far from bland delight in the joys of travel. I found myself on the Evangeline Trail, a main highway passing through Grand-Pré, Nova Scotia.

In 1847, Longfellow published the poem *Evangeline, a Tale of Acadie,* recounting the fictional story of Evangeline and Gabriel, French Acadian lovers about to be married when all Acadians were deported.

The poem brought the plight of the true-life Canadian Acadians to a wide audience. And the Grand-Pré Memorial Church continues to tell the story. A bronze statue of Evangeline rests in the entrance to the stone building. Hand-carved wooden doors lead to a stained glass window in bright shades of blue and green, streaked with red lighting to symbolize the rending of a people from their land.

Evangeline represents the strength and perseverance of the Acadians who, in the early 1600s, settled around the Bay of Fundy and the Minas Basin. The forty-foot tides deposited a rich variety of nutrients from the sea, but created unusable marshlands. When dikes were built, the tides were controlled and the land, now workable, was exceptionally fertile. The ambitious Acadians created an agricultural society, rich with music and art.

But in 1744, war broke out between the British and French, catastrophically altering the lives of all Acadians. Caught between warring factions, they made every effort to remain neutral. Eventually, however, the British no longer accepted neutrality and demanded that the Acadians sign an unconditional oath of loyalty. When they refused to sign unless they were guaranteed they would not have to join the military, the British confiscated land, burned houses, and deported the entire colony.

They resettled, primarily in New England, Quebec, and Louisiana. The new Louisiana Acadians became known as Cadians, or Cajuns.

The names of three hundred families who once lived in Nova Scotia are engraved in bronze in the Grand-Pré Memorial Church. I told my dear friend, Deb Bourgeois, that her family name is among them, still prominent in this part of the world.

I absorbed Acadian history on the sixtieth anniversary of the Nazi holocaust's ending. Once again I wondered what disease attacks those few who dream up the man-made atrocities. Is it contagious, prompting others to bring them to fruition? And is it a different disease that inhabits those who quietly acquiesce?

The next morning I continued my journey, reminded again what a privilege it is to live in this time, in this place.

Charlottetown
Prince Edward Island

Cavendish
Prince Edward Island

Wood Islands Harbor
Prince Edward Island

Caribou
Nova Scotia

Grand-Pré
Nova Scotia

CHAPTER 27

Raising Consciousness

In Caribou, Nova Scotia, I stopped behind a line of cars waiting to park below deck on the ferry to Wood Islands Harbour on Prince Edward Island. Once on the ferry, I took a seat at an outside table to enjoy the sea, grateful for an opportunity to get from one place to the next without driving. The seventy-five-minute mini-cruise allowed me to read and listen to the soft slap of waves hitting the hull. As we approached land, the lighthouse—now a museum—could be seen.

The population in Wood Islands is so small that it isn't counted. Prince Edward Island, commonly called PEI, is home to fewer than one hundred fifty thousand.

Charlottetown, on the south shore of PEI, shelters about thirty thousand people, and in summer, probably the same number of tourists. It's the largest city on the island, serving the entire area with excellent theater, music, restaurants, and shops.

I continued to be surprised at the quality of offerings in small Canadian towns, probably, I think now, because US small towns are usually close to bigger cities and rely on them for the arts, museums, and gourmet food.

Walking in and out of stores and galleries, I noticed it was the time of day when the sun would soon slip beneath the horizon, and my stomach told me to find a place for supper. I saw candlelit tables behind a sparkling window, a neatly posted French menu on the door. Couples at each romantic table, absorbed in each other, didn't notice the lone woman in jeans carrying a book. I ordered wine and studied the menu before selecting sautéed chicken breast with crushed almonds covered with baked brie.

In 1864, this city hosted the meeting that led to the formation of Canada. Province House, where the meeting was held, still functions as a public building, its simple stylishness gracing the community. Like Colonial Williamsburg, it celebrates its heritage with historical presentations in period dress and with the dialect of the time, the men and women maintaining their characters throughout the day— a bit like I did in my early years at the Atlanta VA . . .

Heels, hose, and eye shadow by day; jeans, shirts, and sneakers on nights and weekends, hard soles for dancing—the costume appropriate for the activity and time of day, neither telling the whole story.

It's a Sunday morning in 1974. I drive to the address on the back of Doris's business card, anxious about going to a party with lesbians I don't yet know. Am I dressed okay? Will I be able to make conversation? It's one thing to be in a bar, dancing and drinking . . . another to meet gay women in the daylight. Will they all be butch? At least the bagels and lox will be familiar.

I knock. A stranger opens the door, but Doris appears in a second and says, "Wendy, this is the gal with the big-city Jewish voice. The one I told you about when we got back from the bah the otha night." Turning to me, she adds, "But I can tell ya not from New Yawk. Midwest? And remind me ya name."

"Marilyn. Chicago," I say.

"Well, come on in and meet everybody."

And I meet Carole and a half dozen others.

In a few minutes, I'm munching on an onion bagel with cream cheese and nova, a type of lox (Nova Scotia lox), and circulating easily among these relaxed women. Wendy, though from Brooklyn, says with no accent, "We're starting a consciousness-raising group. It'll be these women. Want to join us?"

The way she says it, I'm thinking I should know what it is. So I ask.

"I'm surprised you don't know. These groups started in New York and Chicago."

"I've lived in college towns since I was seventeen," I explain.

"Ah. Well, you'll pick it up right away, but the general idea in most CR groups is to raise consciousness about women's lib. We're still not there, you know. And since we're all lesbians, we'll focus especially on gay lib. We'll share our stories."

The first meeting is at Doris and Wendy's. Of course we eat, but oh how we talk. I've never heard stories like these, at least not the details, and had told mine only to a therapist. Some of these women have come out to their families— the ones who were forced to do so—but most not yet.

Carole tells us she was with a bunch of gay friends in a park in Greenwich Village. She was sixteen—the others older. The police came over to ask their ages; Carole lied. They told her they didn't believe her, took her to the police station, and called her parents to come for her. Carole told her parents they had to pick up her cousin at a gay restaurant called Pam Pam's. The game was over. Her parents were devastated. She adds that her mom now loves her friends . . . but it took some years. Wendy, who has been married and divorced, believes her mom and dad would be shocked and distressed if they knew. Her partner, Doris, is butch, but they don't seem to notice.

For the first time, I don't feel alone. I truly understand the oppression we live under—vast numbers of us, together in hiding. We still live in secret and worry some might guess.

I'm living a double life, similar to the way I lived as an adolescent. The difference is that in childhood one life was real, the other only in my head; now both are in the real world, just not at the same time of day.

I moved from the unthinking cruelty of the seventies to the kindness of 2005 when I found Mr. Magic.

The never-used TV hanging from the roof of my van's living space, the bottom of which was four feet from the floor, prompted frequent accidental head banging. In Charlottetown, I hit it one time too many. This time I shattered one hinge, causing it to hang askew.

The hinge had been loose since before I left home, but the mechanics in Atlanta declared it "unfixable." I thought the only solution was complete removal of this expensive device, a.k.a. Marilyn's Folly. Yet, Mr. Magic (a.k.a. Eric Bowlan), who owned an electronics shop and wore two hats, both of which were magic, was able to fix it perfectly. He even entertained me with a few tricks. Although I stood not more than two feet away, staring at his hands, I couldn't see how he made a scarf disappear and reappear. No wonder he was called "Mr. Magic."

Like the campground manager who didn't charge me because he hadn't formally opened, and the locksmith who charged me five dollars for time and expertise, Mr. Magic, delighted with my van's living space, charged me nothing for his skill and entertainment.

The Confederation Center of the Arts is the showpiece of Charlottetown, and perhaps of PEI, a place where the arts, history, and multicultural character of Canada are brought together.

There I saw a production of the long-running and always sold-out *Anne of Green Gables*, an adaptation of the novel written by PEI's famed author, Lucy Maud Montgomery—born and raised in Cavendish, twenty-five miles from Charlottetown.

When New York produces an international celebrity, it's no big deal; when a little province does so, it prompts accolades and tributes. In addition to the annual sold-out play in Charlottetown, Cavendish proudly displays the Green Gables homestead and abundant gift shops dedicated to Anne.

From Charlottetown to Cavendish I took the long way, by the sea. It was a dream, like driving through a series of paintings: meadows and rivers, storybook villages, and waves of pale gray mist. Along the way, I stopped at a country inn and sat at a wooden table to feast yet again, this time on seafood that had come off the boat an hour earlier.

I wore a T-shirt that captured my feelings, in print too small to read from a distance, "Life should not be a journey to the grave with the intention of arriving safely in an attractive and well-preserved body, but rather to skid in sideways . . . totally worn out, screaming, 'WOO-HOO, what a ride!'"

O'Leary
Prince Edward Island

Cavendish
Prince Edward Island

New Glasgow
Prince Edward Island

CHAPTER 28

After the Storm

The darkening spring sky promised rains to drench New Glasgow and its highly rated campground: a perfect time and place to stop and relax.

On one rainy day, the forecast predicted a few hours of partial sun. Wearing my already dirty hiking shoes and waiting for this respite, I sat reading in a deli by a trailhead, eating homemade chili with black bean, corn, and turkey. When the sun peeked through a hole in the clouds, I set out on a muddy hike.

Two hours later, thick clouds beginning to form, I returned to the van, got in, and quickly closed the door. Seconds later, the first raindrops slapped the windshield. By the time I returned to the campground, it had eased long enough for me to park and walk the few yards to the lodge. A blazing fire in the woodstove sent tall dancing shadows rising and swirling against rich butterscotch walls and ceilings.

Later, warm and dry in the van, I heard plump drops hit steel, first with short pauses, then faster and faster until a tempest crashed against the metal roof. I watched the storm and remembered days long gone . . .

Barb introduces me to Jane—a slim, elegant psychotherapist fifteen years my senior. She has an upper-crust accent, a deep sexy voice, a position in Emory's Department of Psychiatry, and a private practice specializing in gay men. Jane and I, each without a partner, and neither interested in the other sexually, quickly become "running buddies." We go to parties, and have dinners out almost every night, sometimes with a group and sometimes alone.

In 1976, she introduces me to the Pride march, still in its infancy. I'm thirty-six. She tells me the name "Pride" doesn't mean we are proud to be gay. It means, like everyone else, we respect our efforts and achievements and value our personal character. Unlike many others on that sunny afternoon, we don't wear bags to cover our heads. If my photo is taken and shown on the news, seen by my colleagues or my family, so be it. That would be an easy way to come out. Now that I'm in therapy with a lesbian, working hard to accept my sexuality, I find it more difficult than ever to be in hiding. On the other hand, if no one sees me in the march, I'll be "safe" until I find the courage to come out.

I join a lesbian bridge club—and meet Elise. Her eyes are an intense ice-blue, yet somehow soft, and her long slender fingers are striking. I'm safe until one day she tells me she dreamed about me and gently touches my hand with her graceful fingers. I fall into her inviting eyes and drown as we begin a torrid, yet agonizing affair. We have dinners in great restaurants, spend time with her interesting friends, and have fascinating conversations, but she's drawn to numerous other women and a few men. She tells me she loves me. I'm attracted to no one but her. She's everything I wanted: bright, attractive, and well-liked.

Jane, who I continue to see on the many days Elise has "other commitments," encourages me to end the relationship. She tells me my lover has been flirting even with her. But I'm besotted, addicted, needing Elise as another might crave heroin. In spite of my distrust, I don't leave her. We have screaming fights, all initiated by me. Again and again those eyes lock onto mine and convince me I'm her love.

On one of Mom's trips to Atlanta, I introduce her to Elise. My petite mother puts out her hand to shake. She tells me later she doesn't like my "friend" and explains that the handshake was weak. I don't disagree out loud, but knowing Elise's innate kindness toward elders, I think she was afraid to hurt my petite mom.

After three agonizing years, I find the courage to rip myself from this relationship. Infatuation dissolves like clouds after a storm . . .

It was several years before Elise and I met again and this time became friends. She was an intelligent, interesting person—just not a good partner for me. Elise had been my first lover since leaving Bloomington. From the minute she looked into my eyes and told me she dreamt about me, I experienced my first intense feelings since Chris in Ann Arbor. After losing Chris, I had the feeling there would never be someone I could care about deeply. And now, Elise. There seemed no way out.

During the years we were a couple, I went through the motions at work and gave little thought to my family.

Now, sitting in the car, waiting for visibility to improve before driving, my thoughts wandered over their lives in those years and a storm in Chicago—one that changed my parents' lives . . .

Dad is a roving manager for Polk Brother: a furniture, television, and appliance company that was his main competition before his bankruptcy. Although he is near seventy, he still works long, hard hours, and when it snows in Chicago, his work ethic forces him outside in his overcoat to scrape snow and ice from the car. He then drives to a distant location, opens a store, manages it during the storm, and simultaneously substitutes for any missing salesmen. One night in a particularly bad blizzard, he closes the store, anxious to get home. But the highways are slippery, and rapidly falling flakes block visibility. Cars move at incredibly slow speeds, the roads too bad to navigate. Dad tries to continue, but soon cars jam the entire highway. Police come down the midline and shoulders to pick up stranded motorists. Schools and churches shelter men wearing wrinkled suits, perspiration-drenched shirts, and smelly, wet wool overcoats.

The next day Dad makes it home; Mom and Dad ask each other why they put up with Chicago winters.

Their beloved grandsons, Marty and Gary, are in high school, active and clever. They no longer have much time for their grandparents, and their lives go on tangents away from family. My brother Jeff and his attractive wife, Susie, have moved to a suburb of Atlanta. He is the associate brand manager for Coca Cola. Their baby, Kim, is growing up far from Chicago. My mom and dad are empty-nesters. They make plans to move to an inexpensive condo complex in Florida. They both plan to get jobs to supplement their income—Dad in a drug store and Mom a dime store. Jeff does the driving and will assist as they make the transition, just as he did for me when I moved to Bloomington.

On the way, they stop in Atlanta. My current housemate, Patrick, is obviously gay and clearly much younger than I. Neither Mom nor Dad asks me anything about him. As they are about to run an errand, their car won't start. After jump-starting fails to work, Patrick lifts the hood and fiddles with something. Satisfied, he closes the hood and starts the car. None of us have a clue about what he has just done, but I can see my parents are impressed, gay man or not . . .

As I rested in the van on Prince Edward Island, I realized I belonged not only to the past, but to this night, the raging rain, the present, and tomorrow. Sleep interrupted my reveries and many hours passed before I awoke to a weak sun behind dispersing clouds.

My campground was close to the middle of PEI, allowing day trips to almost anywhere on the island. Here, fishing villages and potato fields provided the two main industries, and together they attracted tourists, the third source of income. A few of the old homes had become marine museums and arty gift shops. The rest remained as they'd been for hundreds of years.

Recent plantings had produced dark-red furrowed fields that often lay next to fallow green meadows. Or one might see a silver pasture—an illusion created by light shining on hay, strewn about to protect seedlings. Fields were often separated by rows of evergreens in lieu of fences. And always, serpentine blue rivers meandered through valleys.

The Potato Museum, in the town of O'Leary, amply demonstrated that potatoes are a primary source of income on PEI, much like the

Henry Ford Museum showed the automobile's value to Detroit. There were displays showing the origin of the potato; its history on the island; growing and harvesting; the development of strains that produce quantity, quality, disease resistance, and ease of growing; and research on curing potato diseases they can't yet prevent.

Sharing land with potato exhibits were several other small museums, all presenting items common in the nineteenth century and well into the twentieth: a one-room school; the Log Barn, housing century-old farm implements; an original telephone office displaying oak boxes with batteries and a power crank; and the Community Museum with a collection of items used in daily life. A chamber pot reminded me of my portable device. In lieu of an electric machine, a contraption was inserted in socks to allow air to circulate. Medical equipment included an iron lung for polio victims and an antique operating table in use until 1980.

So much history saved with so much care in the town of O'Leary with a population fewer than nine hundred hardy people.

Spirits of my grandparents roamed with me as I strolled among objects of their lives while, at the same time, a cell phone rested in my pocket and my navigation system waited in the van, ready to be detected by the nearest Global Positioning Satellite.

Baddeck • Louisbourg

O'Leary ⊙ Iona • Cape Breton

Prince Edward Island Nova Scotia Nova Scotia

CHAPTER 29

Anna

When I left home a year ago, Atlanta was flaunting her glorious spring—a rainbow of intensely hued flowers, bushes, and trees with bright pinks, vivid reds, stately whites, and royal purples. From tulips to azaleas to dogwoods, Atlanta blooms until the gold-green leaves of spring make way for the emerald foliage of summer.

Now it was tulip season in Cape Breton, Nova Scotia—bright colors a sharp contrast to winter's gray skies, icy precipitation, and snow-covered trees. All of Canada becomes a garden in the spring, more blossoms with each passing day and flower-filled planters in front of each home and shop.

The main road on Cape Breton hugged the ocean. As deep blue waters licked multicolored rocks, the pungent sea smell reached me through open windows, and soft morning light sent rays dancing across ripples.

The comfortable breeze, sweet aromas, and brilliant colors of Cape Breton brought poignant memories of meeting Anna Goodman in a long-ago spring . . .

I'm at my desk, studying the application of a young woman coming from out of state to interview for a position with the psychology department. I have been asked to be one of the interviewers. Her submission intrigues me: she's thirty-four, grew up in Tennessee, and went to school in Ohio, but she wants an appointment at the Atlanta VA—and her favorite hobby is rappelling.

She arrives on time, an attractive woman with fashionable glasses and a trim figure, dressed in a tailored light-gray suit, short blonde hair perfectly styled. I stand; she looks directly at me and extends her hand. Her grasp is firm, but not bone-crushing. I think Mom would approve of this handshake. After a brief but substantive conversation, I take her down the hall to be interviewed by another member of the team.

The interview committee decides to offer her a job.

I see her often.

It's not long before I'm attracted to this young woman, but I have no idea if she's gay, much less interested in me. I'm forty-eight; she's thirty-four—not an impossible age difference, but she is a junior colleague.

One evening Anna comes to my house. We eat sandwiches and have several glasses of wine as we chat. When it's time for her to go home, we both realize she should not drive. My guest room is a mess. I start to straighten it. She puts her hand on my shoulder and says she doesn't mind sharing my queen-sized bed. My thinking is wine-fuzzy. We go to bed—one bed. She reaches for me and kisses me, the gentlest kiss my lips remember.

Each night, Anna enfolds me in her arms in a spooning position. In my other relationships, I preferred separation for sleep. But with Anna, this is our position of choice, and we both sleep soundly.

Anna is assigned to another VA for the summer. We talk by phone each night after her roommate goes to sleep. She writes me that being away reminds her how much I add to her life.

While she is gone, I make simple changes to my house to better accommodate two people. She returns. We settle into a life together. My friends meet her and approve. My plants, always delicate before Anna, now thrive.

Anna comes from a religious Jewish family, and her mother is strongly opposed to homosexuality, and my parents, well, I've never told them. Her parents and mine assume we are roommates. But I cannot continue this way without telling Audrey, my colleague and friend. I take her to a picnic lunch and confess to being a lesbian and also to my relationship. Although she accepts a gay male friend, she has trouble with the idea of two women together. She discusses this with her husband, Wade—they rapidly come around and not only accept my orientation, but also my relationship with Anna. They invite us to dinner. Soon we hang out with them much as we do with our gay friends.

Lee, too, likes Anna. Everyone likes Anna. We also spend time with Lee and his partner, Evan. We're invited out more than I was when single. I'm part of a couple now, and Anna is popular . . .

I arrived at the Highland Village Museum in the Nova Scotia town of Iona. Sixty miles from O'Leary, this museum presented another glimpse of early nineteenth- and twentieth-century life, this one Scottish. Memories of my history were replaced by total immersion in the way of life of another time, another place.

Of great interest to me was the model of a log house from 1790: it was one room, built of sod-covered rocks with a sod roof, shared by not only the entire family, but also livestock! A cooking pot hung over a small fireplace in the center of the room, and a bed was built into a cupboard on the wall. Even though people were smaller then, I was incredulous thinking of them in this miniature bed.

A sixty-mile drive would have taken me from Iona to Louisbourg, but since it left the ocean road to cut across land, I chose the route embracing the sea, adding an hour of joy to the drive.

Louisbourg is the site of a reconstructed French fort with stone buildings demonstrating skilled architectural designs from the early eighteenth century. This location on Cape Breton was selected by the French in 1713, chosen not only because it was defendable, but also for its abundant fish.

Though not needed immediately for defense, several hundred soldiers were stationed here to handle anticipated future invasions and Louisbourg became a prosperous trading and fishing community. Continued wars between the British and French finally resulted in a

British takeover in the mid-eighteenth century. The fortifications were destroyed, and Louisbourg slowly crumbled.

In 1961, the Canadian government began a historical reconstruction of Louisbourg and its fortifications, rebuilding them as they would have been at their pinnacle. To accurately replicate the structures, the builders learned eighteenth-century French masonry techniques.

Every detail was reconstructed, from the drawbridge over a moat, to the firing holes at the top of the forbidding wall, to the barracks and chapel, shops and homes.

Character actors portrayed bakers and blacksmiths, aristocrats and roughnecks, soldiers and merchants. Shops and restaurants provided the goods and services of the time. One touch I loved was the spotless but unironed, tablecloths.

A few more miles took me to another century—to 1889, when Alexander Graham Bell built a mansion on the tranquil lake in the town of Baddeck. Reminding him of his Scottish Highland birthplace, it was his favorite home. As is the habit in all of Canada, the town honors the memory of its descendant, this one with an information-packed museum on the lake he loved.

The displays were reminders that Bell—an effective teacher of the deaf—not only invented the telephone, but also designed some of the fastest early airplanes, developed a device to remove salt from sea water, created a probe to locate a bullet lodged in a body, and founded Bell Labs, a renowned research center.

Spending the month of May pulling my consciousness through these histories—relaxing in almost every town in Nova Scotia, visiting tiny art galleries, seeing *Anne of Green Gables* and touring her home on Prince Edward Island, touring the Gampo Alley monastery, viewing the history of Longfellow's Evangeline and the Acadians in Grand-Pré, and wandering through Bell's accomplishments—diminished the importance of my own history, at least for a while. I truly looked forward to the next stop—the month of June in Newfoundland.

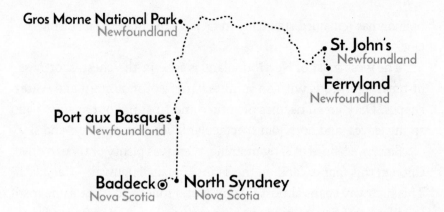

CHAPTER 30

Sea-Change

Few bridges span the ever-present waterways in Nova Scotia; instead, ferries are as much a part of the road system as highways. Some meander across streams so narrow they use rope pulleys instead of motors. A skilled expectorator could spit to the far side.

Unlike the hand-operated boats, the six-hour ferry from North Sydney, New Breton, to Port aux Basques on the southwest tip of Newfoundland required a hefty motor. Sitting in my van in line to board, I watched dozens of mammoth trucks traverse the ramp and disappear under the passenger decks.

Once aboard, I read by a window, repeatedly looking up to see if land was yet visible. A heavy fog slowly lifted as we drew near the dock, like a theater curtain rising to reveal an exquisite set. We arrived at six thirty in the morning, Newfoundland time—six in Nova Scotia. Newfoundland time is half an hour later than Nova Scotia. A *half* hour!

I had to ask a steward. He told me this time zone exists because Newfoundland is exactly three and a half hours from Greenwich. Public opinion has remained staunchly in favor of maintaining its distinctive clock.

The west coast of Newfoundland is ache-in-the-chest, shortness-of-breath gorgeous with an infinite variety of mountain and water shapes. Dark green needles of spruce and fir stand out against pale spring leaves, and both join spectacular blues of waterways and sky.

Since we landed in early morning, there was plenty of time to drive through this fantasyland on the Trans-Canada Highway—Canada 1. This highway spans almost five thousand miles and is the same road I used when I first crossed the border a year ago, the same road that has taken me to, or near, each of my Canadian destinations.

Newfoundland villages were built on hills overlooking the ocean, houses huddled together as if for warmth. When fog and clouds descend to mountain peaks, earth and sky are temporarily intertwined, the mists adding to the unique beauty of winding roads, ocean, and mountain landscape—a mysterious, almost magical place.

I stopped in a small-town antique store where I was greeted by a butch woman. No gaydar was needed to strongly suspect she was a lesbian. We conversed, first about antiques, and then when I admired a particular dish set, her response erased any doubts. She said that set was not for sale; she was taking it home for a special dinner she and her partner, Irene, were preparing for their best friends—two guys who were celebrating their twentieth anniversary. She asked what I was doing in her one-street town, and I told her about my solo journey. We were frequently interrupted by customers who entered, bought something, and chatted with her as she rang up the purchase. Overhearing discussions about their book club, a party at Ben and Joan's, and an upcoming buffet supper, it was clear that she and her partner were accepted in this town.

In this gorgeous setting, there was no problem finding a satisfying campground. Shortly after breakfast, I took my first Newfoundland hike, this one through a burnt-out forest. The bent gray ghosts of once-living trees not only reminded me of the fragility of the woods, but also of people . . .

Mom and Dad settle into a condo in Sunrise, Florida, a retirement commu-
nity on the southeast coast. The door to each apartment opens onto a communal
walkway. Neighbors meet on the way to the elevator and parking lot. They
stop to chat and bask in sunshine felt only in summer in the north.

Most residents are small and either bald or white-haired. I think "Sunset"
might be a more appropriate name.

It's been a few years now, and I notice Dad is becoming more rigid. If Mom
is driving, he might insist that she is going the wrong way. If he is corrected,
he repeats himself with certainty. He often repeats questions, even those Mom
answered ten minutes ago. He walks slowly and only looks happy when I
arrive. Mom handles the bills but puts money in his wallet. In restaurants,
when the check comes, he mentions the price of a typical dinner thirty years
ago and shakes his head. I wonder if losing the present forces him to hold
tighter to the past. Mom works hard at patient, loving responses day after day;
it must be exhausting.

But when he shops with me, he wants to pay for my clothes, cosmetics, or
earrings—he's still the dad.

She visits me in Atlanta, leaving Dad with pre-prepared meals and neighbors
ready to handle any unexpected problems. When she meets Anna, she extends
her hand, just as she did with Elise. This time though, she smiles.

Anna sleeps on the living room sofa, my mom in the spare bedroom. As
the visit ends, Mom tells me she is so happy I have a nice roommate. She was,
she adds, afraid I would always be alone. Her comments, though positive, are
ambiguous. I don't know what she thinks—or knows—but I'm afraid to ask . . .

It was easy to let my mind wander while hiking, or sitting by a
fire, but my reveries were easily broken when I embarked on the next
activity. Back in the van, a few hours on the road brought me to Gros
Morne National Park, where I took my second Newfoundland hike—
this one just two miles—always facing massive, snowcapped, craggy
cliffs with spraying waterfalls emerging from rock.

Eager to see St. John's, I took off the next morning and drove eight
hours across this island to reach its southeastern tip. First settled by
the French in the early seventeenth century, the capital of Newfoundland, its only major city, rises from a protected harbor, and the wooden

houses and shops are tightly packed on narrow, curving roads. I strolled on sidewalks, looking in shop windows, each bearing an unfamiliar name—a far cry from a walk in our malls.

Numerous row houses were brightly painted—tangerine, lavender, fuchsia, burgundy, and turquoise—all with contrasting trims. As I've done many times before, I stopped to ask for the local story. I learned the style is called "jellybean," and there was more than one explanation about how this fashion began. The most often told was that distinct and vivid colors made it easier—after a few drinks—to locate one's home in the dark and fog. Another theory was that long, iron-gray winters and chill winds require cheerful color to brighten the spirit.

It was no surprise that a Canadian metropolis like St. John's, population 175,000, is home to several museums. At one end of the town was a tower honoring Danny Cabot, the first man to land here five hundred years ago. The building housed exhibits on the first trans-atlantic wireless transmission sent in Morse code from a station in Cornwall, UK, and received on St. John's by Guglielmo Marconi in 1901.

In this remote and forbidding part of the world, such notables as Alexander Graham Bell, Amelia Earhart, and Marconi made massive leaps in early telephone, aviation, and telegraph technologies.

A geologic museum built over and around rock greater than five hundred million years old—the Rockies are only fifty million years old—also houses an exhibit on the collision of the *Titanic* with a Newfoundland iceberg, outlining in detail the many things that went wrong, most of which were preventable. Alongside magnificent achievement, intelligence, and effort, sits a memorial to greed and stupidity.

I stayed south of St. John's on what is known as the Irish Loop. Most of the residents still have a lovely brogue, with musical tones that originated long ago across the ocean. Celtic music played on the streets, in restaurants, and in shops. Men and women alike called me *m'love* and *m'darlin,* the phrase echoing the warmth shown in every setting.

The Irish, now nearly half the population, migrated to this prolific fishing community in the early sixteenth century. Ships were sent back to Ireland with consignments of local fish. Large numbers of Irish settlers continued to arrive throughout the seventeenth and eighteenth centuries, becoming the dominant culture in this part of Newfoundland.

This coastal road is also famous for bird watching and historical sites. I took a boat tour to an island known to have about two million birds. The main attraction was the provincial favorite, the puffin, a funny looking black-and-white bird with tiny wings and a vivid orange-red beak. Although puffins are capable of flight, their chubby bodies and tiny appendages make airborne activity difficult. They bounced along the ocean surface, slapping their wings against the water, propelling themselves forward.

Farther south on the Irish Loop is the Avondale Peninsula and the town of Ferryland, the location of an archaeological excavation that revealed artifacts dating back as far as four hundred years: extravagant pottery, stone bases of homes, a blacksmith's forge, and an original cobblestone street.

In a seventeenth-century kitchen, a costumed woman explained the art of making bread while a tantalizing aroma drifted from a loaf in a pot over a working fireplace.

Anna would love this, I thought. She relished our travels, appreciating scenery, ethnic food, and unfamiliar cultures. I remembered our vacations, the most exotic of which was to China . . .

We are among the early tourists to visit China. Lee and Evan are with us. They have moved to California, and we haven't seen them for a few years. Lee's appearance is shocking. He's emaciated, with sallow skin and sunken eyes. On the long plane ride, he and Evan sleep with arms around each other, spread over the length of three seats. Evan is a novelist and never needed to hide his sexuality. Lee, on the other hand, still works for the federal government— and has been hidden for years. Now he is the living picture of advanced AIDS. There's nothing to hide anymore.

Anna and I still pretend to be no more than friends. In the bar of one hotel, we meet some Chinese women, staff of the Chinese delegation to the United Nations. And everyone is tipsy. A few Asian women are on the small dance floor; they beckon us to join them. We do, and so do a few men from our group.

One man fastens himself to Anna and one to me. My fellow wants to take me to his room. I awkwardly sputter that I'm attached to Anna.

In spite of my disclosure, our group continues to be congenial. Anna and I continue to enjoy China, the country I'd always known was reachable only by digging down to the other side of the earth. And we're here together.

We have a Chinese tour guide and are taken to the most famous places: the Great Wall, Tiananmen Square, the Forbidden City, and Beijing's Summer Palace. Bicycles fill the length and width of Shanghai streets, and people bargain in the crowded shopping district in Hong Kong. Our guide is proud of the hospitals and takes us to one. We love most of what we see, but are horrified to see examination rooms looking like hundred-year-old pictures of our infirmaries, spotlessly clean but ill-equipped by our standards . . .

China's evolution since our visit resembled that of the last century in the US: quantum leaps in technology and medicine and concomitant decreases in poverty and disease, but at the cost of vast increases in pollution and angst. Newfoundland, however, had absorbed the benefits of progress, including ease of living and increased longevity, while maintaining a clean environment and relatively peaceful lifestyle.

Improvements can be a blessing, population growth often a curse.

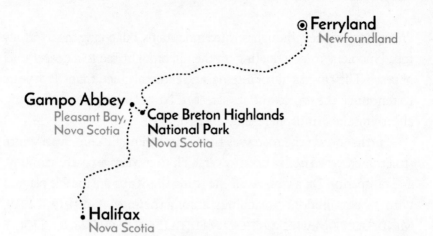

Ferryland
Newfoundland

Gampo Abbey
Pleasant Bay,
Nova Scotia

Cape Breton Highlands
National Park
Nova Scotia

Halifax
Nova Scotia

CHAPTER 31

New, Old, and Ancient

While waiting for the ferry from Newfoundland back to Nova Scotia, I realized it had been more than a year since I slept in my own bed, had breakfast in Atlanta, or detested a rush hour. Every day brought a new experience; every day was unique. This vagabond life was the norm, and I loved it.

The ferry dropped me in the northernmost portion of Cape Breton, the home of Cape Breton Highlands National Park, and not far from my next destination, Gampo Abbey, a renowned Buddhist monastery near the southern portion of the park. The roller-coaster ocean road, carved into the sides of tree-covered mountains, climbed to magnificent elevations, descended to the Gulf of St. Lawrence, and then back up again.

In less than an hour I reached the monastery—almost hidden, tucked away at the end of a long dirt road beside the sea. The abbey announced itself silently with monks in dark-red-and-gold robes strolling up the hill from the water. I thought I'd been relaxed and content driving to the abbey through isolated mountains, but seeing the colorfully robed monks virtually floating up the hill brought me to a deeper level of peace. They lived a life of internal and external quiet, trained for years to renounce the world and its stresses. Now I was here with them, absorbing the atmosphere they created.

Further down the road was the Stupa of Enlightenment, a white structure crowned with a brass tower, built to encourage peace, harmony, and prosperity. On a stone wall encircling the Stupa are marble plaques with Tibetan Buddhist teachings, among them: MAINTAIN A JOYFUL MIND. DON'T MALIGN OTHERS. MEDITATE ON RESENTMENT. DON'T WALLOW IN SELF-PITY.

How I loved these. How I yearned for the peace of these monks. Since my childhood days in hiding I had maintained a nearly constant tension, a tightness in the muscles of my chest, abdomen, and back. In college I learned of Eastern philosophy and occasionally practiced solitary breathing exercises and meditation. It was effective during my ritual, and perhaps for a short while after, but I never learned the secret of these monks . . . I never learned to live a tranquil life.

Some years after I returned to Atlanta, I came across an article by American Tibetan Buddhist nun, Thubten Chodron, in which she described "the attitude that causes anxiety." She wrote that Buddha explained the cycle of "constantly recurring problems in which we are . . . trapped," and asserts that the cause is a focus on "Me. *My* problems. *My* life. *My* family. *My* job. *Me, me, me* . . . We want to take care of *ourselves*. We want to be *happy*. We like *this*; we don't like *that*. We want *this* and we don't want *that*. Everybody else comes second. *I* come first." With this self-centered attitude, even small things cause stress.

In a psychology course in Ann Arbor, I learned of Viktor Frankl, an Austrian Jew who spent three years in Nazi concentration camps, far from Eastern thinking. It was during those dreadful years that he began to formulate the foundations of the renowned Logotherapy and Existential Analysis. The rest of his life was devoted to a philosophy based on our freedom of will and a search for meaning in any situation. He said, "Everything can be taken from a man or a woman but one thing, the last of human freedoms: to choose one's attitude in any given set of circumstances, to choose one's own way."

Life can be meaningful, Frankl believed, even in the most desolate circumstances, but, as the Buddha asserted, not if the emphasis is self-centered and insists on altering an inflexible condition. Frankl wrote, "When we are no longer able to change a situation, we are challenged to change ourselves."

Given that I've known these truths for decades, it's odd that in times of difficulty I do not think of them, always remaining self-centered—and anxious—until I consciously remind myself of the contrast between my relatively tiny problems and the great suffering that exists in the world. Only then do I recall the Buddha's philosophy and Frankl's admonition to change myself.

I'm at home, waiting for Anna before I put a meatloaf in the oven—a perfect meal for a rainy April day. It's prepared and sits in the fridge. The instant she arrives, loaded down with tote bags and books, I know something is bothering her. I don't have the good sense to wait until she has settled down before I ask her what's wrong. Her eyebrows move toward each other, furrowing skin above her nose. "Later," she says.

While she settles in, I put the entrée in the oven and then busy myself setting the table and defrosting some vegetables. We eat slowly, in near silence. After dinner, we clear the table, and Anna says she has something important to tell me.

The only significant downside to our relationship was that I was extremely compulsive. Anna—not so much. I also had a temper. When her behavior didn't suit my standards, I criticized, hoping to cause her to change. When faced with confrontation, she withdrew. I escalated. I knew it couldn't go on this way, but I had no idea how to fix it.

In the past weeks, the distance between us has been growing, but I didn't want to admit it. Now I can no longer avoid it. My chest tightens, and I'm filled with fear. We return to the table. She takes my hand in hers. Her expression is gentle, eyes soft, but her meaning is clear. It's over.

I don't feel anything. Her words had cut the nerves from my ears to my brain.

"I'll get an apartment," she adds.

"Okay, but wait until the weather is warmer. It'll take days, if not weeks, to find an apartment and even more to move all your stuff. It'll be easier in nice weather." She agrees. I'm hoping for a change of heart.

She opens her bags and continues her preparations for the next day. I go to a movie—something nominated for the upcoming Academy Awards. When I return, we exchange ordinary words, and I go to bed. An hour or so later, when she finishes her tasks, I'm still awake. To my surprise, she doesn't go to her room, but joins me in our bed. She enfolds me in her arms, as always before. We don't have sex. Not then. Not ever again.

As spring slides away, we live as though nothing has changed. We decide not to tell our friends until she is ready to move out—we don't want to live the breakup until it's complete. I remain numb until she actually moves.

She's gone. The house is empty, silent.

Emotions come alive again—nonstop grief. Tears come unbidden during any activity—one moment I'm laughing over a joke at dinner, the next moment the waiter sees quiet tears or hears noisy sobs. My friends tolerate every mood, invite me out as always.

It doesn't seem possible this wound will ever heal. The Buddhism I've studied is forgotten, Frankl a distant memory, the ache in my chest the only reality. A year passes before it even crosses my mind that there might be escape from me, my problems, me, me, me and my insistent pain.

I visit a friend with two new kittens, and watch her sitting cross-legged on the floor with a toy in each hand. The kittens romp on and across her knees, joyously, boisterously . . .

Leaving the monastery, I wondered how Anna would relate the story of our time together and especially those final days. The nature of a relationship and its demise depends on your point of view. I was older than Anna and had experienced life with other partners. I no longer expected a perfect pairing and was willing to accept a loving life, in spite of my partner's flaws. But I had not yet learned the art of quietly expressing my feelings. My temper wasn't tolerable to Anna who, I believe, still wished for something better. For me, this was a far deeper love than I had experienced before—not an addiction, but equally compelling. This love was based on mutual interests as well as attraction. The time we spent together fulfilled me, rounded out my life. With Anna, I had not walked my path alone . . . I had a warm, loving companion.

For six years, when I awoke in the night, Anna had always been there beside me, arms wrapped around me, the sweetest peace I had ever known. There was nothing like this for me before Anna . . . nor after.

Not until it was time to leave the monastery did I became aware that though this memory was accompanied by sorrow, there was no anxiety, anger, or regret—no tension in my muscles. This journey had enhanced my acceptance of life's vicissitudes. Had I reached a state of constant peace? Not a chance. But certainly there was progress.

One way to forget about *me* was to immerse myself in the world of other beings. Remembering my delight in the kittens, I hunted a Nova Scotia version: whale watching. I joined five people on a small, fast boat, all passengers provided with conspicuous orange-and-black flotation suits should we happen to fall out of this swiftly moving craft. The outfits were one size—super size. Velcro straps at the sleeves and ankles caused the fabric at my arms and legs to fold, bulge, and flutter. My companions were greatly amused.

The captain explained that when the whales come up for air, we would see a "blow" in the distance. The powerful boat moved rapidly, allowing us to reach the whales before they moved on. He found a dozen razorbacks, each perhaps a hundred tons. Thirty or forty feet from us, four or five would gracefully rise together, and then slowly descend—repeatedly, for over an hour.

All my attention focused on these magnificent beings, there was no "me" in this world of "other."

Almost half of Nova Scotia's million people live in greater Halifax. Beautiful new structures blend with the timeworn; glass buildings adjoin those of stone. New rooflines are taller than the old, but set at the same angle. On the bay, a many-masted schooner rides alongside a bullet like speedboat.

Just outside the city, however, the neighborhoods were exactly like those in Cleveland or Omaha—strip malls and fast food—jarring and disappointing.

A ferry took me across the bay to Dartmouth Harbor, in the shadow of the Citadel—a British fort, never successfully attacked, at the top of a steep hill overlooking Halifax harbor—to the World Peace Pavilion, a simple monument created by the Metro Youth for Global Unity. Rocks and artifacts from eighty countries were on display to "symbolize the natural world, shared by all humanity." *Oddly placed—but perhaps intentional—so near the fort of war.*

While wars raged, artisans thrived near the fort, learning the craft of fine, mouth-blown and hand-cut crystal, which was still produced and sold on the wharf where musicians and puppeteers entertained. Stalls all along the boardwalk display exceptional art and unique jewelry.

Also in Halifax, the Art Gallery of Nova Scotia proudly displays the work of Maud Lewis, a folk artist educated only through the third grade, with no art training whatsoever and extreme arthritis in both hands. Maud was born with almost no chin and spent most of her time alone. To provide an activity, her mother gave her material to begin painting. After the death of both parents, Maud married a poor fish peddler who took care of the house while she, in spite of her severely impaired hands, brought in money with her paintings. She began by painting brightly colored flowers on almost every surface of her cottage, including walls, windows, and even the wood-burning stove. Her front door was always open to visitors curious about the flower-covered exterior. As her reputation grew, people stopped to visit and purchase her work. Her house has been restored and the entire structure moved inside the museum.

Though her hands became increasingly deformed, she continued to paint, holding a brush between fingers bent at improbable angles. Maud Lewis epitomizes the ability to find meaning in difficult circumstances with art that displaced self-pity.

Halifax
Nova Scotia

Yarmouth
Nova Scotia

CHAPTER 32

Reflections

I had left Biddeford Pool on the first of May. Most of the following month was spent in Nova Scotia, and June slid by in Newfoundland. As I headed toward Yarmouth and the ferry that would take me from Halifax to Bar Harbor, I reflected on these months in Nova Scotia and Newfoundland.

This portion of my journey provided me with joy and sadness in equal measure. I saw the overwhelming beauty of uninhabited mountains, streams, oceans and forests, as it was in the time before humans. I also saw contrasts between natural beauty and occasional strip malls, and between frequent art displays and nearby forts designed to protect the island from invaders.

These contrasts reminded me of the feelings I had in Calgary's Glenbow Museum with the same disparities artfully displayed in one place: fabulous art works created on several continents across the centuries and our world's history of wars and rebuilding. Someday, I think, we will wonder about ugliness, hatred, and destruction in the same way we now wonder how mankind lived before electricity.

When I lived in any one place, every site was no more than background to a busy life. But while moving from place to place, the views were foreground; each scene was new, and I noticed everything, good and bad. I could not escape the jarring disparity between the dreadful and the beautiful, adjacent to each other again and again.

About two hundred years ago, essayist and critic William Hazlitt said humans are the only animals "who laugh and weep," for we are the only ones that are "struck with the difference between what things are and what they ought to be."

We are the ones who imagine what life could be like . . . and we are the ones who cause the failure to achieve it.

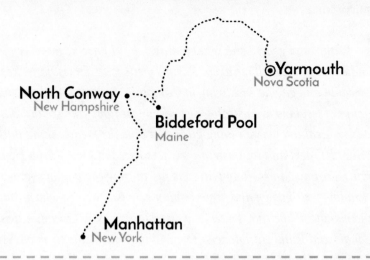

CHAPTER 33

From Mountains to Manhattan

A few hours after leaving Canada on the ferry, driving down the ramp in Maine, I felt a thrill of belonging. Not only was I re-entering the country of my birth, but I had neighbors, friends, and a home in Maine.

Automatically turning on satellite radio to hear CNN 24-hour news, I felt a sorrow that replaced good feelings—London was bombed. On July 7, 2005, four London-born Islamist extremists detonated three bombs on subways across the city and one on a double-decker bus, killing themselves and fifty-two civilians. As always, the shock of devastation created a jarring emotional shift.

I stopped for a cup of coffee and forced my mind back to the present and the enjoyment of this day. With a troubled mind and melancholy heart, I continued being alive. How I wished I could do something . . . anything to help. Perhaps, if I were traveling with a companion, conversation might help me regain perspective. Not all of my journeys since Anna had been alone . . .

With Anna gone, I still want to travel, but I have no travel companion. Andie and Nancy tell me about Robin Tyler's tours for lesbians. Robin is a comedian and gay activist living in California. I travel with them and small groups of lesbians to Australia where I bungee jump and see the coral reefs, to New Zealand where I hang glide and hike the breathtaking thirty-mile Milford Track, and to Amsterdam where I see the Anne Frank House and watch the gay games. Robin attracts fascinating companions for her tours, including well-known and brave lesbian activists, women who are unafraid and making a difference. I meet Jody and Marilyn, New Orleans activists, and Connie and Ruth, trailblazers from Manhattan. I saw them on The Phil Donahue Show *in 1988, long before I met them. All those years ago, Ruth sued the New York City Board of Education causing them to offer health coverage to the partners of gay and lesbian teachers. I am awestruck by their courage as they lead the way to a better future for me.*

When I left Maine for Nova Scotia almost two months earlier, trees were bare, and roads lightly occupied. I returned to thick-leafed trees and numerous cars, cyclists, and hikers on each side of the road. This time I was to stay at Beth and Ada's, but Michael, helping with the summer business, was housed in the guest bedroom. A consistently amusing man, he said of me, "She's like a person, only smaller." So I slept comfortably in my van, parked in the meadow beside their home, and joined the group for supper and evenings.

Many new faces: the summer people. But all my winter friends were still around, warm and welcoming. "Downtown" Biddeford Pool, with its few businesses and the post office, is on the waterfront. Last winter everything was closed except the post office; in summer, people wandered on the narrow street, and groups ate at tables outside the Pool Lobster Pound, facing the boat-filled harbor.

Kayaking, boating, and bird-watching replaced snowshoeing and ice skating, but Union Church is open all year. Jan, the minister, provides moral leadership all four seasons. A cartoon hanging in her office showed two snails and a tape dispenser shaped a bit like a snail. One snail says to the other, "I don't care if she is a tape dispenser. I love her." If a snail can love a tape dispenser, perhaps a British Muslim can love a Christian

Londoner, and a Palestinian might love an Israeli, and maybe, just maybe, a woman can love a woman.

Heather and Erv, who last winter introduced me to shoes resembling tennis rackets and taught me how to walk on soft white snow, now introduced me to kayaking on their river. Heather, many inches taller than I, sat on the dock, put one foot in her boat and had no trouble landing gracefully on the seat. When *I* sat on the dock, my foot swung in the air—several inches too high. To get in the craft, I had to drop into it. I landed off-center, tipped over the boat and fell, fully clothed, into the water. I climbed back on the dock, hair plastered to my face, shirt and jeans dripping. We laughed, Heather still in the water. And then I slowly, carefully boarded the kayak.

A philanthropic art auction was held Sunday evening, the profits of which were donated to Biddeford Pool's Wood Island Lighthouse. Seventy artists were assigned locations, each to produce an original painting to be sold that evening. An elegant event, it began with elaborate hors d'oeuvres, eaten while wandering through a tent displaying the paintings. We were filled with excitement as one painting after another found an owner. And in the typical light-hearted Biddeford Pool manner, a brightly colored Hawaiian shirt was removed from the wearer and auctioned off, selling for five hundred dollars.

Lee and Evan would have loved this affair. Lee was an amateur painter in his spare time, and Evan a writer of novels and editorials. Lee, who continued to work for the VA, also served as Evan's agent, successfully marketing his work to newspapers, magazines, and publishers. But I remembered, when Anna and I were in China, Lee was in the advanced stages of AIDS. Not long after that shared adventure, Audrey phoned to tell me Lee was dead. Evan had remained at his bedside for most hours of those last dreadful weeks. My mind was expecting this news, but my heart was not.

Soon after the auction, I was to stop for a three-day visit with Eleanor in her summer home in New Hampshire. While on my way I thought, as I had many times before, of what it must have been like when Helen, her lifelong companion, died. Eleanor was then in her mid-eighties, and although certainly people knew they were close, no one knew it was her *spouse* who died. When Anna and I separated, my gay friends understood the pain. When I mentioned to family that my "roommate" moved out, I didn't know what to expect . . .

I call my sister Donna—a routine hello—and when she learns Anna has moved out, she responds with "I'm so sorry, Marilyn," her voice filled with concern. I don't know what to think. It reminds me of when, after meeting Anna, Mom told me she was happy I have a nice roommate, adding that she had been afraid I would always be alone. What do they think? Did I miss any clues that they know?

Was it the same for Eleanor? When Helen died, did she fail to get comfort from friends and family because no one could say, "I know you and Helen were more than friends. This must be dreadful for you."

I never had a "coming out." Instead, I tell one friend and one group at a time, everyone now but my family. I think my siblings, their spouses, and their children will be accepting. They may have already guessed. But I fear that if I confirm their suspicions, someone will leak it to Mom or Dad. My parents' lives are sad. Dad has Alzheimer's. Constantly unhappy, he knows he is not well; Mom, highly anxious, takes care of him. For many years, their lives have been grim. I cannot bring myself to cause more sorrow, and I don't trust the rest of the family to understand this.

Though the country is more accepting now than when I was growing up, most parents are devastated when told their kid is gay. Sometimes the child is thrown out of the house and other times tolerated with great pain. Thousands of us have come out, and now hundreds of thousands know we are their respected colleagues, friends, cousins, and neighbors. This realization has changed the hearts and minds of many, but I think Mom and Dad would be distraught to know about me.

In 1993, I march in Washington. Let people see us in all our variations. Let them count us—over half a million lesbian, gay, bisexual, and transgender people on the Mall—and know that we represent only a fraction of our number.

I march with many of my Atlanta friends. An extreme conservative group— the self-righteous right—stands five-deep on both sides of the street. They carry signs saying "queers go to hell," and push into the street shouting obscenities and threats—a few inches from our faces. It's pandemonium. My friend Lori walks through the marchers, carrying orange T-shirts saying "Marshal." Many accept the shirt, put it on, and are instructed to make a thin line between the marchers and the angry crowd. When she gets to my little group, she doesn't ask; she just gives us the shirts and instructions. We are terrified.

The fear brings back other lines, other protests. I think of the one in Ann Arbor in 1960 when we protested segregated lunch counters and people threw raw eggs at us. They hated the idea of blacks and whites sitting together to eat. I remember 1970 in Bloomington, Indiana, where I stood on a wide street in a thin line of faculty between antiwar protesters and armed police. As someone hits my leg with a sign telling me to go to hell, I recall my younger legs, wet with raw egg and splashed with fake blood. Now, in Washington, I am here for myself, serving as a protective barrier between the determined and the dangerously enraged.

TV cameras are all around us. Unlike my first Atlanta Pride Parade in '76, no one wears a bag to hide their face . . .

Having grown up in her small New Hampshire town in the '20s and '30s, Eleanor knew every street and every story. She escorted me through the region and introduced me to local history. The White Mountains, part of the Appalachian chain, were practically in Eleanor's backyard. Eleanor packed us a picnic to eat beside a pond at the foot of Mount Webster, rising dramatically two thousand feet, almost straight up.

She took me to the nearby Heritage New Hampshire museum where, upon crossing the threshold, we were transported to a seventeenth-century English coastal village. We bought a ticket for the simulated voyage to the new world, knowing we had a ninety percent chance of surviving the crossing. Although *our* passage was brief, real travelers had spent six weeks at sea with bad weather and maggot-infested food before landing in the unspoiled woodlands of New Hampshire.

We disembarked into an imitation forest with oversized rocks and trees, and moved from area to area, each a bit later in history: a winter log cabin with the sound of wind; a trout stream running through the woods; a navy yard with appropriate sound effects; the Portsmouth town square during the Revolution, including the shop that printed the Declaration of Independence and the new country's money; and an 1850s kitchen demonstrating hand-washing of clothes, heating water for every need, churning butter, killing the chicken before cooking dinner, and making bread in the fireplace. Lastly, we entered the "Grand Hotel" where we waited in the lobby for a virtual train ride. After boarding the train, noise and rocking soon convinced us we were traveling, autumn murals passing our windows added to the illusion. Eleanor had given me the gift of all she appreciated in this New Hampshire world. No guidebook could have substituted for her enthusiasm.

When I said good-bye to Eleanor, who was so active and vibrant, I had no way of knowing I would never see her again.

Next stop: the home of Sandy, my dear college friend. A few years after leaving Ann Arbor, she fell in love, married, and had three children, now grown with children of their own. Her husband died young—quite soon after his retirement. Though the shock was devastating, Sandy slowly resumed her life—managed her business, remained involved with her children and grandchildren, and continued her relationships with many friends, her rich life with Frank always in the background.

The White Mountains of New Hampshire, the Green Mountains of Vermont, and the small towns of upstate New York led me to her home near Manhattan, the mega-city crush of people, skyscrapers, and slivers of sky between tall, slim structures.

First, lunch with D'vorah, a.k.a. Doris, the woman I met many years ago in an Atlanta lesbian bar, the woman who invited me to the bagels-and-lox party where I met women who were still my friends. Then a walk through Times Square on the way to the show, *Movin' Out*, based on the music of Billy Joel and choreographed by Twyla Tharp. It won 2003 Emmys for both choreography and orchestration. Dramatic scenes of war and spectacular choreography with astonishing lighting making me believe an enormous building burned onstage. What did I expect? It was *Broadway*.

Sandy's daughter, Kathy, and her kids, came to meet me. The children played in my van, loving the miniature house, especially the portable potty. At six, Andrew couldn't resist mounting the toilet seat and assuming the strained expression of someone attempting a bowel movement.

One day Sandy and I were college kids, and later, camp counselors considered cool by the campers. But fifty years had passed. Sandy had grandchildren.

The years drifted by like dust on a windy hill.

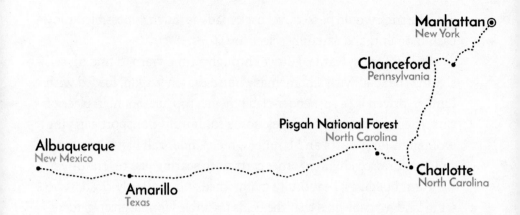

CHAPTER 34

Santa Fe Opera

In August, I received an email from Carol Fillman expressing her hope that I could make it to Albuquerque in one week; she had tickets for *The Barber of Seville* at the renowned Santa Fe Opera House. I had planned to meander across the country for a couple of months before spending the last few weeks with Carol in New Mexico. But I was still in eastern Pennsylvania.

I thought about asking her to invite someone else in my place, but this was an opportunity to see a world-class theater in a spectacular desert setting. Because I would be arriving earlier than planned, she also offered to let me stay as long as I wished and travel the southwest from her home in Albuquerque.

Two thousand miles in a week? That'll average nearly three hundred miles a day. Not bad. But last year I promised myself I'd never rush anywhere again, never focus on a destination. On the other hand, I really want to see the Santa Fe Opera House. Okay, I'm going to do it.

The trick would be to travel back roads as much as possible, enjoy each moment, and carefully select my stops.

Still in Pennsylvania, I drove through a time warp to find myself sharing the road with a homemade horse-drawn wagon, loaded with lumber, driven by a suspender-clad boy in a top hat. Soon, in place of cars, there were more carriages, some for family transport carrying women in long skirts and bonnets, men under tall black hats, and similarly dressed children, other carts with seating just for the driver.

Farm buildings, beautifully maintained and spotlessly clean, were set in land so manicured that the fields resembled formal green gardens. Hope Acres, an Amish farm and restaurant, was one of the few shops on the road. I sat at a shiny wooden table and devoured a large plate of oven-fried chicken with crisp crust, rich whipped potatoes with creamy yellow gravy, and corn and green beans steamed until tender, salted, and then browned in butter.

Its literature said the farm "combines old-fashioned traditions with the best in dairy-science technology . . . one of the first farms to introduce robotic milking practices to the United States." The cows are pampered "with waterbeds and backscratchers." The people in this community don't scorn *all* innovations; they use only the few they consider true enhancements.

These Amish, who believe that peace, prayer, and negotiation will eventually solve anything, live only a short distance from Gettysburg, a town that re-enacts the pivotal battle of the Civil War. History buffs swarm this area where the philosophy is that some evils will never end without war.

Once again, peace and war, were side by side.

I drove through the Appalachian Mountains, avoiding Midwestern industrial views, heading west and south to Carol in Albuquerque. As I approached North Carolina, I thought about my nephew Marty and his wife, Stephanie, who lived in Charlotte. They each had their fortieth birthdays a few days earlier, so why not celebrate? I loved my attractive and talented niece, nephews, and their wives. I didn't see any of them as much as I wished.

Remember, Marilyn, I said to myself, *you are never again to make the destination the whole point.*

Marty and Stephanie have known I was gay since Mom died and absorbed the news that I was gay with no problem. They asked how Anna was doing and if I was looking for a new partner. I told them I was now happily single. We discussed Marty's books, Stephanie's professional success, and life after forty. It was family, warm and comfortable, no topics out of bounds now.

They mentioned a forecast for rain and asked if I'd like to spend the night. But I intended to drive a couple hundred miles after lunch and returned to the road. In a few hours, the threatened rain became a torrential storm on this curving mountain highway, my windshield like a frosted shower door coated with steam. Everyone drove slowly. Cars stopped, half-on and half-off the shoulder, further narrowing the already slim road.

Hmm, I thought, *it's lovely in this part of North Carolina; I think I'll stay the night and make up the time tomorrow.* A nearby campground looked appealing. I stopped to register and was told the campers were participants in a religious convention, the theme of which was to discuss new ways to change the sexual orientation of gay teenagers. They said I could join them, but I grimaced, in a manner intended to communicate, and shook my head slowly from left to right.

Following signs to a bed-and-breakfast, I drove deep into Pisgah National Forest, tall trees on each side of the road leaving only a narrow strip of sky, similar to that between skyscrapers in Manhattan. Repeated sharp curves in the narrow road made me wonder what I would find when the B&B finally appeared. Perhaps a mountain shack and a few goats.

Then the Inn on Mill Creek materialized.

With gardens, a stream, trees taller than the house, and a small waterfall, the exterior views foreshadowed the beauty of the rooms inside. I took a suite with a Jacuzzi and a private deck; wooden ceilings; wall-to-wall and floor-to-ceiling windows; and huge oval mirrors with hand-carved frames above each of the bathroom sinks. Every window in my room looked upon lush green trees or the stream below. *Just think, I could have been in a campground trying to become heterosexual.*

Serendipity.

I'm in line at the VA's Federal Credit Union—my bank. The woman in front of me is perfectly coiffed and dressed in a stylish business suit. As we wait, I ask, "Are you a new staff doctor?"

She turns and responds with an Australian accent, "No, I'm Carol Fillman, the new Associate Director. And you?"

"Marilyn Berman, Chief of Audiology and Speech Pathology."

We do the nice-to-meet-you routine, complete our business, and go our separate ways.

The next day, I get a call from her secretary, asking if I will co-chair Dr. Fillman's newly forming committee to design a year-long training program for upwardly mobile clinicians and administrators. I tell her I'd love to.

Carol sets a meeting time for the two of us. Awestruck by her prominent position in the hospital, I'm anxious when we meet in her spacious, top-floor office. Paying no attention to time, we develop an outline of tasks to be accomplished. I remain tense until Sheila comes in without knocking. She's in charge of new construction, currently a large clinical addition which will include an expanded audiology and speech clinic. I've met with her several times. She gets the job done while remaining pleasant to her staff and colleagues. With hands on hips, she looks at both of us and says, "It's past the end of the work day time for a drink." And off we go.

The more I socialize with Carol and Sheila, the more edgy I become about hiding my sexuality. I'd long ago told my staff that I'm gay, and I'm sure they've told others. I wonder how my new friends will feel when they hear the gossip. Carol is married to Bill Fillman, another VA administrator currently working in New Orleans. Sheila is single and hetero. Both would be vulnerable to gossip if people thought they might be gay.

I make appointments with each, intending to break the news. Sheila is first. She sees my nervousness. "What's wrong?" she asks, her voice expressing concern and her expression serious. When I stammer through my confession, she laughs and says she'd been told soon after meeting me. And she told Carol weeks ago.

I learned over time that they were friends who could always be counted on for anything, no matter how inconvenient, even if the recipient was a lesbian . . .

On the way to Albuquerque, I was invited to spend the night in Amarillo, Texas, at the home of Meredith, Carol's daughter, and her husband, Tim. I arrived in time to join them for dinner. We were to go in Tim's new truck. He opened the door for me, and I stood for a moment, realizing there was no way for me to get my foot on the running board or grab the handle to hoist myself into the seat. Tim, a tall and heavily muscled firefighter, smiled, picked me up with no apparent effort, and deposited me in the plush seat.

After dinner, we relaxed in the den and flipped on the TV. New Orleans. Katrina. A reporter was telling the story of a woman in a nursing home repeatedly calling her adult son and asking when someone would come. Due to the flooding, he was unable to do anything, but he repeatedly told his mother someone was coming. The residents were all frightened, waiting desperately for rescue. The reporter broke down and cried, sobbing for several seconds before he could continue. They didn't come. The mother died. All the residents died waiting for rescue.

Through moist eyes, I looked at Tim, who sat motionless with a tear sliding silently down his clean-shaven cheek.

Asian tsunami, London bombings, and now, only nine hundred miles from where I sat, the surge-protection structures in New Orleans that failed to protect.

Filled with impotent rage, I donated money—again—this time to Katrina victims, and continued on my way.

Four hours after leaving Amarillo, I entered New Mexico and soon noticed how highway retaining walls and expressway underpasses had here been transformed into art exhibits. Smooth tan blocks, decorated with carvings and paintings of horses, windmills, geometric shapes, and teepees, replaced gritty, gray concrete. Brilliant!

In my earlier days—the time of destination-focused wheel-gripping road trips, staring straight ahead except for periodic glances at the clock— I wouldn't have noticed the museum-quality art on the highway.

And if I stayed on the expressway, I would not have passed through an Amish community, nor would I have found the Inn on Mill Creek. I enjoyed all this *and* arrived in time for *The Barber of Seville.*

We left early in the evening because Carol heard the highway would be heavily congested like Atlanta's roads leading to a Falcons football game. As we approached the opera house, traffic slowed and then slowed again. We reached the parking lot with ten minutes to spare, enough time to notice the graceful structure set in the Sangre de Cristo and Jemez Mountains. Adobe walls blended with high-desert terrain, and the merging arches of the two roofs matched the curves of the hills, as if the building had not been formed by human design, but rather had sprung from the sand. The stage and seating area were covered overhead, but the sides of the theater and the rear of the stage were open to mountain views and warm breezes, colors enhanced by the setting sun.

The Barber of Seville is a comedic opera about wealthy Count Almaviva and his efforts to make the beautiful Rosina love him and prevent her from marrying her elderly ward. I traveled across the country to see this opera house and to hear the thrilling tenors, contraltos, and sopranos. They didn't disappoint. Nor did the acoustics. I wondered what genius was needed for architects and engineers to provide superb sound quality with no walls and two overlapping roofs.

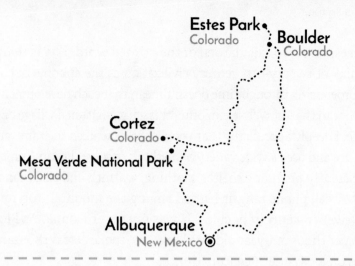

Estes Park•
Colorado •Boulder
Colorado

Cortez
Colorado•
Mesa Verde National Park
Colorado

Albuquerque
New Mexico⊙

CHAPTER 35

Don't Ask

I left Carol's house in Albuquerque for a three-week trip to Colorado. First stop: Mesa Verde National Park in the southwest corner of the state. With its rolling sage plains, massive mountains, enormous canyons, and ancient villages, it's listed by *National Geographic Traveler* as one of fifty must-see places.

Here, the Anasazi, also known as Ancestral Puebloans, lived for hundreds of years in cliff dwellings. Cliff Palace, a multilevel adobe pueblo, is tucked in a huge alcove protected by an overhanging natural roof. Estimates are that it housed up to one hundred fifty people. This Anasazi version of condominiums is built entirely of clay bricks blending perfectly with the rock face.

The skilled builders made tools, dwellings, ladders, art, and furniture, all from natural materials by earth and animals. Thus everything matched everything else.

The engineering and architecture were as stunning as the Santa Fe Opera House, but here it was accomplished without university degrees, access to calculators, or the printed word. It was tempting to think of twenty-first-century civilization as the epitome of culture, but progressing through time doesn't mean that each development was superior to the last. While exploring this great, shattered village of Mesa Verde, I deeply appreciated that people like us walked the same ground long ago and used a wide variety of methods to solve the same problems, consistently providing shelter, clothing, warmth and sustenance.

My cell phone rang as I stood among the mountaintop ruins of two twelfth-century pueblos. It was my sister Donna. As I looked down at thousand-year-old dwellings, we spoke across thousands of miles on a twentieth-century device.

A few minutes from Mesa Verde is the 1909 Anasazi Heritage Center in Cortez, Colorado. There I found a museum of archaeology and American Indian culture, and shivered as I touched timeworn handmade pottery, imagining the man or woman who made this piece with eternal aesthetic concepts—a common bond across eons and cultures. On one exterior side of the building is a mural, painted to look like adobe cliff dwellings. It's perfect.

In the painting are four terraced levels of houses, each recessed to make an area of rooftop available for walking and for ornos—pottery ovens resembling large beehives. Exposed logs, called vigas, hold up the roof and protrude from the front and back of the buildings—a most practical design still used in Southwest architecture. A ragged pile of firewood looks exactly as though it is sitting on top of one of the ledges. I felt I could climb the painted ladders and walk from one home to the next. Perhaps a younger me would have wanted to hang on a viga.

I was here to see an evening play: Sharon French in her one-woman drama, *Black Shawl,* an adaptation of her long-running pageant, *Anasazi, the Ancient Ones.* An outdoor theater-in-the-round was on the patio beside the painted wall. Stone steps for seating circled a tan stage, also of stone. As I waited, the sun approached the horizon, increasing the illusion that I sat beneath an adobe apartment complex, watching residents nearing the dinner hour.

I was trying to remember the French word for this type of realistic art when a boy seated behind me said to his parents that it looked "so real—like real adobe houses stacked up," and the mom replied, "This type of painting has a name. It's called *trompe l'oeil,* and it means 'to deceive the eye.'"

Thanks, Mom. Good timing.

And then the play began. It was originally written for a full cast, but in this version, Sharon performed *all* the parts—male and female, all ages. Although her costume remained the same, she changed dialect and voice, posture and walk, as rapidly as dialogue switched from character to character. Like the painting, the illusion of each character was complete. As Sharon willed it, the transformations were rapid and flawless.

At the end of her phenomenal performance, I joined the audience in a standing ovation with wild applause.

The next morning I traveled north to meet my friend Sandy in the town of Estes Park, the gateway to Rocky Mountain Park. Tourists, eager to get to the mountains, often bypass this town. But although it caters to visitors, there is more charm here than neon. We strolled on the Riverwalk, browsing in the shops and galleries that lined the peaceful narrow waterway. We were still in Estes Park when we saw, a few feet from us, an entire herd of elk meandering down a neighborhood street, eating the shrubs of their human neighbors. Growing up in Chicago, the only large animals I saw were in Brookfield Zoo, but in these traveling months, I have seen so many, so close.

As we walked, it occurred to me that I'd never asked Sandy if she knew I was gay when we were in college. She said it had crossed her mind, but since I was dating a man, she didn't give it much thought. Neither of us remembered how or when I told her, but we knew it was many years ago, perhaps when I went to the Pride march on Washington in 1993. She reminded me that Congress passed "Don't Ask, Don't Tell" later the same year . . .

President Clinton announces his intent to keep his campaign promise: he will end military discrimination based on sexual orientation. But congressional leaders soon threaten to override any executive order on this subject. There is no way he can accomplish all he promised.

He devises a compromise, a baby step. One can be homosexual in the armed forces, as long as no one knows. Homosexuality is no longer grounds for involuntary discharge . . . as long as it's a secret. It sounds like there is no change. But the entire name of the bill is, "Don't Ask, Don't Tell, Don't Pursue."

And Congress passes it, changing military life a bit. In the past, if someone was suspected of being homosexual, an investigation could be initiated.

If you are a lesbian or gay man, you must still remain in hiding. You cannot tell. If someone suspects, they cannot ask you, nor can they institute any kind of investigation. If they break the rule and ask you anyway, an affirmative response is cause for discharge. If you are looking for someone to date, well, hmmm—you may not appear to be looking and you may not tell any of your buddies.

All these offenses are considered "homosexual conduct," still reason for dismissal . . .

This was progress at the time, especially the "don't pursue" portion, but how do you find a partner when you can't appear to be looking? How do you find a real friend while pretending to be other than who you are? We continued to have double lives in the military, like Clark Kent changing clothes in a phone booth. Even Superman had problems hiding his true identity.

Sandy drove us to Rocky Mountain National Park, where Trail Ridge Road, the highest paved road in North America, ascends to twelve thousand feet above sea level, curving as it climbs to spectacular views of high red cliffs, serpentine rivers, jagged mountains, and colorful valleys. Even in August, there were snowfields and glaciers.

Near the top, we parked at a trailhead and walked, listening to the song of nuthatches and the squawk of jays and watching the play of light and shadow on the mountain tans and forest greens—a feast for my senses. Looking down ever higher and steeper slopes, across ponderosa-filled valleys to the mountains on the other side, I rediscovered the deepest relaxation, the sweetest peace.

Overlooking a vista, a small child said, "Hey Mom, this is *awesome!*"

Even after all the beauty I had seen, the drive from Rocky Mountain National Park to Boulder was remarkable. Though it's one of the two largest cities in Colorado, it has less than half a million people. Its many attractions draw tourists and locals alike.

The Pearl Street Mall runs for twelve blocks in the downtown area. Big-name shops, local boutiques, chic galleries, and relaxed cafes share sidewalk space with entertaining street performers.

Boulder also has an adopted sister city, Dushanbe, the capital of Tajikistan. In 1990, Dushanbe sent a teahouse to Colorado in two hundred crates. Four Tajik artisans helped assemble the structure in Boulder.

We climbed gorgeous mosaic steps to enter its richly ornate interior. In the center was a grand fountain, surrounded by seven bronze statues of women. Even the folds of the gown and windblown hair were done in bronze. We sat at a table facing the fountain, and while our eyes feasted on handmade furniture and the stained-glass ceiling, we sipped the sweet white tea I'd discovered while it rained in Stratford.

In return for this stunningly beautiful gift, a team of volunteers from Boulder raised money to build the Cyber Café and Friendship Center, sent to Dushanbe in 2009. Equipped with the latest solar and computer technology, it represented the most modern research accomplished at the University of Colorado, contrasting with the ancient art and culture of Asia in the teahouse, just as my sister's phone call had contrasted with the Cliff Palace adobe village.

The old and the new: two cities who could admire each other's way of life. Can we learn from their example?

While driving back to Albuquerque in September 2005, I thought again about "Don't Ask, Don't Tell," still the law of the land. We knew when it was instituted that it wasn't enough, but we were also realists. There had to be more acceptance in the population before politicians would take risks. And for that to happen, more people had to know who we were. It was up to us.

We knew we had to come out in ever larger numbers. And we did. The *New York Times* reported that over thirteen thousand men and women were discharged for being gay during "Don't Ask, Don't Tell"— many deliberately outing themselves to challenge the law, all finding it increasingly difficult to live secret lives.

The more who come out, the more who will accept us. The more who accept us, the more who will feel safe coming out. It hasn't been quick; it hasn't been easy.

And now, in 2005, it's not done.

Taos
New Mexico

Santa Fe
New Mexico

Albuquerque
New Mexico

CHAPTER 36

Curved Corners

In Carol's typical "road-runner" fashion, we rose each weekday at five o'clock to hike in her neighborhood, the foothills of the Sandia Mountains. Though we walked on local streets, mountain views were ever-present. Carol, younger and stronger than I, walked ahead, periodically turning around to rejoin me for a few minutes. On weekends, we hiked in nearby mountains and took side trips to Taos and Santa Fe.

And we frequented the many fine New Mexico restaurants, some on stone patios with greenery blocking the view of cars or, when farther out of town, with mountain views. The patio at Tamaya Resort was at the foot of a mountain thirty miles north of Albuquerque. Our wine was served on a round copper table near a smoothly curved adobe fireplace. We faced an expansive lawn and a low line of trees followed by the Rio Grande River. On the other side were more trees and, still farther, the mountain. We drank and dined as the sun set, lengthening the shadows on the craggy peak.

During one of those dinners, Carol reminds me of the day she drove Mom and me to the Kiss-Ride stop—to the train that would take us to the airport. That was when Mom whispered to me, seriously asking if she should kiss the driver. That was the beginning of the saddest time, the years of Mom's progressive dementia leading to her death . . .

I'm sixty years old. Dad's been dead for five years. Now Mom is ready to join him. Donna and her husband Chuck, their sons Marty and Gary, and Jeff and his wife Susie all sit by her bed. After a long day's vigil, no clear end in sight, everyone leaves for dinner. Donna returns alone. Tears slipping down her cheeks, she lies beside our mother, holding her as her spirit slowly leaves her body.

Sometime after the funeral, I phone Donna and Chuck, then Jeff and Susie. I tell them the long-hidden truth and ask them to tell their children and spouses. Now it cannot accidentally be told to Mom or Dad. No one seems surprised. Maybe they all knew. Maybe even Mom and Dad. Maybe I could have told them years ago. Maybe everything would have been fine, and maybe we could have been closer or less uncomfortable sooner. Or maybe none of that is true. I don't know what the past was or what the alternate timeline could have been. But from my perspective, in this reality I have lived, it's the first time I have no secrets.

For me, unlike many of my gay friends, there had never been one "coming out." It was a slow process. First I told a few college friends, then a few colleagues in Indiana, a few more colleagues in Atlanta, and later, all of my colleagues.

I told Carol years ago, not long after we met. But my family was the last to be told, marking the final end of my double life. For the first time all conversations could be open. There were no strained silences when relationships entered the discussion. I didn't have to worry about where any subject was leading. I could relax. My siblings and their families became true friends—every aspect was now more comfortable.

New Mexico stunned me, not only its natural beauty, but also its distinct contrasts with the northeast. Stone and adobe structures in old-town Albuquerque, Santa Fe, and Taos seemed to grow out of the tan landscape.

When wall meets wall in buildings, instead of turning at ninety-degree angles, "corners" are often curved. Gentle lines and soft colors provide the illusion of tranquility, even in busy southwestern cities. Bare mountains show their geological history and are dotted with wildflowers, cactus, piñon, and sage, while northern ranges are more often covered with tall pine, maple, ash, and spruce.

Every view—people, buildings, and vistas, city or country–is different from the northern US and Canada; the architecture, people, and views are foreground. In Albuquerque, the Sandia Mountains dominate the horizon . . . jagged, rugged, and multi-tanned; sunlight paints bright beige strips on the rocks, while crevices create black shadows. The skies are often a brilliant blue; the clouds, if any, bright white. At night, stars and city lights shine with a sharpness and clarity rarely seen through the haze of industrial cities. The entire mountain often turns red just before sunset. Whether looking up from the city, riding the tramway to the top, or looking down from the crest, the beauty of the Sandias is both vibrant and subtle.

Populations in small northeastern towns and rural areas are mostly white, and the cities have a wild mix of every color and nationality; while in New Mexico, Hispanic, Native American, and various Caucasian groups make up the majority. Diversity is especially apparent in Santa Fe, where gays and lesbians have settled in large numbers. Do they get along? Well, here you can find bagels with green chili—everything seems possible.

Early in 2004, long before marriage became explicitly legal in New Mexico, a small number of same-sex marriages were licensed in Sandoval County, which is immediately adjacent to Santa Fe County. The practice was halted a few hours later when New Mexico's attorney general filed a lawsuit to stop the practice.

Carol was also tour guide on day trips to Santa Fe, Taos, and surrounding areas, autumn drives unexpectedly colorful in these arid lands. The predictable beige is here, but in many shades, usually dotted with piñon and sage, vivid red wildflowers, blazing gold cottonwoods, and yellow aspen, all sparkling under bright sun. Here, the flat-topped mesas contrast with rich dark-green forested mountains, especially beautiful when only the stream shares the narrow valley with the curving road. Hills are decorated with budding shrubs and wildflowers of yellow and lavender. The range of shapes seems infinite, from the rocky vertical walls to the craggy, pointed mountains to the forests of tall green triangles. When the sun shines, the colors light like fire. As it sets, shadows on craggy rocks gradually intensify.

Since leaving home, much of my touring has been unaccompanied. I selected a museum, restaurant, theater, or shop and experienced it alone. Although it was enjoyable to interact only with exhibits, art, or ambience, I often missed sharing opinions and thoughts about the experience. Carol provided the best of both; she processed the event alone, but loved to converse about it later.

On one trip to Santa Fe, we stopped along the way at Cochiti Pueblo village, all its structures made of adobe mud, including a drum-shaped water tower and the ornos I saw in the Cortez *trompe l'oeil* painting—this time real ovens in active use. In this architectural style, roofs and corners are often curved, removing the sharp distinctions created by perpendicular joinings. The curved corners came to symbolize gentle transitions between peoples. I choose to believe this despite the prohibitions on gay marriage in some of New Mexico's Native American tribes.

Carol told me Cochiti is well known for potters, jewelers, painters, and drum makers, the skills passed from generation to generation. Many of the Cochiti artists work out of their homes. Our destination was the home of potter Dennis Anderson. He and his wife, Mary, specialized in tableaux sculptures known as "storytellers." Though Mary and Dennis lived in a simple adobe home, I learned online their montages sell for up to ten thousand dollars in galleries and at auction.

Dennis conversed leisurely, as though we were the most important things in his life. He told us that some think the main figure in each piece is telling a story to the smaller ones, but *he* believes the montage is telling a story to the viewer—the spectator free to imagine a tale that goes with the figures.

As Mary wrapped our purchases in a manner sufficient to survive an earthquake, Dennis shared his philosophy of life and art: we have no real notion of who God is, but we are all from one God. We are alike, even though our cultures are unique.

"We may not understand each other," he added, "but we can show respect."

Though I had no idea if Dennis included sexual orientations different from his, I chose to assume he did and willed his words to be broadcast on the winds of Earth.

Soon after leaving the Cochiti village, we arrived in Santa Fe. Carol told me zoning here didn't allow high-rises, and all buildings had to be constructed in the pueblo style: Arby's, I-HOP, Walgreens, and the School for the Deaf—all adobe. On this day, the destination was another modern adobe building, the Georgia O'Keefe Museum with three thousand pieces of her work. As I examined her bright images of flowers, rocks, shells, southwest landscapes, and New York skylines, I was reminded of all that I've recently seen. She captured not only the image, but the spirit of everything she painted.

On another trip, I visited *El Rancho de las Golondrinas*—the Ranch of the Swallows, a living-history community on two hundred acres, just south of Santa Fe. Here, three-hundred-year-old buildings were restored or brought in from other locations, and old foundations were used as underpinnings for authentic new structures. There were over fifty cabins, lean-tos, and mills, including a threshing ground, blacksmith, a shop where wool skeins were dyed with local plants, a winery, and water-driven pulleys used to grind flour—everything needed for Spanish colonial life in the 1700s. Villagers, clothed in the style of the time, demonstrated life on the early New Mexico frontier.

I again experienced deep respect for the diverse solutions—providing shelter, clothing, and beauty for another moment in time, another culture, another location.

Carol and I toured Santa Fe's Canyon Road, a street in the city with amazing galleries and art of all types, including extraordinary Native American offerings. Gallery after gallery displayed traditional and unique designs in every art form. We both have an affinity for three-dimensional art—pottery, sculpture, and bas-relief. Most of the offerings on Canyon Road were high quality and beyond the price range of all but Bill Gates and Oprah.

One courtyard displayed several life-size sculptures, including one of Mark Twain reading *Adventures of Huckleberry Finn,* and a man on a bench wearing glasses, legs crossed while reading a newspaper . . . every object in bronze. Nearby was the work of Lee McGary. His sculptures, also in bronze, surpassed any I had yet seen. The unbelievable detail, portraiture, and appearance of motion amazed me. One sculpture is of a slim Native American woman, over six feet tall, leaning into the wind. Her arms outstretched, she is wearing a fringed leather dress and a colorful beaded shawl, also fringed in leather. She carries a multicolored Indian blanket across her back, flowing outward as she seems to move forward. The folds in the "leather" cause the clothing to look exactly like fabric; I had to touch it to know it was metal. Intricately beaded moccasins decorate her feet and a beaded leather sheath holds her knife—moccasins and sheath also in bronze. She wears an expression of peaceful joy, looking as if she was petrified in motion, in this outfit, in this position.

In the Wiford Gallery, we saw Ernesto Montenegro's magnificent bronze sculptures in bas-relief. Like the storyteller dolls of the Cochiti, each piece told a tale, elegant and individual. The work that caused me to stop, stare, and hold my breath was a three-dimensional, framed work depicting Anne Frank. In the foreground, on the right, she was the child we know, and deeply recessed on the left, the old woman she would have become. Whether intended or not, I found the inclusion of Anne Frank to represent one of many symbols of Santa Fe's refusal to accept discrimination of any type.

Deb, in town on a temporary work assignment, joined me for an October evening of storytelling in Taos. The highlight was a woman who had revised *Beauty and the Beast* and told this old tale with deep tenderness toward the plight of Beast; we were motionless, riveted, and profoundly moved. Her second story was of a summer night of waitressing in Martha's Vineyard, an unusually busy night with many quirky customers. She told it rapidly, and with hurried gestures, giving us a vivid picture of how hectic it was. We laughed so hard we wept. The quality of her performances reminded me of Sharon French's one-woman show in Cortez. I would gladly have paid Broadway prices to see either of these artists.

Deb's longtime friend Nancy Marshall was visiting in Santa Fe, as were Patrick and Edwin. An easy ride from Albuquerque, I joined Nancy for lunch at La Fonda on the square and had dinner with the two men. Driving back to Carol's house, savoring memories of the day with Nancy, Patrick and Edwin, I knew my world to be rich in human contact. Over the years, I formed many deep friendships, including my family—especially my brother and sister. These special ones remained through the stages of our lives. Much of the time we came together for conversation and laughter, but the unique virtue of these relationships lies in mutual support and concern, understanding and compassion, trust and love.

When I was physically alone, friends and family were always in the background. Men and women—gay and straight—they know my sexual orientation, temptations, and transgressions, just as I know theirs. We understand each other—assets and flaws—and love anyway, most of all during times of suffering and times of joy. They added value to my journey, to everything in my life. Nothing would be the same without them.

In the sweetness of true friendship, there is no double life, no secret identity, no hiding . . . only truth.

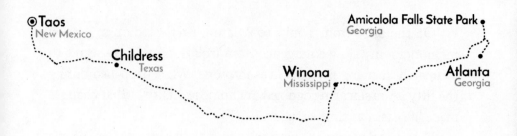

CHAPTER 37
Strictly Rationed Chocolate

I left New Mexico and began my journey home Friday morning, November 25, 2005. I had been away for eighteen months. Living on the road had become the norm. One part of me didn't want it to end, wanting to wander through my remaining years. But I also would be glad to be in the place I'd called home for over thirty years, back with people who were in my blood, my breath.

Slowly, slowly I re-entered my old world.

Choosing back roads, I went through towns such as Childress, Texas, and Winona, Mississippi. I took even smaller roads through Tennessee to Toni's cabin in the Smoky Mountain foothills. Knowing I'd need a transition before big city chaos, she invited me to stay with her for a few days before going home.

The day after I arrived we drove to nearby Amicalola Falls State Park, where we hiked to the dramatic waterfall—just seventy miles from Atlanta, yet in wilderness. After so many months away, the splendors of nature, art, and culture near home were new again.

I had it all here, if only I can remember to use it.

On the drive from Toni's to Atlanta, I reflected on my travel memories—my slow emergence from isolation with my secret to ultimately merging my two lives into one. What happened during the fifty years since I recognized my homosexuality? What changes made life easier as time slipped away?

I knew little about the long and convoluted history of gay people across the world, a history in which, depending on time and place, we might be murdered . . . or tolerated . . . or even honored.

A liberal point of view prevailed in the 1920s and homosexuality was accepted, at least in the big cities. But by the time I was born, bigotry had once again replaced tolerance. Homosexuals went back into hiding to escape scorn and even imprisonment.

Though Berlin had been tolerant in the '20s, by the '30s homosexuality joined Judaism as an odious attribute. And the Holocaust treated those groups similarly. In the camps, while Jews wore the yellow Star of David, gays wore pink triangles—both intended as badges of shame. But when Jews were released at the end of the war, gays were often imprisoned for many more years.

If I had been a Jewish lesbian in WWII Germany, I would have been the lowest of the low. But I was born in the United States in the year the war began, and a few years later, instead of wearing a yellow star or a pink triangle, I was safe beside my mother, holding hands as we walked to find strictly rationed chocolate . . .

It's 1944 and Mom holds my five-year-old hand as we walk to a neighborhood tavern to buy a chocolate bar. Donna, my three-year-old sister, skips along on her other side. We pause at a familiar poster, a photo of a muscular, short-haired member of the Women's Army Corps wearing a tight-fitting tailored uniform. I want to grow up to be her.

Later I see an ad for Fleischmann's Yeast showing another WAC, this one riding a motorcycle. I read aloud, "This is no time to be . . .¿" Mom finishes for me, saying "frail." I want to hang out with this one.

In seventh grade, I'm with friends resting from a bike ride. Someone refers to "queers." I ask and learn the meaning. I think, *Oh, I will never love a boy. I will never get married. Ohhhh.*

I'm thirteen in 1952. There is very little in the newspapers about homosexuals, and nothing on our four-channel television. But I am somehow aware that homosexuals are considered a "security risk" because they can be blackmailed into revealing secrets, and if identified, they are fired from government jobs.

One night, on our way to dinner, a few flamboyant men cross our paths. Mom says to Dad, "Oh, Joe. I would be so worried and sad if we had such a child." Dad nods then shakes his head. I begin my double life, dating boys with my robotic body while my shadow-self loves girls.

In 1954, I read the *Chicago Tribune* Dad left on the kitchen table and learn about Alan Turing's suicide. A British mathematician now widely considered the father of computer science and artificial intelligence, Turing had worked at Britain's WWII Bletchley Park where he devised techniques for breaking German naval codes.

Near the bottom of the article, it says Turing's homosexuality resulted in a criminal prosecution in 1952, when same-sex physical intimacy was still illegal in the United Kingdom. As an alternative to prison, he accepted treatment with female hormones—chemical castration.

Turing took cyanide and died in 1954, two weeks before his forty-second birthday.

I'm sixteen in 1955, and driving alone, late at night, looking for homosexuals who might be on the street as they go from one Chicago bar to another, but I don't try to meet them . . . I'm discovering my first lesbian friends on the pages of the classic *Well of Loneliness* . . . watching my well-to-do father, a victim of embezzlement, go into bankruptcy, open a small hardware store, and work twelve-hour days while I take a job in a ladies' clothing store . . . watching my mother and father watching television, never going out in the evenings, never receiving invitations from the friends they once knew, gritting their collective teeth to bear it.

I can't tell them now.

At seventeen, I'm leaving home for college in Ann Arbor, not realizing the sacrifices that would be made for me to attend an expensive, out-of-state school . . . beginning therapy to be treated for my "illness" and finding it difficult to tell my therapist why I'm there, watching her motionless face as I tell her I'm a lesbian in need of a cure, wondering what she's thinking. When the hour is over, she tells me our next appointment time. I feel relief. Someone knows my secret . . . dating boys and reading lesbian paperbacks, knowing they can't arrest you for reading but hiding the books anyway . . . seeing a few "normal looking" brave couples come out to the world, appearing on television talk shows; hearing a few people mention homosexuality once in a while . . . thinking I can't let my parents know while they're so sad . . . losing my virginity and sleeping with many of the boys I date, trying to be something I'm not.

It's 1959 and I'm twenty. Masculine-looking gay men look for effeminate men; "lipstick lesbians" look for butch women. How else can we find each other to pair up? Our loves are seen as a result of mental illness; our actions can put us in prison. In some countries, we can be put to death.

Some men hunt for sex in public restrooms. Police launch undercover operations, seduce, and then arrest them. The arrests appear in the Ann Arbor paper, and the "guilty" are expelled from the university.

Only a few come out in public, or heaven forbid, to their parents.

There is an active war on gays. We were no threat when the only ones out of the closet were wildly effeminate boys and totally masculine women. But now that people realize there are at least a few more of us hidden among them—we are a problem.

In 1963, the penalties for sodomy in the various states are imprisonment for up to ten years, or a fine, or both.

Chicago, New York, and San Francisco have secret bars dedicated to gay people. But I live in Ann Arbor, Michigan, where there is no such place.

At twenty-nine in 1968, I take a job as an assistant professor in an even smaller town—Bloomington, Indiana. No such bar in this town either.

I meet Mandy. She's also a professor. I think she might be interested and hint until we kiss. We don't love each other, but we make good companions and adequate sexual partners. We know no other gay people. We act like roommates. It's Indiana in 1969; we can go to jail for what we do in our bedroom, and they wouldn't put us in the same cell. We would be two demure faculty ladies, standing before a black-robed judge looking sternly down from his raised desk, flanked by flags, lecturing us on our morals.

It's June of 1969 when police raid a popular gay bar, the Stonewall Inn in Manhattan's Greenwich Village. On this night, the patrons have had enough. "You don't allow me in your places, why must you come to mine? Why should I be arrested in my place?" Surprising the police, the transsexuals fight back with courage and strength, soon followed by the other gay boys and men. Officers quickly lose control of the situation. A crowd gathers outside; the protest spreads and becomes a riot. In the following days, more protests, all aimed at having places for gays and lesbians to be together without fear of arrest.

In 1973, I leave Indiana and move to a job in Atlanta. I go to gay bars, discos, and drag shows. I join a lesbian bowling league and frequent the pool at a gay hotel.

In 1974, the American Psychiatric Association declares that homosexuality is not a mental illness, but they have no control over the laws. Consensual sex between two men or two women is still illegal in most states. Police raid gay bars. I still live two lives, but my shadow-self is coming closer to my physical body. My professional persona appears daily in heels, hose, and lipstick to see patients. Every evening, my shadow materializes in jeans, goes to bars, and dances with women.

I'm in therapy again. This time, my psychologist is a lesbian. The goal is to adjust to being gay in a nonaccepting world. Most therapists, gay and straight, now see this as an appropriate outcome. But some religious groups still wish to convert us to heterosexuality. Often they use aversion therapy, small electric shocks applied as the patient looks at photos of attractive same-sex models.

In 1976, I march in my first Atlanta Pride parade. Only a few hundred people are out today. Unlike a few others, I don't cover my head with a bag, but I have mixed feelings about being caught by TV cameras. On the one hand, my double life would be over. On the other hand, my double life would be over.

The lesbian and gay revolution begins. We form counseling centers, churches, and synagogues, organize marches, and fight for anti-discrimination laws.

Life continues to improve. Raids stop. We go to our bars without fear of arrest. More and more people come out. I'm less afraid. I tell a few more people at work and I don't worry that they might tell others.

In 1982, Anna moves in with me. Her Orthodox Jewish mother, Gwen, visits. She believes homosexuality is a sin. We straighten the office to make it look like Anna's bedroom and turn it over to her mom. Anna sleeps on the sofa. It's clear that Mom thinks we are nothing more than good friends. She gifts me with a small Old Testament Bible. In it, she writes, "To my other daughter, Marilyn. May God richly bless you. I love you. Gwen." I'm honored by her gift. I love her, too. But she would be horrified if she knew the truth.

Also in 1982, Lee, my colleague and dear friend, visits my office, sits down, and tells me about AIDS, a new disease among gay men. One or two cases are diagnosed every day. There are no medications—there's no money for a "gay" disease. No one survives.

Through the rest of the '80s, more and more gay men get sick and die. Nobody knows how it's transmitted and fear grips the gay world. Many physicians have no interest in studying this "perversion-caused" disease; some religious leaders preach that this disease is God's way of punishing gay men. Since the disease finds its way to heterosexual men, and then to their female partners, lesbians declare that we must be God's chosen people.

The president is silent about the AIDS epidemic. Gay activists form foundations, demand research funding, and provide education to hospitals, doctors and clinics.

In 1983, twenty-year-old Bobby Griffith jumps to his death from a freeway bridge in Portland, Oregon. His mother, Mary Griffith, tried throughout his adolescence to "pray away" his "gay nature" with the result that he came to despise who he was. Now, after his death, she realizes that God saw nothing wrong with Bobby and renounces the rigid beliefs that kept her from accepting him during his lifetime.

In 1985, President Reagan announces half a billion dollars for AIDs research. A month later, actor Rock Hudson dies of AIDS.

Lee has the disease. Effective medication will be too late for him.

In 1989, the drug AZT is shown to slow progression in HIV-positive patients. But the high cost is prohibitive for many.

1990 brings the death of young Ryan White. Infected with HIV via a blood transfusion, he was prohibited from attending his public school due to fear of contagion. He faced ghastly prejudice and hostility as he fought for the rights of children with AIDS.

1991 saw popular basketball player Magic Johnson diagnosed as HIV positive. He said ". . . sometimes we think, well, only gay people can get it . . . And here I am saying that it can happen to anybody, even me."

In 1993, African American Arthur Ashe, Wimbledon winner and number-one-ranked tennis player worldwide, dies of AIDS. Just like young Ryan White, he contracted the disease from a blood transfusion. Ashe, Ryan, and Magic Johnson make it clear, to those willing to see, that AIDS is not punishment for sin.

Clinton presents "Don't Ask, Don't Tell, Don't Pursue," his compromise between an increasingly powerful homosexual population demanding equality in all work places and a homophobic military establishment worried about unit cohesiveness and afraid of being scrutinized in the shower.

But, at the VA Medical Center, I'm allowed to tell. So I do. I discover that everyone who recognizes "the short woman in the white coat" already knows I am gay.

My two selves are almost merged now. Only my family hasn't been told.

In 1996, Congress passes the Defense of Marriage Act, explicitly defining marriage as a union of one man and one woman, implicitly declaring gay marriage a menace to family life. I don't understand. If I marry a woman, how do we threaten the heterosexual marriage next door? Why does that marriage need a defense against us?

In 1997, Jim Wheeler, a gay high-school student in Pennsylvania, commits suicide after constant harassment and physical abuse at school.

Shortly after midnight on October 7, 1998, twenty-one-year-old Matthew Shepard, a gay student at the University of Wyoming, meets two men who are pretending to be gay. They introduce themselves to Matthew and strike up a conversation. Later, after offering to drive Matthew home, they take him instead to a remote, rural area, tie him to a fence, then burn and torture him—leaving him to die.

It's 1999. I'm sixty years old. Mom dies in Donna's arms. After the funeral I tell my family the long-hidden truth. It's the first time I have no secrets. I had a half-century with a secret life, at first all alone, then known to a few, then many—fifty years with two lives, slowly merging into one.

In 2003, the Supreme Court invalidates the remaining sodomy laws. And the people of Massachusetts grant the right of same-sex couples to marry in their state. With this law, Massachusetts announces its rejection of the Defense of Marriage Act.

But also in 2003, thirteen-year-old Ryan Patrick Halligan commits suicide in Vermont after suffering repeated bullying from classmates who sent him homophobic messages, threatened, insulted, and taunted him incessantly.

And, in this same year, the infamous Westboro Baptist Church transports its hate-mongering from its home in Topeka, Kansas, eleven hundred miles to Harrisburg, Pennsylvania, to protest a documentary about Jim Wheeler, the gay student who committed suicide in 1997 because of persistent gay bashing.

As I write these words in 2014, I am free to live a transparent life, but the job is not yet done. Though attitudes and laws have greatly improved, gay children still fear coming out. Some commit suicide to escape bullying or parental rejection.

While same-sex marriage is legal in many countries and several states, homosexuality is a death penalty crime in some nations. Our war is not over.

Will mankind ever agree to accept differences?

There are those who look at things the way they are, and ask
    why…
I dream of things that never were, and ask why not?
—ROBERT KENNEDY

Gros Morne National Park, NL

St. John's, NL

Ferryland, NL

Port aux Basques, NL

Cape Breton Highlands National Park

Baddeck, NS

Gampo Abbey, Pleasant Bay, NS   Iona, NS
North Syndney, NS   Cape Breton, NS
New Glasgow, PE   Louisbourg, NS
Cavendish, PE
                                        Charlottetown, PE
O'Leary, PE   Wood Islands Harbor,
                                        Prince Edward Island
                                    Caribou, NS

CANADA

Quebec City, QC
              Levis, QC
                              St. John, NB
Agawa Bay, ON   Acadia
Sault Ste. Marie, ON   National
                              Park   Halifax, NS
Montreal, QC   Grand-Pré, NS
              Ottawa, ON   Bridgton   Digby
Park   Freeport
Manitoulin Island   Portland   Yarmouth, NS
                          North   Camden
Stratford, ON   Conway   Biddeford Pool

Chicago

Manhattan

Chanceford

ATLANTIC

OCEAN

Pisgah National Forest   Charlotte

Amicalola Falls State Park

Atlanta

Tybee Island

Orleans

THE BAHAMAS

exico

EPILOGUE

"Where Have All the Flowers Gone..."

They're gone now, so many gone. Others are sick, but defiant.

Jane, my friend of many years, is dead from a lengthy, debilitating lung cancer. And Eleanor, also from cancer. Maureen's friend Amos died at his cabin in Minnesota. Both Judy and Bob MacGillivray—Bob in Biddeford Pool surrounded by friends, while Judy was cared for by her daughter in Texas—each without the other. And Carol Fillman is now terminally ill.

Kevin died long ago during a robbery in Canada; Chris, still drinking heavily, died in her early seventies; Lee succumbed to AIDS years before effective medication was available. Audrey surrendered to an inherited defect of collagen, the "glue" that holds everything together. After twice fighting for life in her sixties, she submitted at seventy-four, not long after visiting me in Maine.

Others, despite battling severe illnesses, currently live full, rich lives. Had they been treated by physicians in the mid-nineteenth century—

when we were still using the butter churns and ice-harvesting tools now displayed in Canadian museums, when modern medicine was a toddler and cancer treatment still in its infancy, when surgery was performed with crude anesthesia and vague knowledge of tumor location, with neither electricity nor effective antibiotics—none would have lived long after diagnosis.

And me?

The dementias and deaths of my beloved Mom and Dad opened this book. I wondered then if I would follow in the paths of my parents, my vitality slithering away in small, humiliating episodes. A few years later, that question still unanswered, I decided to get on the road while physically and cognitively intact.

Before my sojourn, I experienced the world's glorious panoramas mainly in movies and auto ads. The physical reality was mine only rarely and briefly—a few tasty appetizers leaving me wanting when the view was again asphalt and neon. Now I have partaken fully, dining often at the extravagant tables of natural and man-made feasts.

The challenges and distractions provided by this journey not only decreased my anxieties, but also enhanced my self-reliance and belief in my ability to handle anything life could present, no matter how difficult. And indeed, three years after my return to Atlanta, life did offer complications.

IMMORTALITY

Deep in my bones a silent conviction:
I'm immortal. No contradiction.

Routine mammo this morning. Doc gazes at me
And pauses; I wonder, *What did he see?*
"We need more tests." I fail those too.
With surgery and radiation my breast is born anew.
Energy restored, a sigh of relief.
Immortal again—but the pardon is brief.

No sign of recurrence, pleasant hours and days.
Then a fearful warning: my eyes will not liaise.
Every day's a little worse, and I am asking *why*.
A specialist assures me, the cause is not the eye.
This dedicated doctor requests a special test.
It shows a tumor in my head, there is no time to rest.

To destroy this stealthy enemy, surgeon wields his knife.
He is a mighty soldier in this battle for my life.
"I think I got it all," he says. "But it might recur."
The fantasy of endless time disperses in a blur.

Weeks and months slide by as eye functions mend.
One face in the mirror. I dare to hope for tumor's end.
Once again I visit—now I know it's as a guest—
The land of immortality for a transitory rest.

Though invisible on fancy tests, miniscule tumor specks remain.
Unknown to all assessors, it's still lurking in my brain.
It will not come back, I yet resolve, as if reality yields to decision.
Certainty comes with sad acceptance when I wake again with
double vision.
Two more times I need the knife
To save my vision, to lengthen my life.
Then forty days of proton beams,
This radiation—never in my dreams.
Prognosis good, I live again
But now I know there is an end.

Acknowledgments

This book has been greatly enriched by the efforts of the many people who influenced the days of my life and those who offered ideas and suggestions.

My first thanks go to Carol Fillman, Ruth Leutwyler, and Audrey Lowe, the friends who encouraged me to write this book and made major contributions all along the journey. Audrey died long before my book came to completion, but I could hear her cheering along with Ruth and Carol as the last pages were written.

Thanks to: my beloved parents, Lenore and Joseph, who wanted only good things for their children; my brother and sister, their spouses, and children, who accepted and loved me at each phase of my life, even before they were told the specifics; and the friends who shared my days—successes, failures, sadness, and joy.

And to Harriet, Wendy's mom, who accepted her daughter and all the friends with her typical love and grace when she was told about Wendy's sexuality. Now in her nineties, she continues to be a vibrant force in all of our lives. Ros, Carole's mother (now deceased), who learned by accident when Carole was sixteen, also became a loving and valued mother to all the friends.

Long before *Traveling the Two-Lane* was imagined, my journey was supported by Audrey and Wade Lowe, Nancy Miller, Deb Bourgeois, Wendy Nelson, and Cindy Maynard. This group of friends stored large objects, helped with van preparation, and agreed to manage my house, renters, and mail during my absence.

I also thank the skilled members of my writing groups who listened to my chapters, freely offering opinions and suggestions that continuously enhanced my efforts: Ron Aiken, Jim Butorac, Chuck Clark, Tara Coyt, Angela Durden, Rebecca Ewing, Carolyn Graham, Chuck Johnson, Greta Reed, Stan Waits, Sandie Webb, Fred Whitson, and Aimee Wise. And thank you to my expert teachers and editors: Rosemary Daniell and Jedwin Smith.

Before the manuscript could be submitted for publication, I requested still more feedback from gifted reviewers Chuck Clark and Garrett Marco, whose enthusiasm and editorial comments strengthened the manuscript immeasurably.

And finally, the early readers and supporters from Biddeford Pool, whose encouragement spurred me on to publication: Lisa Barstow, Beth Baskin, Carol Bassett, Anita Coupe, Brad Coupe, Erv Davis, Heather Davis, Ada Goff, Jan Hryniewicz, Heather Locke, and Polly Nodden. A special thanks to Heather Davis for coordinating early readings.

When I thought all was ready, BookLogix added still more. I truly appreciate the editorial contributions made by the talented editors Kelly Nightingale and Daren Fowler. Thanks must go out to Ellina Dent and her design team, especially Laura Kajpust for the enticing cover and gorgeous maps. I also thank Caitlin Wells, marketing manager; Jessica Parker, senior publishing consultant; Angela DeCaires, publishing director; and Ahmad Meradji, the president and leader of the team.

As I thank my family and friends, I must note that our memories sometimes differ. Marcel Proust said it best when he wrote, "The remembrance of things past is not necessarily the remembrance of things as they were." Any errors are my responsibility. And to protect the identities of several people, I have changed names and details of their lives.

ABOUT THE AUTHOR

Marilyn Berman

Marilyn Berman received her PhD in Communication Disorders from the University of Michigan. She was a faculty member at Indiana University before accepting a position as Supervisor of Speech Language Pathology at the VA Medical Center in Atlanta and, later, as Chief of Audiology and Speech Language Pathology at the same hospital. She also taught part time at Emory University and Georgia State.